Menschenaffen wie wir

Porträts einer Verwandtschaft

Apes Like Us

Portraits of a Kinship

Menschenaffen wie wir

Porträts einer Verwandtschaft

Apes Like Us

Portraits of a Kinship

Jutta Hof & Volker Sommer

EDITION **PANORAMA**

Prolog	7	8	Prologue

AUFTAKTE / UPBEATS

1. Geschichte(n) *Die Entdeckung unserer Verwandten*	36	39	**1. Historie(s)** *Discovery of a Relationship*
2. Primaten *Anleitung zur Selbsterkenntnis*	46	49	**2. Primates** *Know Thyself*
3. Namensgebung *Sind wir „weise Schimpansen"?*	56	60	**3. Namegame** *Are We "Wise Chimpanzees"?*

LEBENSBILDER / LIFESTYLES

4. Orang-Utans *Eremiten im Urwald*	88	92	**4. Orangutans** *Hermits in the Jungle*
5. Gorillas *Milde und wilde Riesen*	98	103	**5. Gorillas** *Mild and Wild Giants*
6. Schimpansen *Keine besseren Menschen*	110	114	**6. Chimpanzees** *Not Better People*
7. Bonobos *Im feministischen Utopia?*	122	126	**7. Bonobos** *In Feminist Utopia?*

HORIZONTE / HORIZONS

8. Intelligenz *Mentale Landschaften*	154	158	**8. Intelligence** *Mental Landscapes*
9. Philosophisches *Die Provokation des Monismus*	166	168	**9. Philosophising** *The Provocation of Monism*
10. Zukunft *Archen in der Menschenflut*	174	178	**10. Future** *Arks in the Great Human Flood*

Anhang / Appendix

Literatur	186	186	Literature
Schutz- und Forschungseinrichtungen	188	188	Conversation and Research Institutions
Die Porträtierten	189	189	The Portrayed
Fotografin und Autor	190	190	Photographer and Author

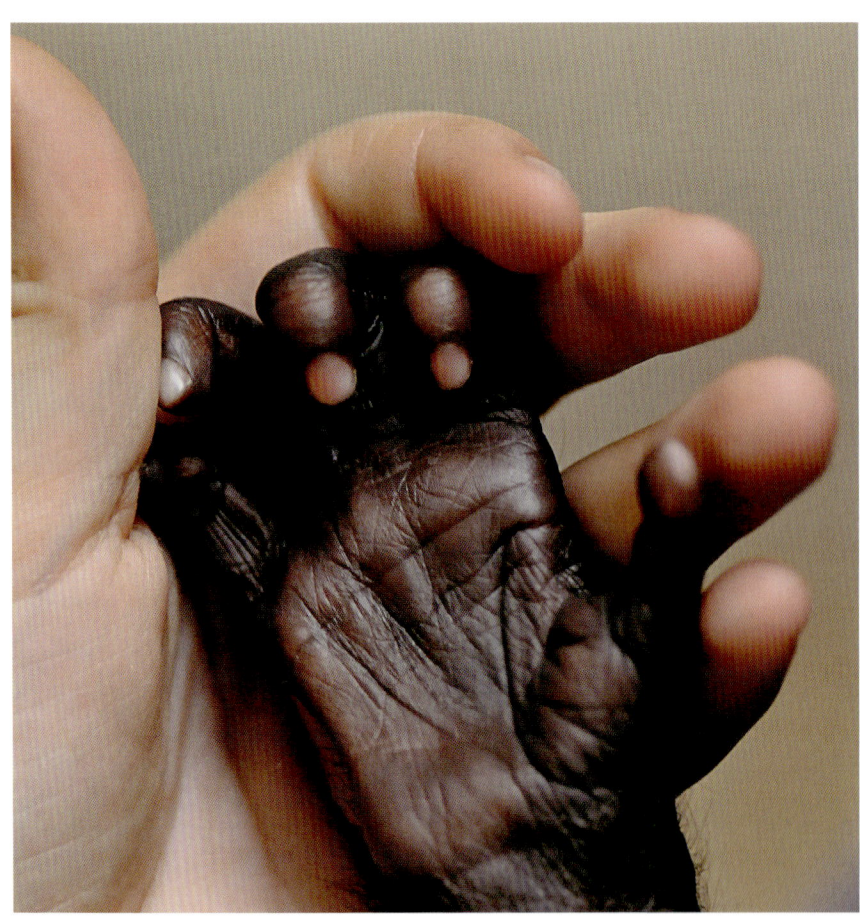

Bonobo / *bonobo*

Prolog

Volker Sommer, Buenos Aires / Argentina, im April 2010

Wer Tiere „vermenschlicht", wird in der Wissenschaft schief angesehen. Denn klare Grenzen soll man nicht verwischen. Und schon gar nicht die zwischen Natur und Kultur, zwischen Instinkt und Denken, zwischen Genen und Erziehung, zwischen Materie und Geist – eben die Unterscheidung von Tier und Mensch.

Außerhalb der Wissenschaft geht es weniger puritanisch zu. Niemand tadelt Frauchen, wenn es erzählt, wie Hundchen sich über ihr Nachhausekommen freut. Oder wie „Waldi" ein schlechtes Gewissen plagt, weil er den Teppich zerkaute. Solchem Anthropomorphismus erliegen wir umso williger, wenn die Versuchung von unseren allernächsten Verwandten ausgeht: den Menschenaffen. Blickt der Schimpanse reglos drein, halten wir ihn für traurig. Den Orang-Utan haben wir im Verdacht, dass er etwas im Schilde führt. Die Bonobo-Mutter krault, so scheint es uns, ihr Baby äußerst liebevoll. Und dass Gorillakinder Riesenspaß beim Balgen haben – wer wollte das bezweifeln?

Derlei Vermenschlichung wird von Wissenschaftlern gern belächelt. Doch der Wind scheint sich langsam zu drehen. Wie einst die traditionelle Anatomie demonstriert nun die moderne Genetik, wie nahe uns speziell andere Primaten hinsichtlich des Körperbaus stehen. Zugleich wird von Disziplinen wie Verhaltens- und Neurobiologie aber auch immer deutlicher herausgearbeitet, dass Affen, ähnlich wie wir, in komplexen mentalen Landschaften zuhause sind.

Einst sakrosankte Grenzziehungen werden dadurch immer fraglicher. Und so dürfen auch akademisch Informierte – unter Wahrung von Augenmaß – genau das tun, was einst als Fehltritt von Laien galt: Tiere anthropomorphisieren (also vermenschlichen) und Menschen zoomorphisieren (also vertierlichen).

Ob und wie wir die Gegensatzpaare aufweichen – oder eben nicht – hängt von unserer Grundeinstellung ab. Die Philosophie des Alles-oder-Nichts sucht nach Einzigartigem und behauptet entsprechend, dass allein Menschen über Denkvermögen, Werkzeuggebrauch oder Kultur verfügen. Diese Weltanschauung identifiziert qualitative Sprünge – und postuliert unüberbrückbare Unterschiede.

Die Philosophie des Mehr-oder-Weniger vertritt hingegen, dass anatomische wie mentale Merkmale eine Geschichte haben, nämlich eine Evolution. Diese Weltanschauung denkt in quantitativen Unterschieden – also fließenden Übergängen. Während also der eher pessimistisch eingestellte Dualist das Glas halb leer sieht, sieht es ein eher optimistischer Gradualist halbvoll. Wer letztere Ansicht teilt, hofft mithin auf längerwährenden Genuss und wird sich wohl recht gerne auf den programmatischen Titel dieses Bandes einlassen: „Menschenaffen wie wir." Die darin ausgebreitete Deutung ist das persönliche Bekenntnis eines Verhaltensforschers, der seit drei Jahrzehnten unsere wilde Verwandtschaft in ihrer natürlichen Heimat erforscht.

Gepaart sind die Texte mit einer anderen subjektiven Betrachtung: der Fotografie. Jutta Hof hat ihre Porträts in Zoos erarbeitet. Dort konnte sie sich Menschenaffen bis auf Zentimeter nähern – denn dicker ist eine Glasscheibe nicht. Den außergewöhnlichen Aufnahmen wohnt die Magie der Identifikation inne. Die Intensität hat einerseits vielleicht damit zu tun, dass Jutta Hof nicht in Grenzen denkt, sondern dass ihre Studien, wie sie betont, in einem Gefühl der Verbundenheit wurzeln. Andererseits vollziehen auch Betrachter die Verbindung intuitiv nach, weil sie auf einem objektiven Tatbestand beruht: Wir können uns in andere Menschenaffen versetzen, weil wir selbst Menschenaffen sind.

Wer möchte, kann die Porträtierten als Botschafter einer modernen Weltsicht verstehen: Eines Naturalismus, der uns selbst wie andere Tiere als Zeugen der Jahrmilliarden alten Geschichte des Lebens auf diesem Planeten begreift. Mit jenen, die gemeinsam mit uns das längste Stück einer langen Evolutionsgeschichte zurückgelegt haben, dürfen wir hier jedenfalls besondere „Augen-Blicke" teilen.

Prologue

Volker Sommer, Buenos Aires / Argentina, April 2010

Those scientists who "humanise" animals are not well liked within their trade. One should not blur clear distinctions, and certainly not those between nature and culture, instinct and thought, between genes and upbringing, or matter and spirit – that is to say, precisely those distinctions between animals and humans.

Outside of science, things are less puritanical. Nobody criticises the pet owner who reports how "happy" her puppy was when she came home from work. And how the next day, when Fido had chewed the carpet to bits, she immediately noticed the "guilt" on his face. We succumb all the more willingly to such anthropomorphism when tempted by our closest relatives: the apes. The motionless chimpanzee who stares to the ground – quite clearly, he is sad. The orangutan, with its pensive looks, is obviously plotting something. The bonobo mother grooms her baby, so it appears, very lovingly. And those playful gorilla youngsters having fun – who wants to doubt that?

Such humanising is often smiled upon – usually patronisingly – by scientists. But the winds are slowly turning. Like the field of comparative anatomy before it, modern genetics continues to demonstrate how close other primates are to us with respect to bodily features. At the same time, disciplines like ethology and neurobiology increasingly reveal that monkeys and apes, like humans, inhabit complex mental landscapes.

Each and every boundary between animals and humans that once seemed sacrosanct is questioned by these recent discoveries and revelations. And so even academics and scientists are – with appropriate measure – permitted to do what once indicated the ultimate blunder of amateurs: to anthropomorphise animals (thus humanise them) and to zoomorphise humans (thus animalise them).

If and to which degree we soften the boundaries between these pairs of opposites – or refuse to do this – depends on our attitude. The philosophy of all-or-nothing seeks uniqueness and claims, accordingly, that humans alone can think, use tools and possess culture. This belief identifies qualitative leaps – and postulates irreconcilable differences. A philosophy of more-or-less, however, argues that physical and mental characteristics have a history, namely an evolution. This belief focusses on quantitative differences – that is, smooth transitions.

The dualist, pessimistically inclined, will thus rate the glass as half empty. While the gradualist, more optimistically, will think it half full. Whoever shares the latter view, therefore, hopes for a longer-lasting treat and probably will rather willingly subscribe to this book's programmatic title: *Apes Like Us*. The gradualist interpretation developed therein is the personal confession of a behavioural scientist who, for the past three decades, has studied our wild kin in their natural homes.

The essays are paired with another mode of subjectivity: photography. Jutta Hof created her portraits in zoos. Here, she could approach apes within an inch – because panes of glass are not thicker than that. The extraordinary visual recordings ooze a magical quality of identification. This intensity may have to do with the fact that Jutta Hof herself eschews boundaries, and so her work, as she likes to emphasise, is grounded in intimacy. But we also experience this connection intuitively, because it reflects an objective fact: we can read the faces of apes, because we are apes ourselves.

Whoever wishes to understand the portrayed as ambassadors of a modern world view can do so via a naturalism that conceives us as well as other animals as living testimonies of a history of life that is billions of years old. Alongside those who were travel-companions on this journey for the longest, we'll share, within these pages, some special souvenirs.

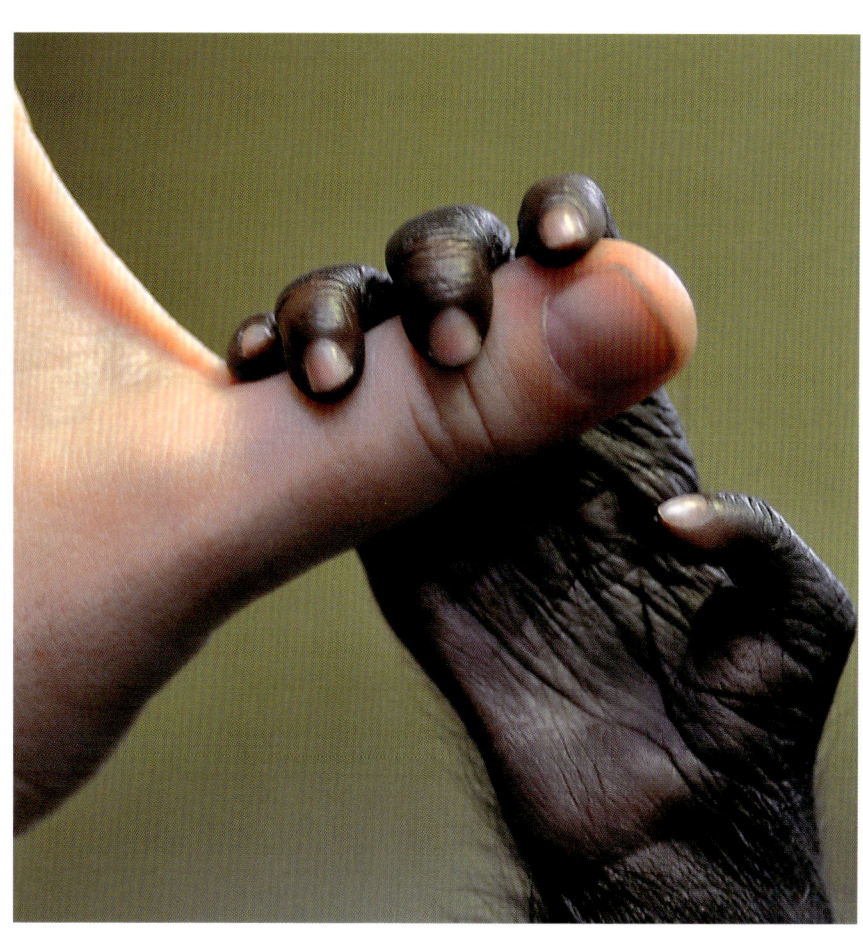

Bonobo / *bonobo*

Orang-Utan / orangutan

Gorilla / *gorilla*

Bonobo / *bonobo*

Schimpanse / *chimpanzee*

AUFTAKTE
UPBEATS

Bonobo / *bonobo*

Schimpanse / *chimpanzee*

Bonobo / *bonobo*

Bonobo / *bonobo*

Bonobo / *bonobo*

Bonobo / *bonobo* Gorilla / *gorilla*

Bonobo / *bonobo*

Bonobo / *bonobo*   23

Bonobo / *bonobo*

Bonobo / *bonobo*   Bonobo / *bonobo*   Bonobo / *bonobo*   Bonobo / *bonobo*

Gorilla / *gorilla*   Orang-Utan / *orangutan*   Bonobo / *bonobo*   Bonobo / *bonobo*   27

Bonobo / *bonobo*

Geschichte(n)
Historie(s)

Bonobo / *bonobo*

Schimpanse / *chimpanzee*

1. Geschichte(n)

Die Entdeckung unserer Verwandten

Von alters her waren Menschen von jenen Tieren fasziniert, die ihnen am ähnlichsten sehen. Nüchterne Naturwissenschaft pflichtet der naiven Ansicht ausnahmsweise einmal bei: Wie wir wurden, was wir sind – in dieser Hinsicht halten uns Affen einen Spiegel vor.

In Indien gelten Langurenaffen auch heute noch als heilig. Denn, so der Epos des *Ramayana,* einer der ihren verhalf dem guten Gott Rama zum Sieg über den Oberdämonen. Als der tapfere Affengeneral Hanuman die Heimstatt des Bösewichts niederbrannte, verkohlte er sich Hände, Füße und Gesicht. Weil das ansonsten silbrige Fell der Langurenaffen genau an jenen Stellen pechschwarz ist, weisen sie sich als Nachfahren des heldenhaften Hanumans aus, und werden von gläubigen Hinduisten in Hainen und Tempeln gefüttert.

Im alten Ägypten wurden Paviane gehalten, die als Gott Anubis den Pantheon bevölkerten und nach ihrem Tod mumifiziert wurden. Auffällig waren die Menstruationsblutungen der Affen. Sie wurden deshalb zu Begleitern des Mondgottes Thoth erhoben, war dieser doch ebenfalls zyklischen Schwankungen unterworfen.

Während die einen Affen vergötterten, wurden sie von anderen verteufelt – speziell von frühen Christen, die sich mit ihrem Monotheismus auch von heidnischen Tierkulten abgrenzen wollten. Die Menschenähnlichkeit der Affen galt zudem als Hybris, als überhebliches und damit sündiges Begehren, sich über seine Bestimmung hinwegsetzen zu wollen. Solch unbotmäßiges Streben zeichnet ja auch den Teufel aus. So heißt es im biblischen Buch *Jesaja* zum Fall Luzifers: „Ich will zu den Wolkenhöhen mich erheben, gleich sein dem Allerhöchsten (*similis ero altissimo*)." Das lateinische Wort *simia* (Affe) wurde deshalb gerne von *similitudo* (Ähnlichkeit) abgeleitet. Analog zum dunklen „Fürsten der Welt" avancierte der „Affe der Welt" zum geflügelten Wort.

Die Äbtissin Hildegard von Bingen hebt um 1150 den verwerflichen Statuskonflikt des Affen treffend hervor: „Weil er eine gewisse Ähnlichkeit mit dem Menschen hat, macht er immer nach, was dieser tut. Er hat aber auch die Tiernatur in sich, so dass er weder vollkommen das machen kann, was der Mensch tut noch was die Tiere tun. Wenn er einen Vogel beobachtet, springt er auf und versucht zu fliegen. Aber weil er seinen Wunsch nicht erfüllen kann, wird er sofort wütend." Der Affe träumt hier gleichsam stellvertretend den frevelhaften Traum des Menschen, sich vogelgleich in die göttliche Machtsphäre zu schwingen. Das wird bereits aus seiner Neigung deutlich, himmelsstrebende Bäume zu bewohnen.

Mit dem Aufblühen städtischer Märkte begegnete der mittelalterliche Mensch lebenden Affen im Geleit von Akrobaten und Gauklern. Wer die Tiere leibhaftig sah, konnte sich einer leisen Sympathie nicht erwehren. Das Image des „Leibhaftigen" bröckelte und wich langsam „humaneren" Deutungen. Der Affe galt alsbald nicht mehr als der Satan selbst, sondern als dessen Opfer. So verweist der Spruch „sich einen Affen antrinken" auf die Neigung zu weltlichen Freuden, der Sünder gerne erliegen. Und als Wunschziel aller „schludrigen" Faulpelze und Schlemmer galt das „Schlur-affenland".

Bis ins Spätmittelalter verknotete sich konkrete Artenkenntnis durch Reiseberichte über Affen und fremde Völker zu einem grotesken Gewirr von zoologischer Information und Legenden. Ausführlich wurde über behaarte aufrechte Wesen fabuliert, die in Höhlen und Dschungeln ferner Länder hausten – speziell ab dem 17. Jahrhundert, als die Kolonialmächte Europas ihre Flotten um den Globus schickten. Erst im 20. Jahrhundert sollte sich die Sage von haarigen Tiermenschen in halbwegs korrekte zoologische Systematik auflösen. Denn erst jetzt wurden Orang-Utans, Gorillas, Schimpansen und Bonobos nicht nur voneinander, sondern auch von kleinwüchsigen Menschenvölkern unterschieden.

Kein Wunder, dass der schwedische Biologe Carolus Linnaeus nur mühsam erste Ordnung in das Chaos phantastischer Affengeschichten bringen konnte. Mit seinem *Systema Naturae* von 1735 erfand Linné eine bis heute gültige Benennung von Pflanzen und Tieren: die „binäre Nomenklatur" aus vorangestelltem Gattungs- und nachfolgendem Artnamen. In der zehnten Auflage von 1758 schloss er mehrere Gattungen zu einer Ordnung der *Primates* zusammen, den „Vorrangigen", im Deutschen noch unbescheidener übersetzt als „Herrentiere". Hierzu zählten die Genera *Homo* (Mensch), *Simia* (Affen) und *Lemur* (Halbaffen). Zu *Homo* stellte Linné *Homo sapiens,* den Menschen, und zunächst auch *Homo troglodytes,* einen „Höhlenmenschen", der Züge der noch weitgehend sagenhaften Menschenaffen trug.

Für den gläubigen Christen Linné hatte ein Schöpfergott die abgestufte Ähnlichkeit der Arten wundersam hervorgebracht. Dennoch war er fortschrittlicher als manche Nachfolger, die Menschen aufgrund ihres aufrechten Ganges und ihrer geistigen Fähigkeiten wieder aus der Ordnung der Primaten ausgliederten. Statt nach Ähnlichkeiten wurde deshalb nach *Humana* gesucht, nach Merkmalen, die unsere Einzigartigkeit belegen sollten. Der Göttinger Anthropologe Johann Friedrich Blumenbach etwa trennte zwischen *Bimana* (Zweihänder) und *Quadrumana* (Vierhänder), während der deutsche Zoologe Karl Illiger die *Erecta* (Aufrechte) einführte und der englische Urzeitforscher Richard Owen die *Archencephala* (überlegene Gehirne).

Diese Begriffe waren allesamt kurzlebig. Genauere Forschung förderte stattdessen mehr und mehr Gemeinsames in der Körperorganisation von Menschen und nicht-menschlichen Primaten zutage. Der vermeintliche Angriff auf die Würde des Menschen erfuhr eine heftige Steigerung in den Werken Charles Darwins, behauptete der englische Naturforscher doch, die Vielfalt der Organismen sei nicht Werk eines Schöpfers, sondern habe sich allmählich aus Urformen entwickelt. Dank Darwin wissen wir nun, *warum* wir anderen Affen so nahe stehen: Wir teilen über weite Strecken eine gemeinsame Stammesgeschichte.

Als Darwin 1859 seine Evolutionslehre ausbreitete, ließ er sein epochales Buch *Über die Entstehung der Arten* so vorsichtig wie programmatisch ausklingen: „Licht wird auch fallen auf den Menschen und seine Geschichte." Darwin zögerte zwölf Jahre, seine Erkenntnisse öffentlich auf den Menschen anzuwenden. Erst 1871 folgte *Die Abstammung des Menschen,* mit der expliziten Behauptung, dass Menschen von affenartigen Vorfahren abstammen.

Bis heute wird Darwins Lehre angegriffen, weil sie ein vertrautes Schema auf den Kopf stellt. Gemäß der Bibel hatte der Schöpfer den ersten Menschen engelgleich geschaffen, und erst die Sünde brachte ihn zu Fall. Darwin kehrte diesen Abstieg von den Engeln um in einen Aufstieg von den Affen. Aus einer schmeichelhaften Devolution machte er eine ernüchternde Evolution. Dagegen polemisierte ein prominenter Zeitgenosse Darwins, der Politiker und zeitweilige Premier Benjamin Disraeli: „Die Frage lautet: Ist der Mensch ein Affe oder ein Engel? Mein Gott, ich bin auf der Seite der Engel."

Wenn Menschen sich gefühlsmäßig wehren, „vom Affen abzustammen", tun sie das oft aus dem Missverständnis heraus, ihre Vorfahren seien unter heutigen Affenarten zu finden. Das ist nicht so. Vielmehr sind wir – wie alle anderen lebenden Primaten – abgewandelte Modelle vormaliger Urformen.

Ebenfalls irreführend ist der Gedanke, die Stammformen seien „Vorstufen" oder „niedere" Kreaturen. Das ist schon deshalb unplausibel, weil Lebewesen zu allen Zeiten, in denen sie existieren, voll funktions- und konkurrenzfähig sein müssen. Deshalb lässt sich Evolution auch nicht mit Fortschritt gleichsetzen. Selbst Darwins Werke sind nicht ganz frei von diesem Stufendenken, war er doch ein Kind seiner Zeit: Der viktorianischen Ära mit ihrer Hierarchie von primitiven und zivilisierten Völkern und ihrem ungezügelten Glauben an stetige technische Verbesserung im Zuge der industriellen Revolution.

Wenn eine veränderte Umwelt eine Umstrukturierung des Köperbaus vorteilhaft macht, wäre das Motto „Wegen Umbau geschlossen" gleichbedeutend mit Aussterben. Nachbesserungen müssen vielmehr mit laufendem Motor vorgenommen werden. Statt wie ein Architekt mit einem brandneuen Entwurf zu arbeiten, muss die Evolution wie ein Bastler vorgehen und das Beste aus verfügbarem Material machen. Das ist übrigens ein schlagkräftiges Argument gegen den Gottesbeweis vom „intelligenten Design". Denn wenn überhaupt, dann zeugt die Konstruktion vieler Organismen von „unintelligentem Design".

Wir Menschen sind ein gutes Beispiel. Der Wechsel zum Bodenleben und aufrechtem Gang gilt als Schlüsselereignis unserer Evolution, doch war der Wandel nur um den Preis einiger Schwachstellen zu haben. Bereits 1770 deutete der italienische Anatom Peter Moscati Leiden wie Krampfadern und Hämorrhoiden als Konstruktionsprobleme eines aufrecht gehenden Wesens. Weil erhebliches Gewicht auf den knorpeligen Verbindungen zwischen den Lendenwirbeln ruht, wird zudem ihr gallertartiger Kern oft herausgedrängt, wodurch sich Bandscheibenvorfälle erklären. Und die schwere Geburt – mit der sich andere Menschenaffen nicht plagen – geht auf die stetige Vergrößerung des Gehirns und damit des Kopfumfangs zurück. Die Alternative – eine Erweiterung des Beckens – würde

Watscheln erzwingen und damit Probleme beim Gehen. Der Philosoph Immanuel Kant kommentierte, diese Ungemächlichkeiten des Menschen entsprängen eben daraus, „dass er sein Haupt über seine alten Kameraden so stolz erhoben hat".

Stammbäume können nicht nur über Fossilien und anatomische Studien rekonstruiert werden, sondern ebenfalls über Vergleiche von Verhalten. Bereits vor 100 Jahren versuchte der Naturforscher Eugène Marais solche Einsichten umzusetzen, als er in Südafrika Pavianhorden beobachtete: „Niemand kann auch nur in die Nähe einer echten Vorstellung des Unbewussten im Menschen kommen, der nicht die Primaten in ihrer natürlichen Umwelt kennt…"

Ein „goldenes Zeitalter" der Freilandprimatologie initiierte Louis Leakey. Der 1903 als Missionarssohn in Kenia geborene Urmenschenforscher ermunterte drei mittlerweile zu Legenden gewordene junge Frauen, Menschenaffen in ihren wilden Heimaten zu beobachten. Die scherzhaft als „Trimates" bezeichneten Forscherinnen fanden in der „grünen Hölle" ihr Paradies. Zunächst machte sich um 1960 die 26jährige Britin Jane Goodall zu den Schimpansen auf, 1967 die 35jährige Amerikanerin Dian Fossey zu den Berggorillas, und 1971 die 25jährige Kanadierin Biruté Galdikas zu den Orang-Utans. Ihre Pioniertaten inspirierten Generationen jüngerer Forscher, die heute in Urwäldern und Savannen rings um den Äquator Affenforschung betreiben.

In dem Maße, wie wir das Leben anderer Primaten verstehen, können wir jene Entwicklung nachzeichnen, die in die „Hominisation", die Menschwerdung, mündete. Denn quasi als „Stellvertreter" spiegeln heute lebende Affen Trends wider, die zu jenem Ast am Stammbaum führten, von dem aus sich die Menschenaffen verzweigten. Diese wissenschaftlichen Geschichten sind mindestens ebenso faszinierend wie die fabelhaften.

1. Historie(s)

Discovery of a Relationship

Since ancient times, people have been fascinated by those animals who look most similar to them. For once, sober science agrees with the naive view. In this respect – how we became what we are – monkeys place a mirror directly in front of us.

In India, langur monkeys have been long considered sacred. The ancient epic *Ramayana* tells how one of them enabled Lord Rama's victory over the demon king. As the brave monkey general Hanuman torched the villain's home, his hands, feet and face were burned. The otherwise silvery fur of langur monkeys is black in exactly these spots. This identifies them as descendants of the heroic Hanuman – and that is why devout Hindus feed langurs in groves and temples.

In ancient Egypt, baboons were kept as incarnations of the god Anubis and mummified after their death. Their conspicuous menstrual bleedings made them also companions of the moon god Thoth, given that this deity likewise underwent cyclical fluctuations.

While monkeys were idolised by certain civilisations, they were vilified by others – especially by early Christians, whose monotheism also served to distance the believers from pagan animal cults. The human-like appearance of monkeys was seen as hubris, an arrogant and sinful desire to defy one's destiny. Such was also the rebellious quest of the devil. Thus we read in the biblical book of *Isaiah* about Lucifer's fall: "I will ascend above the tops of the clouds; I will make myself like the Most High – *similis ero altissimo*". The Latin word *simia* (monkey) was commonly seen to be rooted in *similitudo* (similarity).

The Abbess Hildegard of Bingen in 1150 stressed the monkey's reprehensible conflict: "Because he has a certain similarity with humans, he always imitates what the latter does. He also has the animal nature in himself so that he can neither fully do what man does nor what animals do. When watching a bird, he jumps up and tries to fly. But because he can't fulfill his wish, rage immediately overcomes him." The monkey's dream stands for the outrageous ambition of man to soar, birdlike, into the divine sphere. This is already indicated by the monkey's habit of living in trees that strive towards the sky.

When urban markets began to flourish, medieval minds encountered monkeys in the company of acrobats and jugglers. Anyone who saw these animals in the flesh could not help but feel a slight sympathy and affinity. The image of "the evil one" gave gradually way to more "humane" interpretations. Monkeys were no longer incarnations of the Satan himself, but his victims. Sayings such as "to have a monkey on one's back" for somebody who is drunk refers to those worldly pleasures to which sinners easily succumb. In German, the imaginary abode of those who indulge in luxury and idleness became known as *Schlaraffenland*: "land of lazy monkeys".

By the late Middle Ages, knowledge about particular species and travel reports about monkeys and exotic peoples became mixed into a grotesque concoction of zoological information and legends. Fables about hairy and upright creatures that populated caves and jungles of distant shores were especially popular – particularly after Europe's 17th-century colonial powers sent their fleets around the globe. Only in the 20th century were legends of hairy "manimals" replaced by a more or less correct zoological nomenclature. For now not only were orangutans, gorillas, chimpanzees and bonobos distinguished from each other, but also from diminutive humans.

No wonder the Swedish biologist Carolus Linnaeus struggled when he first tried to bring order to the chaos of fantastic monkey stories. In his *Systema Naturae* of 1735, Linnaeus introduced a method of naming plants and animals still valid today: the „binary nomenclature" of a prefix indicating the genus and a subsequent species name. In the tenth edition of 1758, he subsumed several genera into the order of "primates": the "first" or "highest". These included *Homo* (humans), *Simia* (monkey) and *Lemur* (prosimians). The genus *Homo* not only encompassed the species *Homo sapiens,* i.e., humans, but initially also a *Homo troglodytes,* a "cave man" that exhibited traits of the still largely mythical apes.

As a faithful Christian, Linnaeus believed that God wondrously had created the graded similarity of species. Yet he was more progressive than some of his successors, who once again removed humans from the primate order based on criteria such as our upright posture and mental abilities. Instead of focussing on similarities, they searched for *Humana,* features that should prove our uniqueness. The 18th-century Göttingen anthropologist Johann Friedrich Blumenbach, for example, distinguished *Bimana* (two-handers) from *Quadrumana* (four-handers), while the *Erecta* (Upright) were introduced by his contemporary, the German zoologist Karl Illiger, alongside the 19th-century notion of *Archencephala* (superior minds), conceived by the English palaeontologist Richard Owen.

All of these concepts were short-lived. Instead, detailed research revealed more and more commonalities in the physical organization of human and non-human primates. The alleged attack upon the dignity of man was sharply stepped up in the works of Charles Darwin, as the English naturalist claimed that the variety of organisms had not been created, but gradually developed from primitive forms. Thanks to Darwin, we now know *why* we are so close to other primates: We share a long history of descent.

When Darwin published his theory of evolution in 1859, his landmark book *On the Origin of Species* ended cautiously as well as programmatically: "Light will be thrown on the origin of man and his history." Darwin hesitated for twelve years to apply his findings publicly to humans. *The Descent of Man* appeared in only 1871, with the explicit assertion that humans descended from ape-like ancestors.

To this day, Darwin's theory is under attack because it turns a familiar pattern on its head. According to the Bible, the first human was created as almost an angel, and only primeval sin brought him down. Darwin reversed this relegation from the angels into an ascent from the apes. A flattering devolution was made into a sobering evolution. This invited a polemical retort by a prominent contemporary of Darwin, the politician and occasional prime minister Benjamin Disraeli: "The question is this: is man an ape or an angel? I, my Lord, I am on the side of the angels."

People will often emotionally deny that they "descend from apes" because they wrongly assert that their ancestors are to be found among today's primates. This is not so. Rather, we are – like all other living primates – modified models of past forms.

Also misleading is the idea that these progenitors were "precursors" or "lower" life forms. This is erroneous, because living things must be fully functional and competitive whenever they exist. Therefore, evolution cannot easily be equated with progress. Even Darwin's writings are not entirely free from such thoughts, given that he was a child of his time, the Victorian era, with its hierarchy of primitive and civilized peoples and its unbridled belief in constant technological improvements in the course of the Industrial Revolution.

If environmental changes render a restructuring of the anatomy advantageous, a slogan "closed for renovation" would be synonymous with extinction. Improvements must rather be executed with the engine running. Instead of relying on a brand-new design, as an architect would do, evolution must proceed as a tinkerer and make the most of available material. This is a powerful argument against a proof of God's existence through "intelligent design". Because if anything, many organisms display an "unintelligent design".

We humans are a good example. The switch to a terrestrial and bipedal lifestyle is considered a key event in our evolution, but the change was at the cost of considerable weaknesses. As early as 1770, the Italian anatomist Peter Moscati suggested that conditions such as varicose veins and haemorrhoids were construction problems of a being that walked upright. Considerable weight rests on the cartilaginous joints between the lumbar vertebrae. Accordingly, their gelatinous core is often squeezed out, thereby explaining herniated discs. And a difficult birth – not experienced by other apes – dates back to a steady increase in brain volume and thus of the head circumference. The alternative – an enlargement of the pelvis – would have led to waddling and thus to problems with locomotion. The philosopher Immanuel Kant commented that these discomforts were consequences of the fact that man "raised his head so proudly over his old comrades".

Evolutionary trees can be reconstructed not only through fossils and anatomical studies, but also based on comparisons of behaviour. Already 100 years ago the naturalist Eugène Marais tried to implement such insights while observing hordes of baboons in South Africa: "No man can ever attain to anywhere near a true conception of the subconscious in man who does not know the primates under natural conditions."

A "golden age" of field primatology was initiated by the palaeoanthropologist Louis Leakey, born to a missionary in Kenya in 1903. Leakey encouraged three young women to observe wild apes in their natural habitats. All have meanwhile become legends. Jokingly referred to as "trimates", these researchers found their paradise in the "green hell". A 26-year-old English woman, Jane Goodall, went out to study chimpanzees in 1960. The 35-year-old American Dian Fossey followed in 1967 with investigations of mountain gorillas. Finally, the 25-year-old Canadian Biruté Galdikas began with her observations of orangutans in 1971. Their pioneering work inspired generations of younger scientists who now study primates in jungles and savannahs north and south of the equator.

The better we understand how other primates live, the better we can reconstruct the process of "hominisation", the development of the human race. This is because living primates reflect those trends which led to that very branch on the evolutionary tree from which apes would divert. These modern scientific stories are as fascinating as the antique fables.

Bonobo / *bonobo*

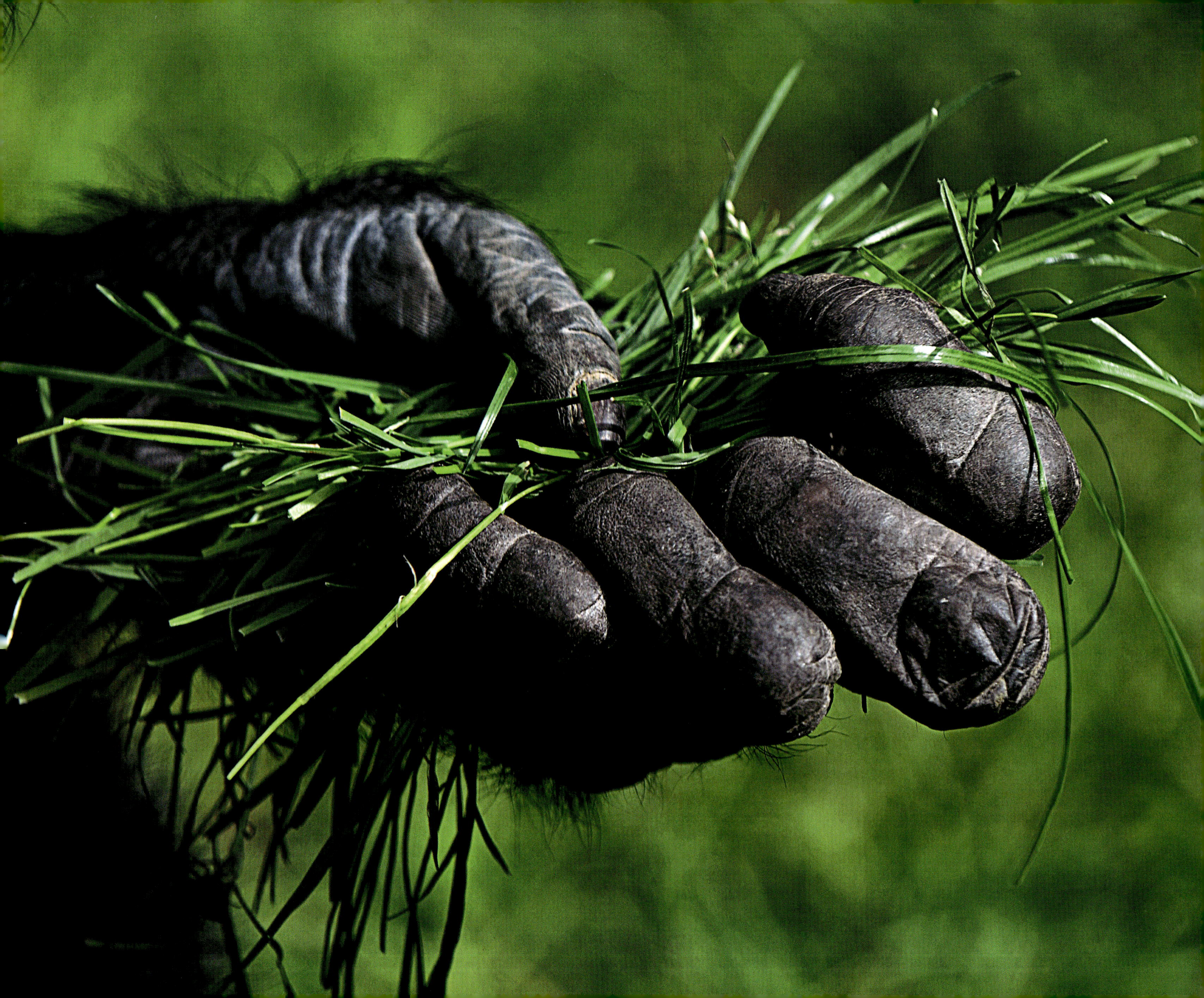

Primaten
Primates

Bonobo / *bonobo*

Bonobo / *bonobo*

2. Primaten

Anleitung zur Selbsterkenntnis

„Nosce te ipsum! – Erkenne Dich selbst!" Die hehre Aufforderung des antiken Orakels zu Delphi stellte Linné der von ihm neukreierten Gattung *Homo* bei, statt sie, wie es der schwedische Naturforscher bei allen anderen Tiergruppen tat, über zumindest ein spezifisches anatomisches Merkmal zu definieren. Linné glaubte nicht, dass ein grundsätzlicher Unterschied zu den Nachbargruppen seines *Systema Naturae* – den Halbaffen und Affen – feststellbar sei. Die separate Gattung *Homo* führte er nur ein, um den zu erwartenden Widerstand gegen die Eingliederung der Menschen ins Tierreich abzumildern. Sein „Nosce te ipsum!" war somit ein Schachzug – der uns in der Tat eine erweiterte Selbsterkenntnis beschert hat.

Zur Gattung *Homo* des Linnaeus zählten Menschen und Menschenaffen. Die Aufmerksamkeit, die wir diesen uns am nächsten stehenden Primaten entgegenbringen, nährt sich auch heute noch über das Interesse am Werdegang des Menschengeschlechts. Die verständliche Selbstbezogenheit sollte uns jedoch nicht hindern, Menschenaffen ihr ganz eigenes Lebensrecht zuzubilligen. Damit gäbe es doppelten Grund, sich mit ihnen zu beschäftigen: Um unserer und ihrer selbst willen.

Wer verstehen will, was Menschenaffen und Menschen verbindet, sollte dies auf dem Hintergrund ihres gemeinsamen zoologischen Erbes tun: Dass sie nämlich Primaten sind. Diese Ordnung der Säugetiere umfasst ungefähr 400 Arten einer breiten und vielfältigen Formenskala. Sie schließt den 50 Gramm leichten Mausmaki ebenso ein wie einen 350 kg schweren Zoogorilla, das nachtschwarze Fingertier ebenso wie den kunterbunten Kleideraffen.

Die Vielfalt spiegelt das evolutionäre Erfolgsrezept der Primaten wider. Weniger als in anderen Ordnungen diktieren starre genetische Vorgaben bestimmte Lebensräume und Lebensweisen. Vielmehr sind Primaten ökologisch, sozial und mental flexibel. Diese Anpassungsfähigkeit ist bei Menschen extrem ausgebildet und erlaubte unserer Spezies, alle Kontinente zu besiedeln.

Als vor etwa 70 Millionen Jahren die Dinosaurier ausstarben, begann der Aufstieg der Primaten – vermutlich, weil die ursprünglich nachtaktiven Säugetiere nun auch tagsüber weniger Konkurrenz hatten. Gegenwärtig in Asien, Afrika und Südamerika beheimatet, lebten nicht-menschliche Primaten vormals auch in Europa, im Mittleren Osten und vom Westen der jetzigen USA bis in die Spitze Südamerikas. Heute finden sie sich vornehmlich in den Tropen. Hier schwankt die Temperatur zwar stark zwischen Tag und Nacht, ist über das Jahr hinweg jedoch relativ konstant. Primaten meiden saisonal harsches Klima. Gleichwohl können manche im Schnee überleben – so die Berberaffen Nordafrikas, die Stumpfnasen im Süden Chinas und die berühmten Japan-Makaken, die sich im Schneewinter zuweilen in heiße Quellen zurückziehen.

Der Stammbaum der Primaten umfasst zwei große Zweige. Der erste Formenkreis schließt die *Feuchtnasenaffen* ein. Diese meist nachtaktiven Arten profitieren von einem guten Geruchssinn, der von Schleimhäuten im Bereich der Nasenlöcher unterstützt wird. Zu ihnen zählen Lemuren, Loris und Galagos, relativ kleine „Halbaffen" in Afrika und Asien. Alle anderen Primaten gehören zum zweiten Formenkreis, den *Trockennasenaffen*. Hierzu zählen zunächst als weitere Halbaffen die nachtaktiven Koboldmakis Südostasiens. Fast alle anderen Arten sind tagaktiv und stellen die eigentlichen „Affen" dar. Die teilen sich wiederum in zwei Gruppen auf. Da sind einerseits die in Latein- und Mittelamerika beheimateten *Neuweltaffen*, darunter Krallen-, Brüll-, Kapuziner- und Klammeraffen. Andererseits leben in Afrika und Asien die *Altweltaffen*. Sie schließen Schlankaffen, Makaken, Meerkatzen, Drills oder Paviane ein, sowie die „Menschenähnlichen", zu denen Menschenaffen und unsere eigene Spezies zählen.

Primaten fehlen übergreifende spezielle Merkmale, deshalb sind sie schwer als eigene „Einheit" gegen andere zoologische Ordnungen abzugrenzen. Alle sind lebendgebärend und Junge saugen Milch aus mütterlichen Drüsen. Das zeichnet jedoch alle Formen von Säugetieren aus. Ein Durchschnittsprimat lässt sich jedenfalls nicht anhand eines Einzelmerkmales charakterisieren, sondern ein ansehnlicher Katalog ist vonnöten.

Beispielsweise wird das Gebiss beim Erwachsenwerden einmal gewechselt. In jeder Hälfte von Ober- und Unterkiefer befinden sich maximal zwei Schneidezähne und ein Eckzahn, sowie drei Vorbacken- und drei Backenzähne (Zahnformel 2.1.3.3.). Altweltaffen einschließlich Menschenaffen reduzierten die Vorbackenzähne auf eine Zahnformel von 2.1.2.3. Derlei verschiedene Zahntypen belegen, dass nicht Spezialisierung das übergreifende Prinzip ist, sondern Verzehr diverser Nahrung, die oft Früchte, Blätter, Blüten, Samen und Insekten einschließt.

Obwohl sich viele Arten sicher über den Boden fortbewegen, steht das Talent, Bäume zu erklettern, an der Wurzel des Stammbaums. Greifhände und -füße, mit denen auch schwerere Tiere Äste sicher umfassen konnten, erlaubten frühen Primaten, Wälder zu ihrer Domäne zu machen. Halbaffen verfügen meist lediglich über einen „Ganzhand-Griff", bei dem sich automatisch alle Handstrahlen zugleich schließen. Die meisten „echten" Affen sind fingerfertiger und können Gegenstände zwischen den einzeln beweglichen Fingerkuppen halten. Bei Menschenaffen erlaubt Abspreizen und freie Beweglichkeit des Daumens einen feinen „Präzisionsgriff". Die ausstellbare Großzehe ging bei Menschen mit dem Wechsel vom Baumleben (Arborealität) zum Bodenleben (Terrestrialität) verloren. Diesbezüglich unterschiedliche Versionen finden sich bei Menschenaffen: Das Baumleben ist bei Orang-Utans am ausgeprägtesten, Gorillas sind sehr terrestrisch, während Schimpansen und Bonobos eine Mittelstellung einnehmen. Anstelle ursprünglicher Krallen traten allmählich Plattnägel. Diese Versteifungen an Fingern und Zehen erhöhen ebenso wie die zahlreichen Schweißdrüsen die Griffestigkeit. Wir helfen dieser Funktion nach, wenn wir vor dem Schaufeln in die Hände spucken. Die Handteller sind zudem mit Hautleisten überzogen, die wie das Haftprofil von Autoreifen wirken und eine sichere „Be-Handlung" und Erkundung von Objekten ermöglichen. Mittels dieses Vielzweckwerkzeuges gewannen schließlich Menschen die Oberhand über die Erde.

Nachtaktive Primaten orientieren sich vornehmlich durch Gehör und Geruch. Bei tagaktiven Primaten inklusive Menschenaffen bildeten sich die Riechschleimhäute des feuchten Nasenspiegels sowie das Riechzentrum im Großhirn zurück. Stattdessen wurde der Gesichtssinn wichtiger. Bei vielen Säugetieren stehen die Augen seitlich am Kopf. Die Sichtfelder überlappen kaum, so dass jedes Auge seine Umgebung flächig erfasst. Für Fortbewegung auf ebenem Boden wie bei Pferden oder Antilopen ist das dienlich. Bei Primaten rückten die Augen hingegen enger zusammen, wodurch die Gesichtsfelder überlappen. Das zweiäugige Sehen gewinnt damit eine räumliche Dimension. Die dreidimensionale Perspektive ist besonders nützlich bei Handhabungen und um Entfernungen im Geäst abzuschätzen.

Die Welt erscheint den meisten Säugetieren ziemlich grau in grau. In der Netzhaut tagaktiver Primaten hingegen sind gewöhnlich die Zapfen vermehrt, jene Sinneszellen, die Farben und scharfes Sehen vermitteln. Ursprünglich mag Farbensehen nützlich gewesen sein, um etwa reife gelbe Feigen besser gegen grüne Blätter ausmachen zu können. Bunte Signale spielten jedoch auch zunehmend im Sozialen eine Rolle. Die Palette reicht jedenfalls von rot-grün-blauen Genitalien der Meerkatzen über den sanduhrförmigen roten Brustfleck des Gelada-Pavians bis zur schrillen Nasenfärbung der Mandrills. Da leuchtende Farben Gesundheit und genetische Qualität anzeigen, ist nur verständlich, dass kluge Tiere wie Menschen sich gern mit fremden Federn schmücken – von Schmuck und Kriegsbemalung bis hin zu Makeup.

Verglichen mit ähnlich schwergewichtigen Säugern ist das Gehirn von Primaten und speziell das von Menschen ziemlich groß. Diese Aussage ist allerdings mit Vorsicht zu genießen. Denn absolut gesehen sind die Gehirne natürlicher Giganten wie Elefanten viermal schwerer als die von Menschen und die mancher Wale gar fünfmal. Primaten sind auch dann nicht unbedingt Spitze, wenn das Verhältnis von Hirn- zu Körpergewicht berechnet wird. Wird das entsprechende Ergebnis für die Spitzmaus gleich 1.0 gesetzt, so erreicht der Mensch den Rekordwert 29. Den Wert für Schimpansen von 11 übertreffen hingegen mit 20 lässig die Delphine – obwohl dies vielleicht nur ein weniger „dichtgepacktes" Gehirn anzeigt, weil mehr Körpergewicht für Wasserbewohner nicht mit entsprechenden „Tragekosten" einhergeht. Als „neuester" Gehirnabschnitt ist die Großhirnrinde bei Menschenaffen und speziell Menschen besonders ausgeprägt und überwuchert andere Teile fast vollständig. Diese „Neurinde" – der Neocortex – ist stark gefurcht und gefaltet, was die Oberfläche vergrößert. Als Grundlage für ein besonders leistungsfähiges Lern- und Erinnerungsvermögen eröffnet dieses Areal erweiterte Dimensionen technologischer und sozialer Rafinesse.

Verglichen mit Säugetieren ähnlicher Größe ist die Schwangerschaft bei Primaten ausgedehnt, die Wurfgröße klein und die Zeit bis zum Erwachsenwerden lang. Zwillingsgeburten kommen zwar bei manchen Halbaffen und den kleinwüchsigen Krallenaffen regelmäßig vor. Alle anderen Affen und Menschenaffen bringen jedoch fast immer nur Einlinge zur Welt. Diese Strategie der Vermehrung setzt also zunehmend statt auf Quantität (was mit hoher Sterblichkeit der Nachkommen verknüpft ist) auf Qualität (was ein verstärktes Umkümmern der Kleinkinder verlangt).

Der Lebensentwurf von Primaten zielt somit auf ein hohes Alter, wofür ein Gehirn gebraucht wird, das sich auf plötzlich wechselnde Umweltbedingungen einstellen kann. Primaten entwickelten dafür einen Lebensabschnitt, der spielerisches Ausprobieren erlaubt und in dem man auf die Nase fallen kann, um sich schließlich umso besser in der Welt zurechtzufinden: das Jugendstadium. Vermutlich erweitern nicht nur Menschen, sondern auch nicht-menschliche Primaten in ihrer Jugend den engen Horizont des Hier-und-Jetzt, indem sie phantasievoll Sphären des Möglichen erproben. Ähnlich wie Menschenkinder mit Puppen spielen, tragen beispielsweise manche Schimpansenkinder kleine Knüppel herum, die sie sorgsam behandeln und mit ins Schlafnest legen – genauso, wie es eine Schimpansenmutter mit ihrem Sprössling tut.

Von Ausnahmen abgesehen sind Primaten ihrer Organisation nach somit Generalisten, sowohl in Anatomie wie im Verhalten. Ihre Spezialisierung ist die Unspezialisiertheit. Dies trifft umso mehr auf Menschenaffen zu.

Ein Artenvergleich innerhalb der Primaten fördert jedenfalls zutage, dass sowohl unser Körperbau wie unser Verhalten und Denken tief in äffischem Erbe wurzelt. Qualitäten, die als typisch menschlich gelten, entstanden in kleinen Schritten über lange Zeiträume und sind keine exklusiv menschlichen Merkmale. Das heißt also, es ist nicht trennscharf auszumachen, wann der Mensch anfing und der Affe aufhörte – und speziell nicht der Menschenaffe.

Bonobo / *bonobo*

2. Primates

Know Thyself

"Nosce te ipsum!" The noble call of the ancient oracle at Delphi was chosen by Linnaeus as a substitute for a description of his newly created genus *Homo*. Instead of defining *Homo* through at least one specific anatomical feature, as the Swedish naturalist did for all other animal groups, Linnaeus believed that one could not identify a fundamental difference between *Homo* and the neighbouring groups of his *Systema Naturae:* the lemurs and monkeys. He only introduced the separate genus to alleviate anticipated resistance to his integration of humans into the animal kingdom. His *"Nosce te ipsum! – Know thyself!"* was thus a tactical move – a gambit that presents us, indeed, with an enhanced understanding of ourselves.

Linnaeus' genus *Homo* included humans and apes. The attention we shower upon our closest primate relatives is to this very date fed by our interest in the evolutionary career of the human race. Such self-reference is understandable, but should not prevent us to concede autonomy to the apes. There is thus a twofold reason to study them: for our and their own sake.

An understanding of what connects apes and humans is best based on the background of their common zoological heritage: namely, that they are primates. This order of mammals encompasses approximately 400 species of a wide and varied scale. It includes a 50-gram specimen of a mouse lemur as well as a zoo-dwelling gorilla that grew to 350 kg and the entirely black-furred aye-aye as well as the fanciful coloured Douc langur.

The diversity reflects the recipe for the evolutionary success of primates. Less than other animal orders does their basic genetic makeup constrain them to a narrow range of habitats and lifestyles. Rather, primates are flexible: environmentally, socially and mentally. Humans express this malleability to an extreme degree, thus enabling our species to colonise every continent.

The ascent of primates began some 70 million years ago, when dinosaurs went extinct – presumably because the initially nocturnal mammals now faced less competition during the day. Currently found in Asia, Africa and South America, non-human primates lived previously also throughout Europe, the Middle East and from western North America to the tip of South America. Today, they are mainly distributed in the tropics. Here, temperatures vary greatly between day and night, but are relatively constant throughout the year. Primates therefore tend to avoid extremely seasonal climates. However, some can survive in snow – for example North Africa's Barbary macaques, the snub-nosed monkeys of Southern China, as well as the famous Japanese macaques, which may at times enter hot springs to escape heavy snow.

The family tree of primates supports two major branches. The first group is called *strepsirhini*, the "wet-nosed" primates. These species are mostly nocturnal and benefit from a good sense of smell, which is enabled by a mucous membrane around the nostrils. They include lemurs, galagos and lorises, relatively small *prosimians* in Africa and Asia. All other primates belong to a second group, the *haplorhini* or "dry-nosed" primates. These include a further type of nocturnal prosimians, the tarsiers of Southeast Asia. Almost all other haplorhine species are diurnal, representing the "true" monkeys, also termed *anthropoids.* These are again divided into two kinds. Species native to Latin and Central America are called *New World monkeys* and encompass forms such as marmosets and tamarins, capuchin, howler and spider monkeys. Species that live in Africa and Asia are called *Old World monkeys.* Amongst these are langur, colobus and snub-nosed monkeys, macaques, guenons, drills and baboons – as well the *Hominoidea,* which include the apes and our own species.

Primates are difficult to distinguish as a separate "unit" from other zoological orders, as they lack typical special features. All give birth to live young who suckle milk from mammary glands. However, these are also characteristics of other mammals. It is therefore not possible to define the average primate through a single trait. A considerable catalogue is required.

For example, primate dentition is changed once during adulthood. Each side of the upper and lower jaw contains a maximum of two incisors and one canine, as well as three premolars and three molars (dental formula 2.1.3.3.). Old World monkeys – including apes – lost one premolar, leading to a dental formula of 2.1.2.3. Such different types of teeth indicate that the overarching principle is not specialisation, but the consumption of various food stuffs, such as fruits, leaves, flowers, seeds or insects.

Although many species can move safely on the ground, it is the talent to climb in which the primate evolutionary tree is rooted. Grasping hands and feet allowed even heavier animals to attach themselves safely to branches, thus making forests their primary domain. If prosimians grip something, all digits of their hand will close at more or less the same time. Most "true" monkeys are more dexterous and can hold objects between individually moveable fingers. In apes, the thumb can often be abducted and freely rotated, thus allowing for a finetuned "precision grip". Humans lost the ability to also abduct their toes during the change from a life in trees (arboreality) to a life on the ground (terrestriality). Various stages of this development are found in apes: arboreality is most pronounced in orangutans, gorillas are the most terrestrial, while chimpanzees and bonobos occupy a middle position.

Claws that assisted early primates with locomotion were gradually replaced by flat nails. These reinforcements on the tips of fingers and toes increase grip security. Sweat glands have the same purpose, and we mimic this when we spit into our palms before using a shovel. Palms are also covered with epidermal ridges that function like the adhesive profile of tires in that they increase the safe handling and exploration of objects. With this multi-purpose tool, humans would ultimately gain the upper hand over Planet Earth that we see today.

Nocturnal primates orient themselves primarily through hearing and smell. Diurnal primates, including apes, experienced a reduction both in the mucous membrane around the nostrils that aids olfaction and in those parts of the brain that process smell. Instead, vision became more important. In many mammals, eyes are located at the side of the skull. Fields of vision thus overlap little, and each eye perceives the surroundings one-dimensionally. This is useful for animals that are active mainly on level ground, such as horses or antelopes. In primates, the eyes moved towards the front of the skull and thus closer together. Such changes added a three-dimensional quality, as the fields of vision overlap. A 3-D binocular view is particularly useful while manipulating objects and estimating distances between branches.

To most mammals, the world appears rather grey. The retina of diurnal primates, however, is populated by an increased numbers of cones. These photoreceptor cells capture colours and provide sharp sight. Originally, colour vision may have aided in identifying ripe fruit against a background of green leaves. But colourful signals soon became more and more important in the social sphere, too. This is exemplified by the red, green and blue genitals of vervet monkeys, the hourglass-shaped red spot on the chest of gelada baboons or the garish nasal colouration of mandrills. Bright colours indicate health and genetic quality. It is therefore quite understandable that intelligent animals such as humans adorn themselves with borrowed plumes – from jewellery and war paint to make-up.

Compared with mammals of similar weight, primates and in particular humans, sport a large brain. This statement, however, should be treated with caution. In absolute terms, brains of natural giants such as elephants are four times and those of some whales five times heavier than those of humans. Primates are also not necessarily the top scorers for relative brain weight, i.e., when the ratio of brain to body weight is calculated. If one uses the value for the tree shrew as a reference point, equal to 1.0, then humans reach a record value of 29. The value of 11 for chimpanzees on the other hand, is clearly outperformed by a score of 20 for dolphins – although this may simply indicate a less "fine" brain because additional weight has less metabolic costs in aquatic animals. The latest addition to the brain, the cerebral cortex, is particularly developed in apes and especially humans, and covers other parts almost completely. This so-called *neocortex* is heavily wrinkled and folded, which increases the surface area. As a basis for particularly powerful capacities of learning and memory, this section opens up new dimensions of technological and social sophistication.

Compared to mammals of a similar size, pregnancy is extended in primates, litter size is small and it takes long to grow to adulthood. Although twin births occur regularly in some lemurs and the diminutive marmosets, all other monkeys and apes almost always produce singletons. Such a strategy of reproduction indicates a shift from quantity (which incurs high offspring mortality) to quality (which requires increased care of infants).

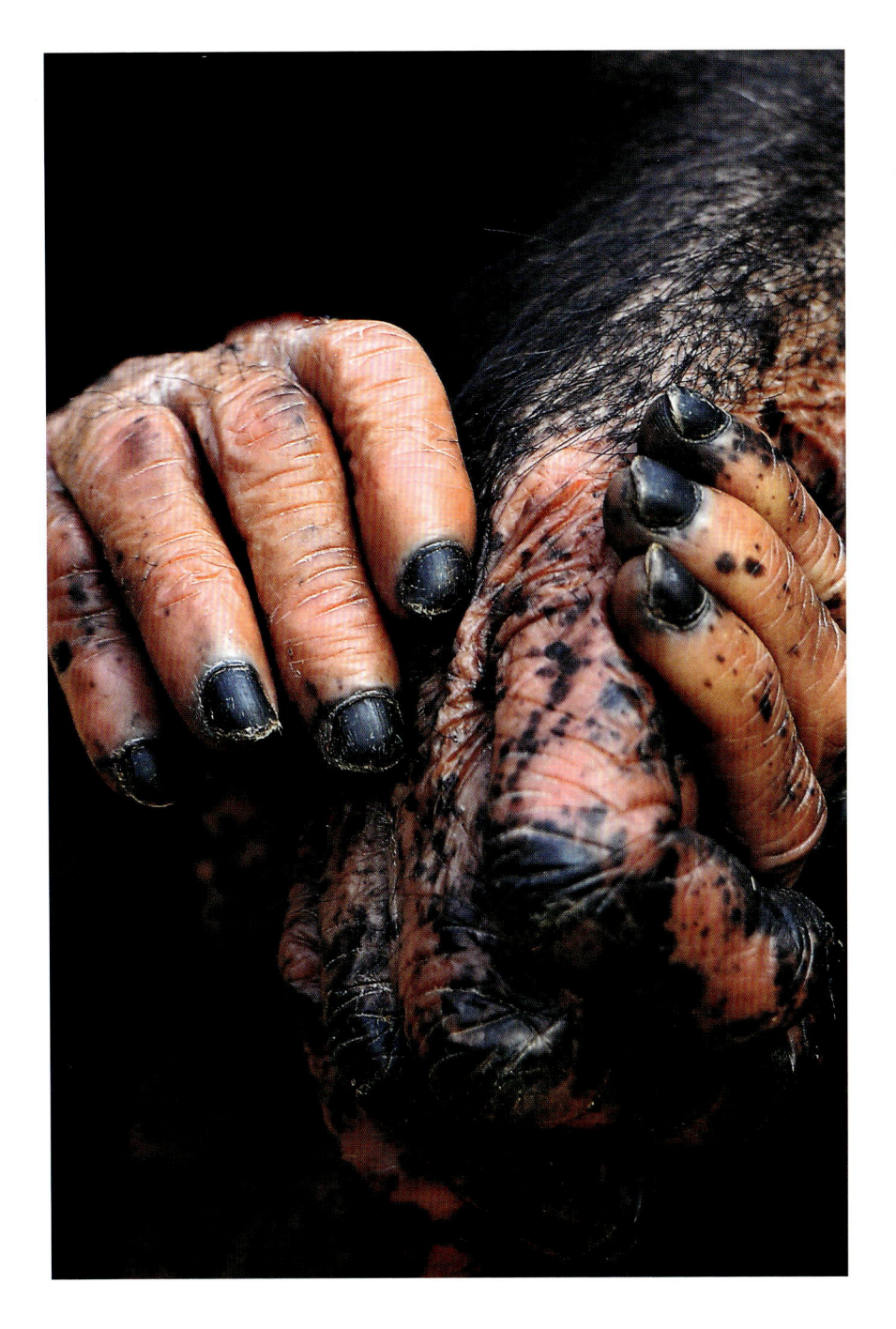

Primate life-histories thus aim to maximise longevity. For this, a brain is needed that can cope with sudden environmental changes. Primates also developed a life stage that allows for experimentation – the juvenile period – because a bloody nose can teach valuable lessons. It is likely that not only humans but also non-human primates expand the narrow horizon of an existence in the here-and-now during their youth by exploring dimensions of possibilities through imagination. For example, while human children play with dolls, young chimpanzees at times carry sticks around; they handle them with care and put them into sleeping nests – just as a chimpanzee mother would do with her offspring.

With some exceptions, primates are therefore generalists, both in anatomy and behaviour. Primates are specialised to be unspecialised – even more so when it comes to apes.

A comparison across the various primate species thus reveals how deeply our body and our mind are rooted in a simian heritage. Typical human qualities evolved in small increments over long periods of time, and they are hardly ever exclusive traits of our species. In other words, it is not possible to pinpoint the exact moment in evolution when we became humans while our inner monkey ceased to exist – and especially not our inner ape.

Schimpanse / *chimpanzee*

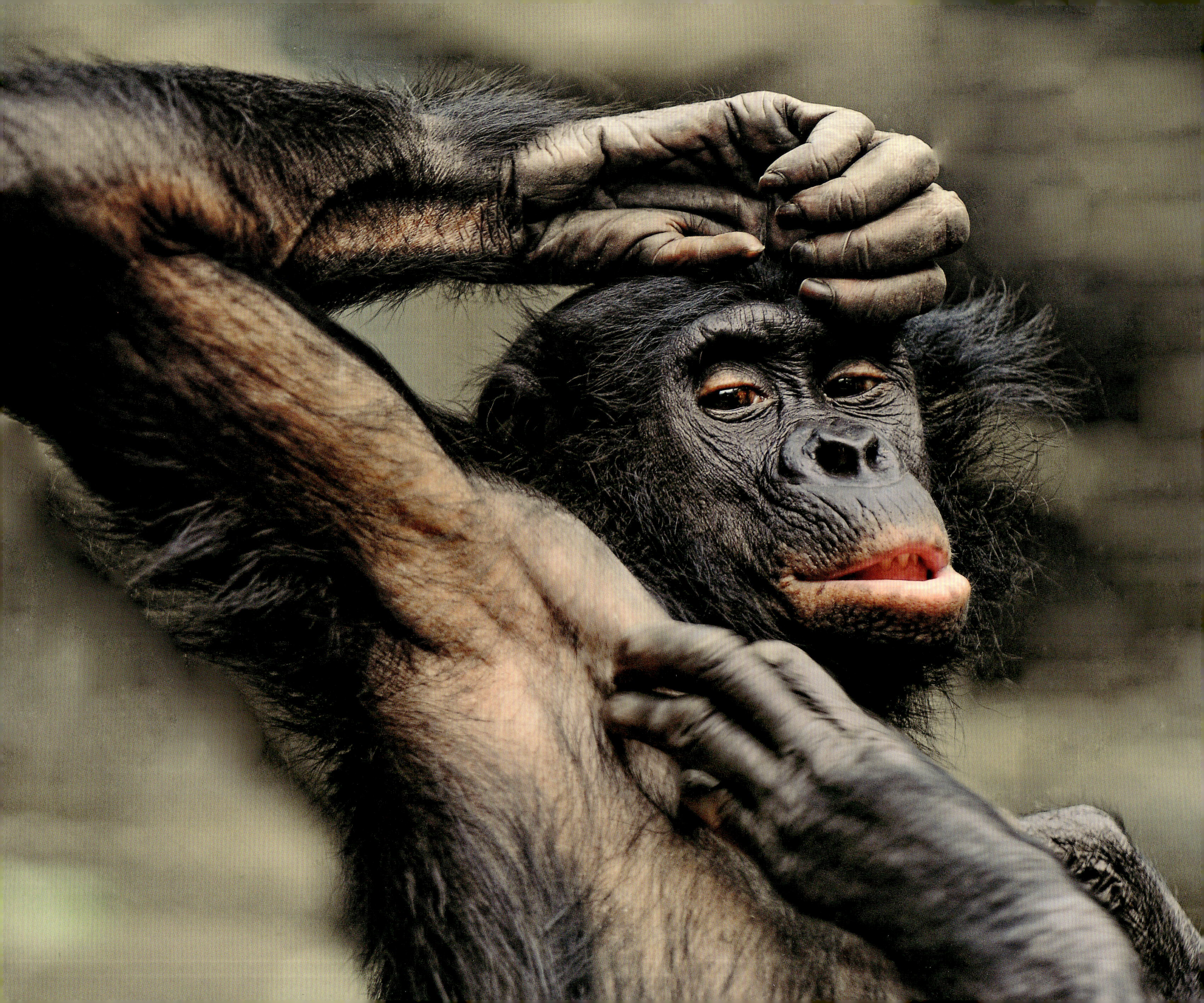

Namensgebung

Namegame

Bonobo / *bonobo*

Schimpanse / *chimpanzee*

3. Namensgebung

Sind wir „weise Schimpansen"?

Im biblischen Schöpfungsmythos benennt Adam die Tiere, „ein jegliches nach seiner Art". Namen verleihen Identität – doch Zugehörigkeit ist zugleich Verschiedenheit von anderen. Wir bedienen uns tagtäglich solcher Schubladen, denn sonst müssten wir unsere Umwelt beständig neu einteilen. Gleichwohl: Namen können auch irreführen oder schlichtweg falsch sein – wofür die Benennung der Menschenaffen ein gutes Beispiel liefert.

Die Ordnung der Primaten schließt eine Gruppe ein, deren Mitglieder – im Unterschied zu „echten" Affen – keinen Schwanz haben. Diese sogenannten *Menschenähnlichen* (lateinisch *Hominoidea*) umfassen *Kleine Menschenaffen* (Gibbons und Siamang), *Große Menschenaffen* (Orang-Utans, Gorillas, Schimpansen, Bonobos), sowie *Menschen*.

Die Bezeichnung „Große Menschenaffen" verschleiert allerdings die tatsächlichen Verwandtschaftsverhältnisse – mit nicht unbedeutenden Konsequenzen für unser Selbstverständnis. Vor ein paar Jahrzehnten wurden, gemäß damaliger Kenntnis, Menschenaffen und Menschen stets säuberlich getrennt. Kleine Menschenaffen wurden in der Familie *Hylobatidae* zusammengefasst, Große Menschenaffen in der Familie *Pongidae*. Diesen stand die Familie *Hominidae* gegenüber, die heutige Menschen und ausgestorbene Formen wie Australopithecus und Neandertaler umfasste. Allerdings wurde schon seit Darwins Zeiten mehr und mehr darauf verwiesen, dass Orang-Utans (*Pongo*), Gorillas (*Gorilla*) sowie Schimpansen und Bonobos (*Pan*) untereinander nicht genügend morphologische Ähnlichkeiten aufwiesen, um sie gemeinsam klar von Menschen abgrenzen zu können. Alsbald machten Fossilfunde klar, dass die zum Orang-Utan führende Linie bereits früh eine Eigenentwicklung genommen hatte. Ein revidierter Stammbaum folgte. Nun wurden alle Formen in der Familie *Hominidae* zusammengefasst. Die bekam zwei Unterfamilien: *Ponginae* mit dem Orang-Utan als alleinigem Vertreter und *Homininae*, in der afrikanische Menschenaffen und Menschen versammelt waren.

Alsbald wurde es jedoch nötig, innerhalb der *Homininae* die Verhältnisse abermals neu zu ordnen. Denn molekulargenetische Befunde sprachen dafür, dass die Stammlinie der Gorillas eine Eigenentwicklung nahm, während *Pan* und *Homo* noch einen gemeinsamen Vorfahren teilten. Somit wären Schimpansen und Bonobos weniger nahe mit Gorillas verwandt als mit uns Menschen.

Widerspricht die Aufteilung nicht dem gesunden Menschenverstand? Beispielsweise sind Menschen „nackte Affen", während andere Menschenaffen dicht behaart sind. Außerdem bewegen sich die Großen Menschenaffen „quadruped" auf Händen und Füßen fort. Orang-Utans stützen sich auf ihren Handflächen ab. Gorillas sowie Schimpansen und Bonobos sind Knöchelgänger, die ihre Finger in die Handflächen hineinbiegen und die Außenseite der Mittelhandknochen belasten. Menschen hingegen bewegen sich „biped" auf zwei Beinen und damit aufrecht fort. Somit fordert der Augenschein eine Dreiteilung zwischen erstens *Pongo*, zweitens *Gorilla* und *Pan*, und drittens *Homo*.

Oberflächliche Gleichform bedeutet jedoch keineswegs automatisch enge Verwandtschaft, wie das Beispiel von Fledermäusen und Vögeln lehrt. Umgekehrt könnten Vögel und Krokodile kaum unterschiedlicher aussehen, sind aber tatsächlich recht nahe miteinander verwandt. Die Verhältnisse innerhalb der *Homininae* lassen sich deshalb so erklären: Der gemeinsame Vorfahre von *Gorilla*, *Pan* und *Homo* pflegte den Knöchelgang. Schimpansen und Bonobos behielten ihn bei, während Bipedie eine spätere Sonderentwicklung des Menschen ist. Damit steht folgender Aufteilung der Unterfamilie *Homininae* nichts mehr im Wege – nämlich in einen „Tribus" *Gorillini* (mit der Gattung *Gorilla*), und einen Tribus *Hominini* (mit den Gattungen *Pan* und *Homo*).

Der Ausdruck „Große Menschenaffen" ist also umgangssprachlich irreführend und zoologisch schlicht falsch, weil er nahelegt, dass alle damit bezeichneten Tiere untereinander näher verwandt seien, als mit den Menschen. Ein einfacher und konsequenter Ausweg bietet sich an – nämlich uns selbst der Gruppe der Großen Menschenaffen zuzuordnen.

Die Revision des Stammbaumes beruht auf Untersuchungen des genetischen

Verwandtschaftsgrades. Die ersten Vergleiche des Erbguts bezogen sich auf Eiweißverbindungen und Chromosomen, doch war es speziell die DNS-Hybridisierung, welche vor 30 Jahren die systematische Einteilung der Lebewesen revolutionierte. Diese Technik macht sich den Umstand zunutze, dass die Erbsubstanz DNS (Desoxyribonucleinsäure) ein doppelsträngiges Molekül ist, die gewundene Doppel-Helix. Um die genetische Ähnlichkeit zweier Arten zu ermitteln, wird deren DNS durch Erhitzen in Einzelstränge zerlegt. Der Schmelzpunkt, bei dem Stränge auseinanderbrechen, beträgt beispielsweise bei Menschen und Schimpansen 86,0 Grad Celsius. Die Hybridisierungs-Technik macht sich die Neigung der Einzelstränge zunutze, beim Abkühlen erneut einen Doppelstrang zu bilden. Das Ausmaß der Aneinanderlagerung und damit die Festigkeit der resultierenden Hybrid-Helix hängt davon ab, wie gut die DNS zweier Arten in ihren molekularen Bausteinen übereinstimmt. Der Hybrid-Doppelstrang von Mensch und Schimpanse etwa schmilzt bereits bei 83,6 Grad, also um 2,4 Grad früher. Ein Absenken des Schmelzpunktes um ein Celsiusgrad bedeutet, dass zwei Arten von DNS sich in etwa einem Prozent ihrer „Gen-Buchstaben" – ihrer zentralen Moleküle – unterscheiden.

Zwischen Mensch und Schimpanse beträgt die so gemessene genetische Ähnlichkeit also 97,6 Prozent. Je früher im Laufe der Stammesgeschichte sich die Ahnenreihen trennten, desto geringer ist die Übereinstimmung. Entsprechend beträgt die genetische Ähnlichkeit mit Gibbons 94,7 Prozent, mit Rhesusaffen 91,1 Prozent, mit Kapuzineraffen 84,2 Prozent und mit Halbaffen wie dem Galago noch lediglich 58 Prozent.

Das Ausmaß der Ähnlichkeiten und Unterschiede an sich sagt noch nichts über den Ablauf der Evolution aus. Um diesen zu rekonstruieren, müssen in einem weiteren Schritt genetische Distanzen nach dem Prinzip der molekularen Uhr in absolute Zeitangaben übersetzt werden. Dabei wird angenommen, dass Änderungen der Erbinformationen auf Zufall beruhen und in winzigen Schritten vonstatten gehen. Zunächst muss aber eine Eichung gefunden werden, also ein Maß für die Rate der genetischen Veränderungen. Fatal wäre es, wenn die Mutationen einmal rascher und einmal langsamer vonstatten gingen. Glücklicherweise scheint das hinsichtlich der Menschenartigen nicht der Fall zu sein. So weisen Große Menschenaffen und Mensch sämtlich dieselbe genetische Distanz zu den Kleinen Menschenaffen auf. Wie bei einer tickenden Uhr sind also die Intervalle der Veränderungen konstant. Die Zeiteinheit zwischen zwei Uhr-Ticks kann durch Abgleich mit Fossilien bekannten Alters bestimmt werden. Unterscheidet sich die Molekülsequenz zweier Arten beispielsweise an 100 Stellen, und wurde der letzte gemeinsame Vorfahre durch Fossilfunde auf 10 Millionen Jahre (MJ) zurückdatiert, dann hätte sich die Erbsubstanz einmal alle 100.000 Jahre stellenweise verändert.

Hinsichtlich der Menschenartigen kommen verschiedene molekularbiologische Methoden zu ähnlichen Schlüssen, auch wenn absolute Angaben oft um ein bis zwei Millionen Jahre schwanken. Gemäß einer Studie trennten sich Altweltaffen und Menschenaffen vor etwa 23,3 MJ. Die Kleinen Menschenaffen, die Gibbons, spalteten sich vor 14,9 MJ von der Linie der Großen Menschenaffen und Menschen ab. Orang-Utans schlugen vor 11,3 MJ einen Sonderweg ein, und Gorillas vor 6,4 MJ. Der letzte gemeinsame Vorfahre von Schimpansen und Menschen wiederum lebte vor 5,4 MJ. Schimpansen und Bonobos schließlich teilten sich vor etwa 1,5 MJ, während vor 200.000 Jahren der „moderne Mensch" auf den Plan trat – anatomisch ausgezeichnet etwa durch hohe Stirn und reduzierte Überaugenwülste und vermutlich mit erweiterter Sprachfähigkeit begabt.

Neue und stetig raffiniertere Labortechniken erweitern unser Wissen über die Familienverhältnisse bei Primaten beinahe täglich. So scheint es, dass die *Pan*- und *Homo*-Linien sich noch bis vor drei bis vier Millionen Jahren immer wieder kreuzten. Vielleicht waren die Linien auch nie komplett getrennt. Einiges spricht dafür, dass sie sich auch heute noch miteinander fortpflanzen könnten. Ob die Produkte dieser Verbindung ein glückliches Leben führen würden, ist allerdings fraglich.

Zweifellos stehen uns Schimpansen genetisch sehr nahe. Doch kompliziert sich diese Aussage dadurch, dass Prozentzahlen auf sehr unterschiedliche Weise ermittelt und gedeutet werden. Beispielsweise gibt es Teile im Genom, die sich nicht hybridisieren lassen – womit die Differenz zwischen Schimpanse und Mensch auf vielleicht drei bis vier Prozent anwachsen würde. Andererseits betreffen zahlreiche Mutationen jene riesigen „stummen" Abschnitte der DNS, die gar keine Eiweiße kodieren – die sogenannte „junk DNA". Diese Mutationen sollten bei den Kalkulationen vielleicht ganz außen vor bleiben. Zudem mutiert die DNS nicht nur in einzelnen Positionen, sondern auch, wenn ganze Abschnitte des Riesenmoleküls verloren gehen (Verlustmutation) oder als Kopien anderswo ins Genom eingebaut werden (Genduplikation). Wenn ein solches Bruchstück 1.000 jener „Buchstaben" enthält, aus denen die DNS aufgebaut ist, zählen manche Wissenschaftler hier 1.000 Unterschiede, während andere die Mutation als ein einziges Ereignis werten. Der genetische Unterschied ist je nach Zählweise entsprechend größer oder kleiner. Die publizierten Werte schwanken entsprechend um einen Faktor 10, nämlich zwischen 6,4 und 0,6 Prozent. Am häufigsten wird ein Wert um 1,5 Prozent genannt in dem sich Schimpansen von Menschen unterscheiden – während übrigens durchschnittlich zwei bis vier Prozent zwischen Menschenmännern und -frauen liegen!

Zudem können überhaupt nur wenige Mutationen bislang mit einem Vor- oder Nachteil in Verbindung gebracht werden. Hierzu zählt das CMAH-Gen, das die Herstellung eines Zuckers fördert. Der ist bei Interaktionen zwischen Köperzellen wichtig, scheint aber die Funktion von Gehirnzellen zu beeinträchtigen. Schimpansen besitzen das CMAH-Gen, während unsere Vorfahren es vor etwa zwei MJ verloren – genau in jener Epoche, als sich das Gehirn der Urmenschen zu vergrößern begann. Umgekehrt wird hinsichtlich einer Variante des FOXP2-Genes spekuliert. Diese fehlt Schimpansen und trat vor etwa 200.000 Jahren erstmals bei „modernen Menschen" auf. Die FOXP2-Variante ist wichtig für die Motorik der Mundregion und grammatikalische Fähigkeiten und mag deshalb mit der Evolution unserer Sprache zu tun haben.

Die evolutionäre Genetik, so atemberaubend ihre Entdeckungen sind, steht jedenfalls noch am Anfang. Mittlerweile zeichnet sich ab, dass die teilweise deutlichen Gestaltunterschiede zwischen Schimpansen und Menschen weniger auf genetische Innovationen zurückgehen als auf Umstellungen in der Regulation des Körperwachstums. So veränderte sich etwa die Aktivität jener Gene, die Wachstumshormone steuern. Dadurch wachsen beispielsweise embryonal flach angelegte Gesichtsprofile bei Schimpansen schnauzenartig nach vorne, während sie beim erwachsenen Menschen ebenmäßiger bleiben. Außerdem wächst bei Menschen das Gehirn über eine längere Zeit hinweg, und wird dadurch größer. Zudem sind die Netzwerke jener Eiweiße verschieden, die die Aktivität bestimmter Gene im Gehirn regeln, was zu einer höheren Dichte der neuronalen Vernetzung führt.

Aufgrund dieser Einschränkungen halten manche Wissenschaftler genetische Ähnlichkeit für ein ungeeignetes Maß, das Divergenzen in Körperbau und Verhalten zwischen Menschen und Menschenaffen nicht im richtigen Verhältnis widerspiegelt. Andere Forscher finden, dass die geringen genetischen Differenzen die Unzuverlässigkeit unserer naiven Wahrnehmung ersichtlich machen – ganz ähnlich wie das „Oberflächenmerkmal" Hautfarbe uns oft dazu verleitet, Unterschiede zwischen Menschengruppen gravierender einzuschätzen als sie sind. Somit schaffen Molekularbiologie und Genomik paradoxerweise für klare Einteilungen mehr Probleme als sie lösen. Denn je besser ein „Vergrößerungsglas" auflöst, desto mehr Unterschiede werden ersichtlich. Es ist aber noch immer weithin in das Ermessen des jeweiligen Wissenschaftlers gestellt, welche dieser „innerartlichen" Variationen als so essenziell anzusehen sind, dass sie eine eigene Kategorie rechtfertigen.

Hinsichtlich *Homo* und *Pan* gilt aber in jedem Fall: Differierte das Erbgut von Käfern um solche Bruchteile, würden sie gewiss nicht alternativen Gattungen zugeschlagen. Somit erscheint eine auf den ersten Blick seltsame Forderung durchaus angebracht – nämlich die, unsere Gattung zu erweitern. Das würde bedeuten, dass Schimpansen in *Homo troglodytes* umbenannt werden und Bonobos in *Homo paniscus*.

Nur wenige Genetiker, Paläoanthropologen und Verhaltensbiologen machen sich derzeit für eine Erweiterung der Gattung *Homo* stark – aber immerhin ist eine engagierte Diskussion im Gange. Würde sich der Vorschlag durchsetzen, wären wir interessanterweise wieder dort, wo Carolus Linnaeus vor 250 Jahren begann, als er Menschen und Menschenaffen unter *Homo* vereinte. Da die Gattung *Pan* erst um 1816 von dem deutschen Naturforscher Lorenz Oken eingeführt wurde, hat der ältere Name vorrang. Ansonsten könnten wir auch in die Situation geraten, uns selbst umbennen zu müssen – in *Pan sapiens*: „weise Schimpansen".

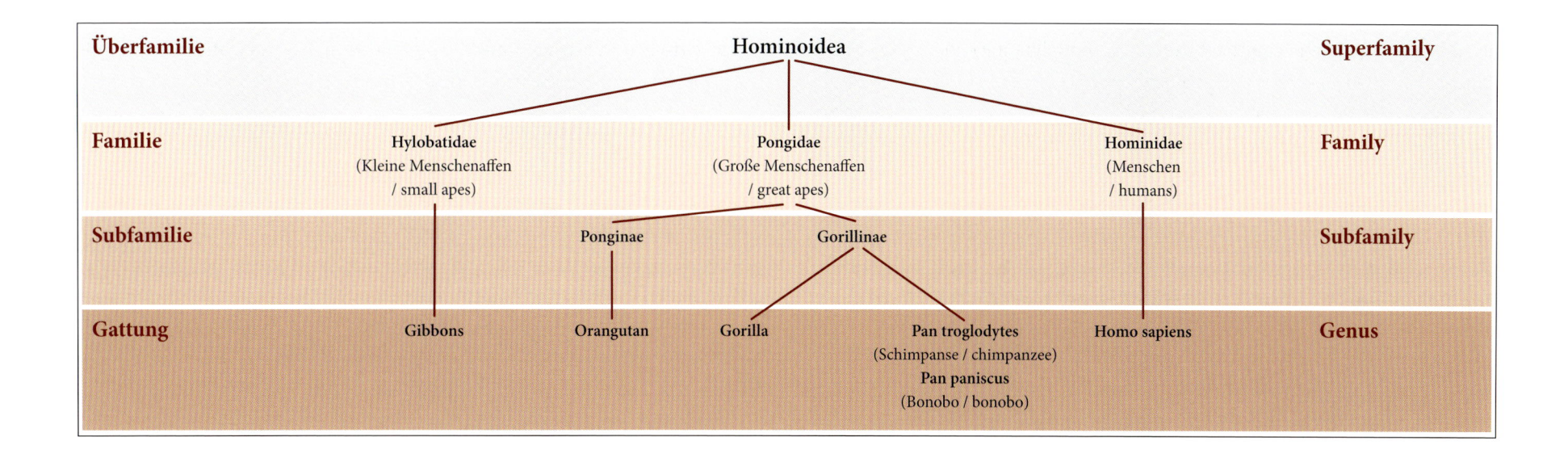

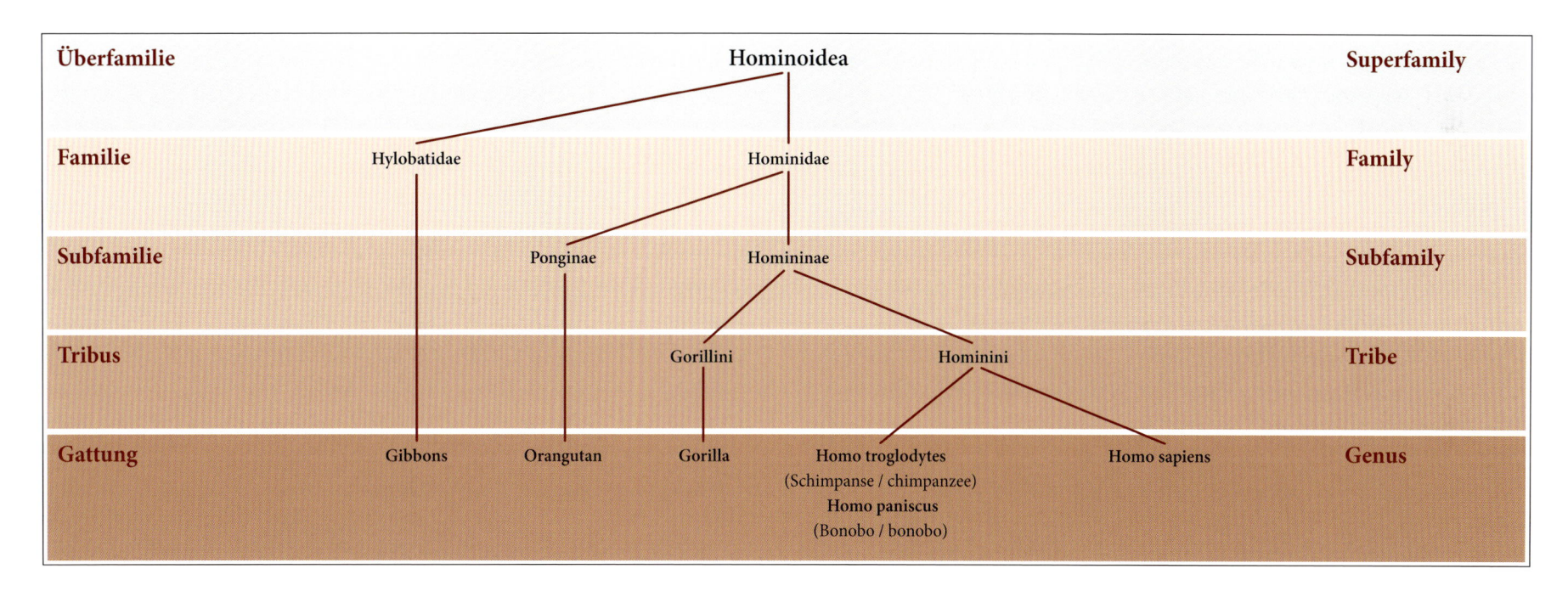

Überfamilie	Hominoidea					Superfamily
Familie	Hylobatidae (Kleine Menschenaffen / small apes)	Pongidae (Große Menschenaffen / great apes)			Hominidae (Menschen / humans)	Family
Subfamilie		Ponginae	Gorillinae			Subfamily
Gattung	Gibbons	Orangutan	Gorilla	Pan troglodytes (Schimpanse / chimpanzee) Pan paniscus (Bonobo / bonobo)	Homo sapiens	Genus

Überfamilie	Hominoidea					Superfamily
Familie	Hylobatidae	Hominidae				Family
Subfamilie		Ponginae	Homininae			Subfamily
Tribus			Gorillini	Hominini		Tribe
Gattung	Gibbons	Orangutan	Gorilla	Homo troglodytes (Schimpanse / chimpanzee) Homo paniscus (Bonobo / bonobo)	Homo sapiens	Genus

Zoologische Einteilung der Menschenartigen: Früher (oben) und neuester Vorschlag (unten) — *Zoological grouping of apes and humans: Traditional (top) and currently proposed (bottom)*

3. Namegame

Are We Wise Chimpanzees?

Adam, according to the Biblical myth of creation, "gave names to every beast of the field". Names provide identity – but belonging also means being different from others. We use such pigeonholes every day, as otherwise we would have to constantly ponder of how to categorise our environment. Nevertheless: names may also mislead or be plain wrong. The designation of apes is a good example.

The primate order contains a subgroup whose members, unlike monkeys, do not possess tails. These so-called *Hominoidea* consist of the "small apes" (gibbons and siamang), the "great apes" (orangutans, gorillas, chimpanzees, bonobos) and humans. However, the term "great apes" conceals the actual evolutionary relationships – with consequences that are not insignificant for our self-understanding. A few decades ago, apes and humans were always neatly separated. Small apes were assigned their own family *Hylobatidae*. Great apes were grouped in the family *Pongidae,* in clear distinction to the family *Hominidae*, which included living humans and extinct forms such as *Australopithecus* and Neanderthals. Still, ever since Darwin, more and more experts pointed out that orangutans (*Pongo*), gorillas (*Gorilla*) as well as chimpanzees and bonobos (*Pan*) were not sufficiently similar in their morphology to distinguish them as a group from humans. Moreover, fossil finds soon revealed that the line leading to orangutans had branched off quite early from all other great apes. Consequently, a new phylogenetic tree was drawn. All great apes and humans were united in a single family, *Hominidae*. It had two subfamilies: *Ponginae,* with the orangutan as the sole representative, and *Homininae,* which encompassed African apes and humans.

Meanwhile, however, relationships within the *Homininae* need to be re-arranged yet again. This is because recent findings of molecular genetics suggest that the line that led to gorillas developed on its own, while *Pan* and *Homo* still shared a common ancestor. Thus, chimpanzees and bonobos are not as closely related to gorillas as to us humans.

Does this division not contradict common sense? For example, people are "naked apes", while other apes are hairy. Also, great apes move "quadrupedally" on hands and feet. Orangutans support themselves with their palms. Gorillas – as well as chimpanzees and bonobos – are knuckle-walkers; they bend their fingers back into their palms while putting their weight on the outside of the metacarpal bone. People, by contrast, move "bipedally" on two legs and thus upright. These traits would call for a tripartite division between first, *Pongo;* second, *Gorilla* and *Pan;* and third, *Homo*.

But a superficial uniformity of outer form does not automatically equate to a close evolutionary relationship – as the example of bats and birds teaches us. Conversely, birds and crocodiles could hardly look more different, but they are actually very closely related. The relationships within the *Homininae* can therefore be explained as follows: the common ancestor of *Gorilla, Pan* and *Homo* used knuckle-walking. Chimpanzees and bonobos retained this mode of locomotion, while bipedalism is a later development of the human lineage. This allows us to break the subfamily *Homininae* into a "tribe" *Gorillini* (with the genus *Gorilla*), and a tribe *Hominini* (with the genera *Homo* and *Pan*).

The expression "great apes" is thus a misleading vernacular and simply wrong in zoological terms because it suggests that all animals denoted by this word are more closely related amongst each other than either of them is to humans. A simple solution would be to subsume humans under this same category. Thus: we are apes.

This revision of the family tree is supported by genetic studies. The first such comparisons related to protein compounds and chromosomes. However, about 30 years ago, the systematic classification of living things was revolutionised by DNA-hybridisation. The technique capitalises on the fact that the genetic material DNA (desoxyribonucleic acid) is configured as a double-stranded molecule, the twisted double helix. To determine the genetic similarity between two species, their DNA is unravelled through heating into single strands. The melting point, when the strands break apart, is, for example for humans and chimpanzees, 86.0 degrees Celsius. The hybridisation technique takes advantage of the tendency of the single strands to again assemble into a double strand, once they cool off. The extent of realignment and thus the strength of the resulting hybrid helix depends on how well the molecular building blocks of the DNA of two species match. The hybrid double strand of humans and chimpanzees melts already at 83.6 degrees, thus 2.4 degrees earlier. A reduction of the melting point by 1 degree Celsius means that two types of DNA differ in roughly one percent of their central molecules, that is to say, their "genetic letters".

The so-measured genetic similarity between humans and chimpanzees is thus calculated as 97.6 percent. The earlier in their evolutionary history the lineages split, the less their DNA sequences agree. The genetic similarity therefore is only 94.7 percent with gibbons, 91.1 percent with rhesus monkeys, 84.2 percent with capuchin monkeys and, with prosimians such as the galago, only 58 percent.

The extent of the similarities and differences in itself reveals nothing about the evolutionary process itself. To reconstruct *when* splits occurred, genetic distances need to be translated into units of absolute time, based on the principle of the molecular clock. For this, it is assumed that changes of genetic information occur by chance and in tiny steps. First, however, a calibration needs to be established, a measure of the rate of change. It would complicate such calculations enormously, if mutations happened more quickly during certain evolutionary periods and more slowly during others. Fortunately, that does not seem to be the case within the *Hominoidea*. Thus, great apes and humans all have the same genetic distance to the small apes. Like with a ticking clock, the intervals of change are therefore constant. The absolute duration between two clock-ticks can be determined by comparisons with fossils of known age. Let us assume that the molecular sequences of two species differ in 100 locations and that the last common ancestor, according to fossil finds, lived 10 million years ago (mya). We can then calculate that partial changes in the DNA occurred once every 100,000 years.

Different methods of molecular biology arrive at similar conclusions with respect to the *Hominoidea,* even if absolute dates often vary by one or two million years. According to one study, monkeys and apes parted about 23.3 mya. Gibbons, the small apes, split 14.9 mya from the line that lead to the great apes and humans. Orangutans went their own way 11.3 mya, and gorillas 6.4 mya. The last common ancestor of chimpanzees and humans lived 5.4 mya. Finally, chimpanzees and bonobos split about 1.5 mya. "Modern man" appeared about 200,000 years ago – anatomically distinguished by, for example, a steep forehead and reduced brow ridges and probably endowed with advanced language skills.

New and ever more sophisticated laboratory techniques increase our knowledge about family relationships in primates almost daily. So it seems that the *Pan-* and *Homo-*lines were still regularly interbreeding until at least three or four million years ago. Perhaps the lines were never completely separated. Even today, they might be able to reproduce with each other. Whether the results of this reunion would lead a happy life, is, however, questionable.

No doubt, chimpanzees are genetically very close to us. But this statement is complicated by the fact that percentages are calculated and interpreted in very different ways. For example, there are parts of the genome that cannot be hybridised. This notches the difference between chimpanzees and humans up, to perhaps 3–4 percent. On the other hand, many mutations affect those enormous sections of DNA that are "silent" and do not code for any proteins – the so-called "junk DNA" – which should therefore arguably not enter into the equation. Moreover, DNA does not only mutate in specific locations, but also when entire sections of the giant molecule are lost (gene deletion) or elsewhere incorporated into the genome (gene duplication). If such a fragment contains 1,000 of those "letters" from which DNA is built, some scientists will count 1,000 differences, while others rate this mutation as a single event. The genetic difference is correspondingly larger or smaller, depending on the calculation method. Published values fluctuate accordingly by a factor of ten, that is, between 6.4 and 0.6 percent. Most commonly, a value of 1.5 percent is given as the difference between chimpanzees and humans – while, by the way, men and women differ on average by 2–4 percent!

Moreover, only a few mutations have as yet been associated with an advantage or disadvantage. These include the CMAH gene, which promotes the production of a particular sugar. While this sugar aids interactions between cells, it seems to impede the function of brain cells. Chimpanzees possess the CMAH gene, whereas our ancestors lost it about 2 mya – precisely during the period when archaic humans developed larger brains. A converse speculation surrounds a variant of the FOXP2 gene. Chimpanzees lack this gene that "modern humans" acquired only about 200,000 years ago. The FOXP2 variant is important for motor functions of the mouth region and grammatical skills, and may therefore have to do with the evolution of human language.

Evolutionary genetics proceeds at a breathtaking pace, but the discipline is still in its infancy. Meanwhile, it becomes apparent that prominent differences between the anatomy of chimpanzees and humans are not so much linked to genetic innovations but to adjustments in the regulation of body-growth pattern. For example, the activity of those genes that control growth hormones changed. Because of this, the flat face of chimpanzee embryos grows forward and attains its snout-like appearance, while the facial profile is less pronounced in even adult humans. In addition, the human brain grows over a longer period, thus becoming larger. Finally, the networks of those proteins that regulate the activity of specific genes in the brain differ, leading to a higher density of neuronal networks in humans.

Because of these limitations, some scientists maintain that genetic similarity is an altogether inappropriate measure that doesn't properly reflect the degree of variance in body structure and behaviour between humans and apes. Other researchers stress that, because genetic differences are so small, this indicates how unreliable our naive perceptions are – similar to how a "surface trait" like skin colour may tempt us to rate inequalities between groups of people as more pronounced than they are. Thus, paradoxically, molecular biology and genomics create more problems for clear categorisation than they solve. This is because the better the resolution of a "magnifying glass" is, the more differentials become apparent. But it is still largely within the discretion of a given scientist to consider which of these identified "intraspecific" variations are essential enough so that they would warrant a separate category.

One thing is certainly true with respect to *Homo* and *Pan*: would the genome of two beetles vary by such fractions, they would certainly not be assigned to alternative genera. Thus, a demand requires appropriate consideration, which might seem strange at first glance – namely, to expand our genus. That would mean to rename chimpanzees as *Homo troglodytes* and bonobos as *Homo paniscus*.

Few geneticists, biologists, palaeoanthropologists and behavioural researchers are currently pushing for an enlargement of the genus *Homo* – but a lively discussion is already taking place. Should the proposal be accepted, then we would be back where Carolus Linnaeus started 250 years ago, when he united humans and apes under the label *Homo*. The genus *Pan* was only introduced about 1816 by the German naturalist Lorenz Oken. Thus, the older name has priority. Otherwise, we could find ourselves in the odd situation of having to rename ourselves – into *Pan sapiens*: "wise chimpanzees".

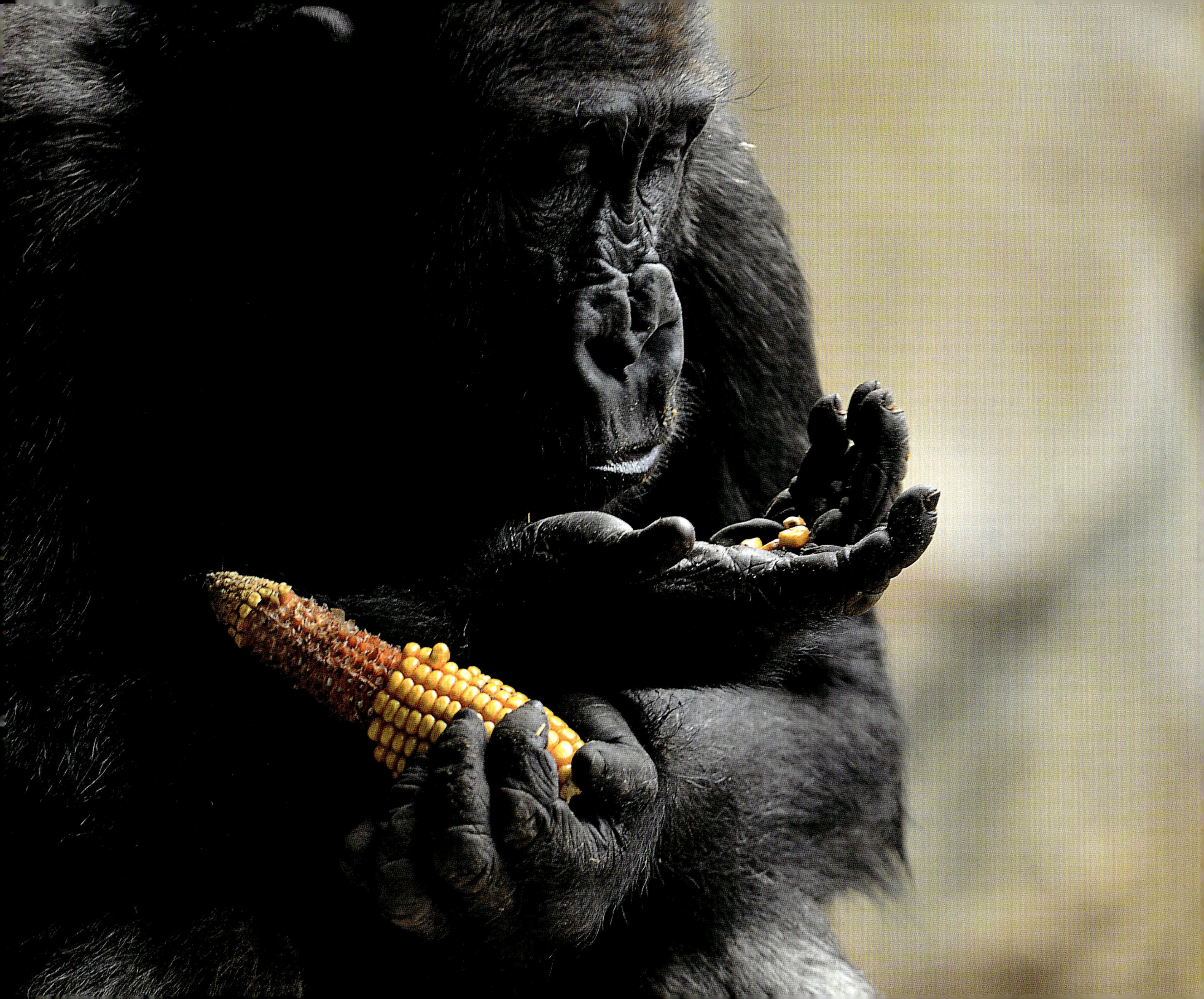

LEBENSBILDER
LIFESTYLES

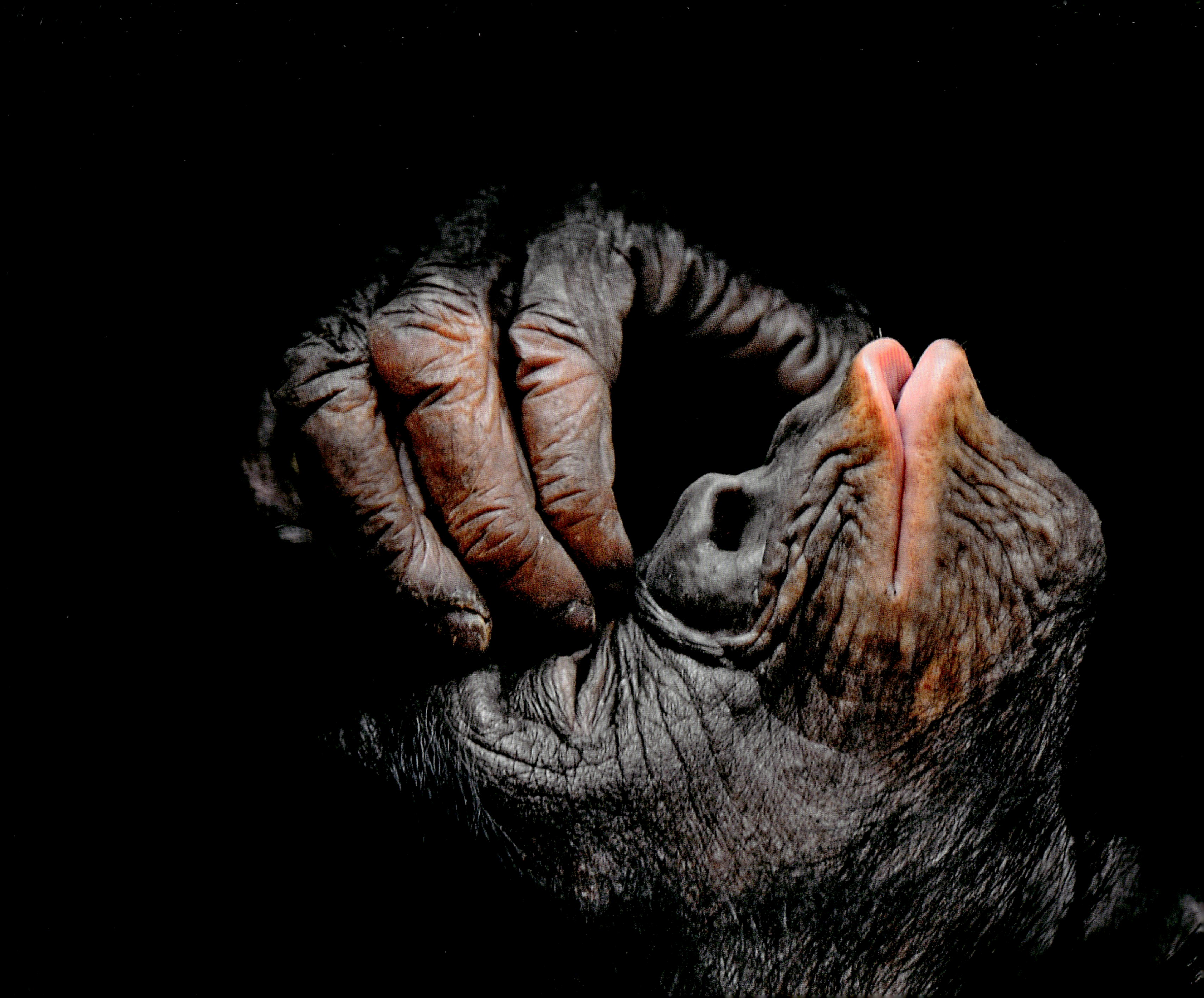

Bonobo / *bonobo*　　　　　　　　　　　　　　　　　　　　　　　　　　　　　　　　　　Gorilla / *gorilla*　　67

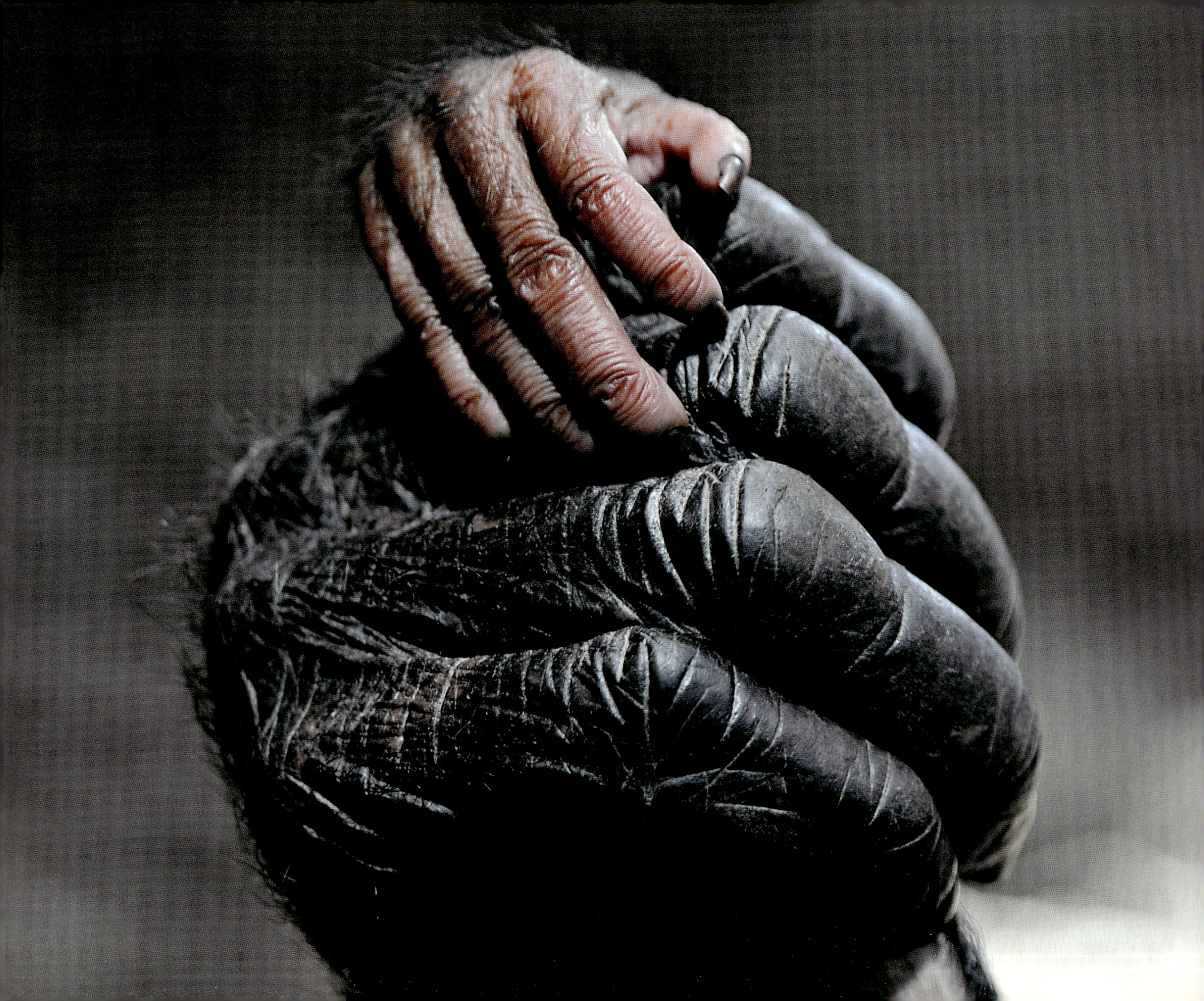

Schimpanse / *chimpanzee*　　　　　　　　　　　　　　　　　　　　　　　　　　　　　　Gorilla / *gorilla*

70   Bonobo / *bonobo*

Bonobo / *bonobo*

72 Orang-Utan / *orangutan* Bonobo / *bonobo*

Bonobo / *bonobo*

Schimpanse / *chimpanzee*

Bonobo / *bonobo*

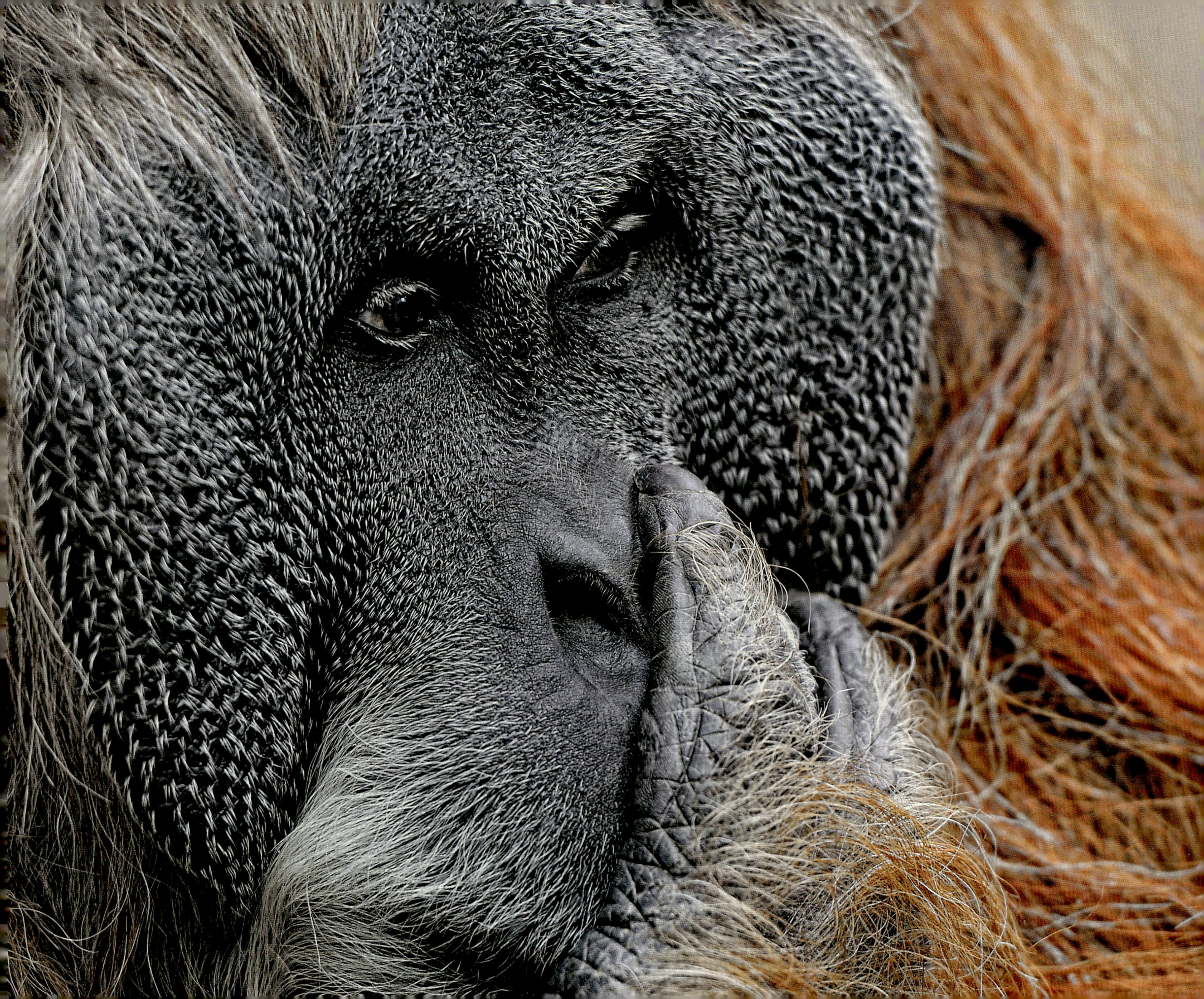

Orang-Utan / *orangutan*

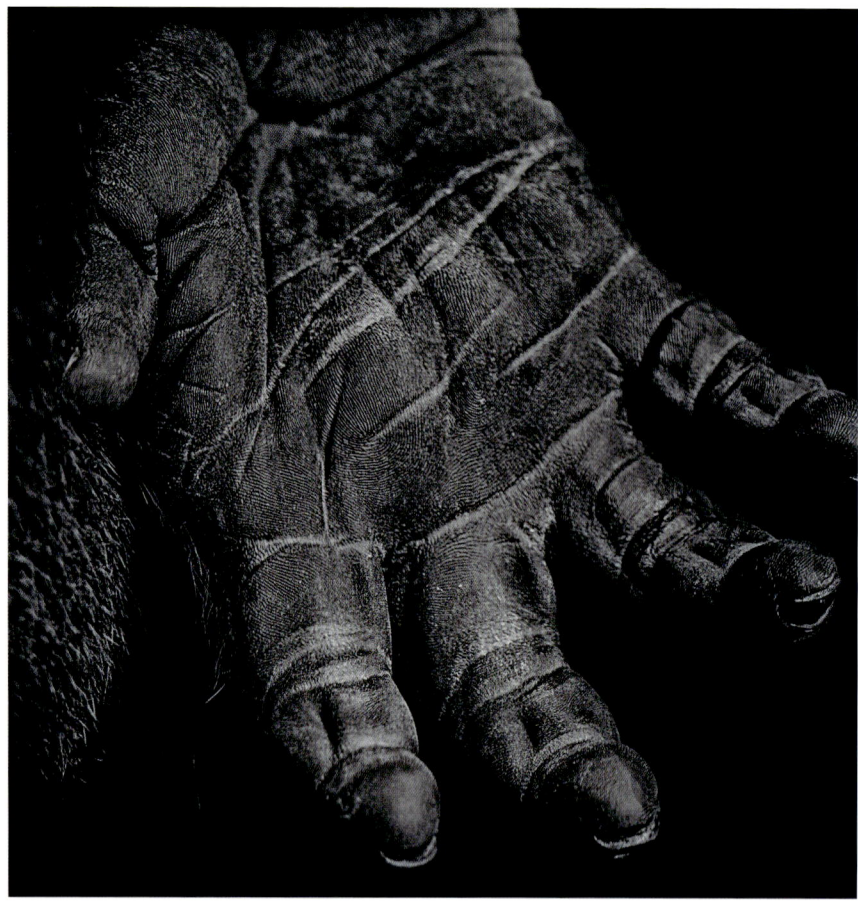

78 Bonobo / *bonobo*   Gorilla / *gorilla*   Bonobo / *bonobo*

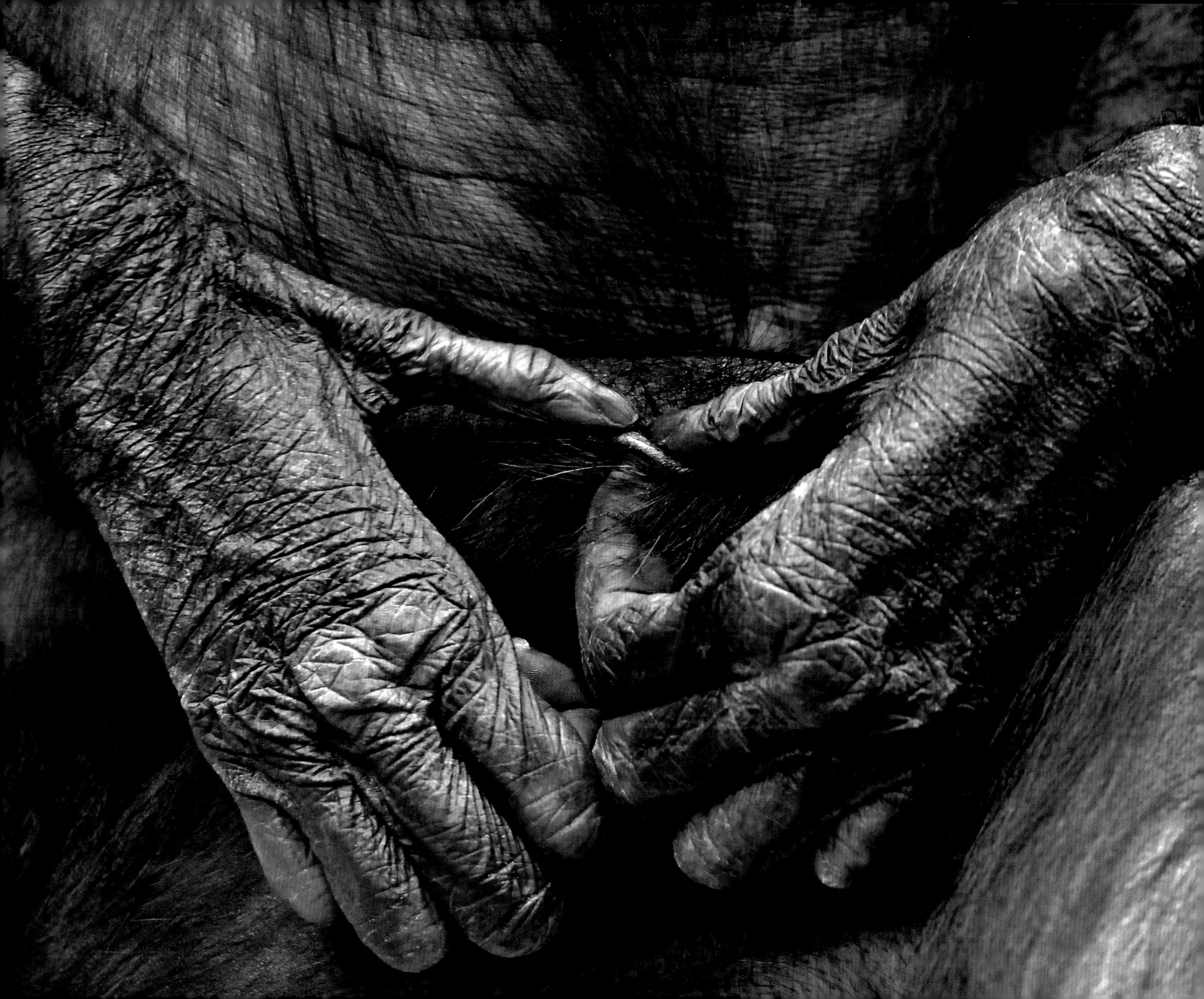

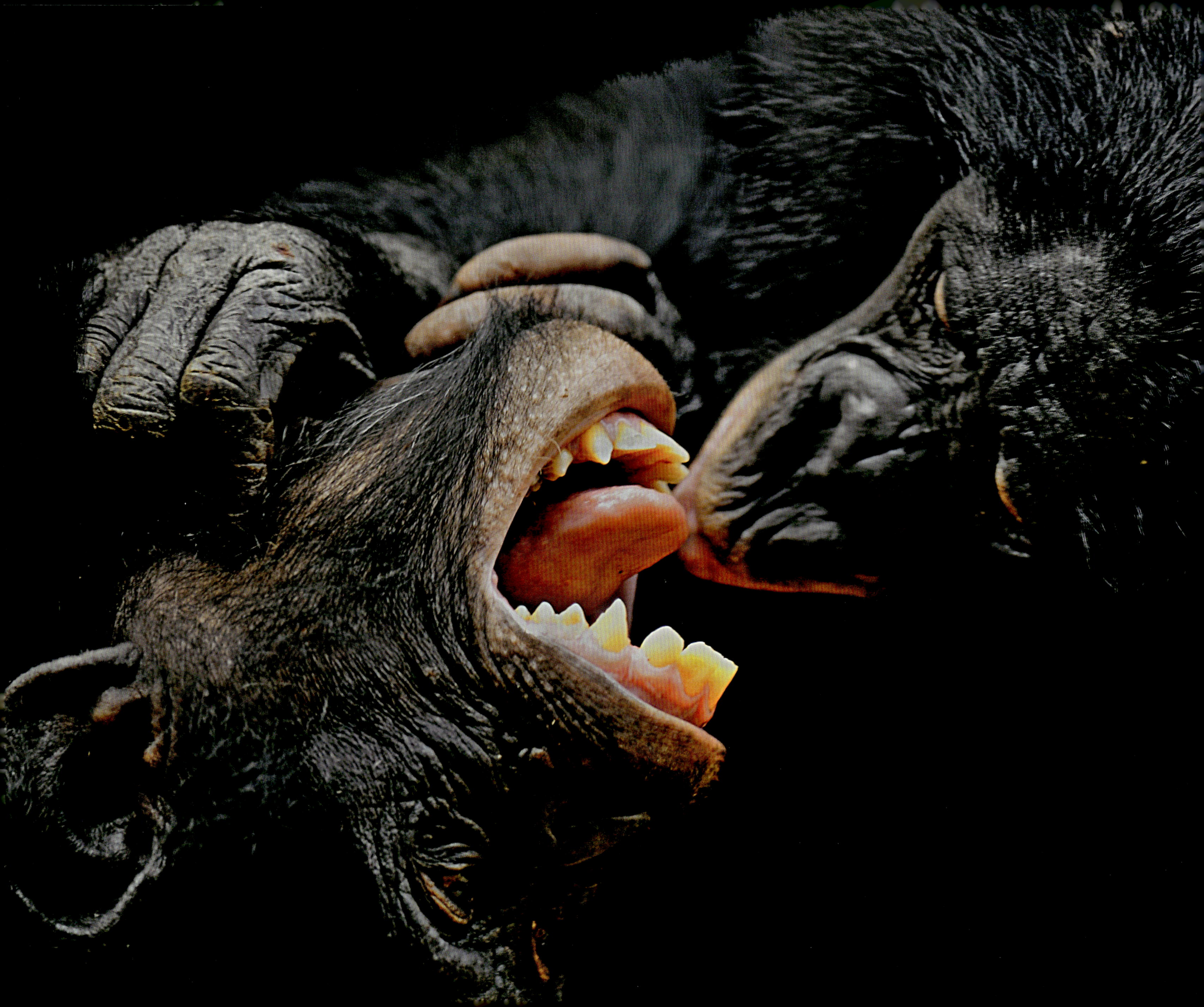

Bonobo / *bonobo*   Bonobo / *bonobo*   81

Bonobo / *bonobo*

Bonobo / *bonobo* 83

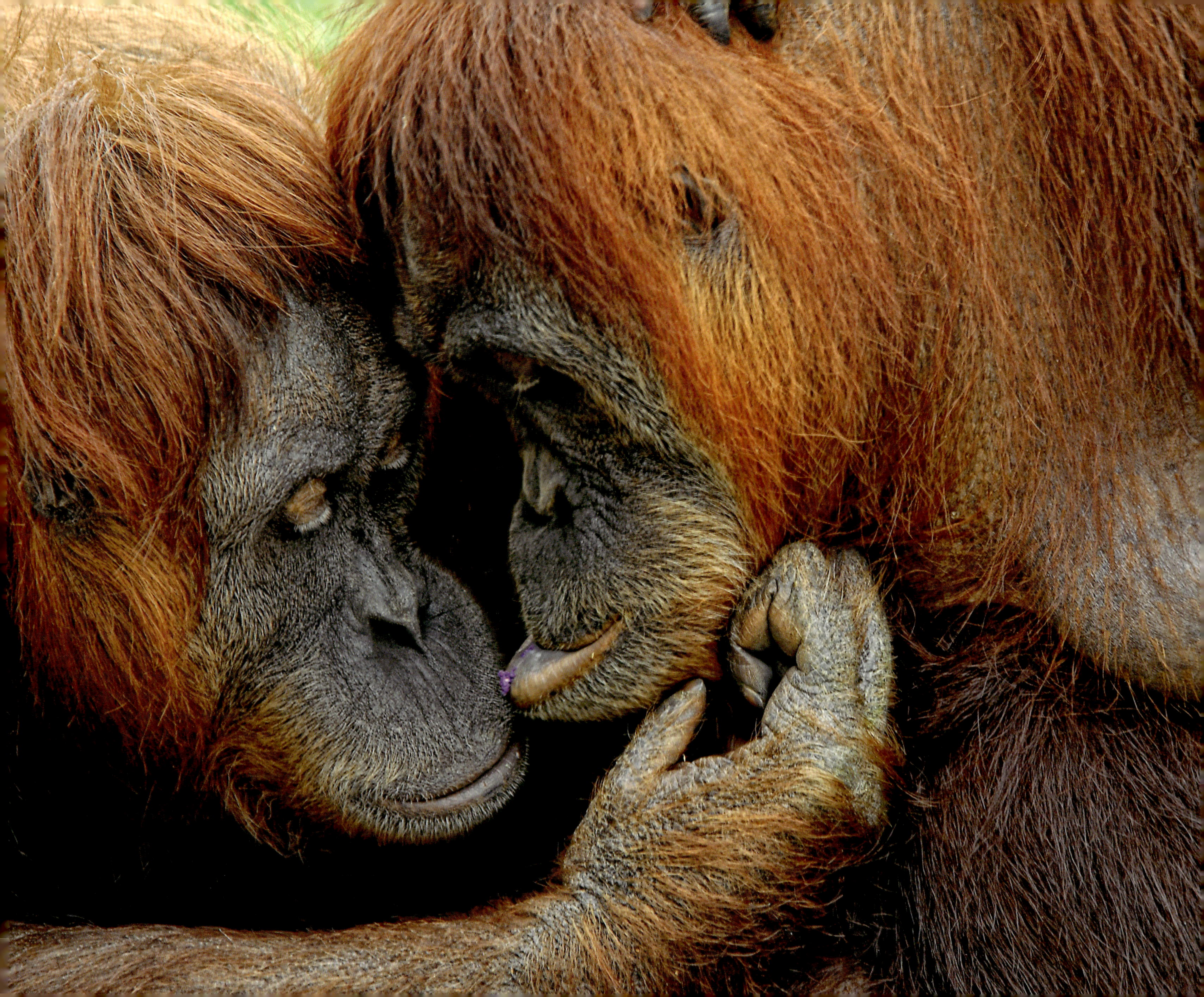

Orang-Utans
Orangutans

Orang-Utan / *orangutan*

Orang-Utan / *orangutan*

4. Orang-Utans

Eremiten im Wald

Ihre Gestalt brachte den rot-braun behaarten „Wald-Menschen" – so die Übersetzung ihres malaiischen Namens – nicht unbedingt Vorteile. Denn die Dayak, Kopfjäger auf Borneo, akzeptierten als Trophäe auch den Schädel eines Orang-Utan. Die Art ist Asiens einziger Großer Menschenaffe. Noch vor tausend Jahren waren sie in Südostasien und China weit verbreitet, wie Knochenfunde und regionale Folklore belegen. Die zuweilen aufrecht gehenden, großwüchsigen Primaten geben überdies einen akzeptablen Prototypen des legendären Yeti ab. Als einziger Menschenaffe zieht der Orang-Utan allein umher, und in der Tat wurden vewandte Fossilien im Himalaya gefunden. Als Menschen das asiatische Festland dichter besiedelten, verschwanden Orang-Utans von dort. Heute überleben sie lediglich auf Sumatra und Borneo, doch machen ihnen Waldrodung und Plantagen auch die letzten Heimatreste streitig.

Eine *Zeltzaame als Zonderlinge Aap sort, Genaamd Orang-outang, van het Eiland Borneo* („Seltsame wie sonderliche Affensorte, genamt Orang-outang, von der Insel Borneo") wurde erstmals 1778 vom Leiter der Menagerie des Prinzen von Oranien beschrieben. Die spätere wissenschaftliche Gattungs-Bezeichnung *Pongo* mag auf „M'Pungu" zurückgehen, kongolesisch für „Ungeheuer" und war ursprünglich auf den Gorilla gemünzt. Der Spezies-Name *pygmaeus* hingegen bezeichnete auf Griechisch einen „zwergenhaften Stamm". Im indonesischen Nordsumatra findet sich die Unterart *Pongo pygmaeus abelii*, während *Pongo pygmaeus pygmaeus* auf Borneo im indonesischen Teil Kalimantan und den malaysischen Staaten Sabah und Sarawak lebt. Manche Wissenschaftler stufen die Formen als verschiedene Arten ein. Die Sumatra-Variante hat langes, wenngleich spärliches und rauhes rötliches Haar, leuchtendorange bei Jungtieren und kastanienrot bei Erwachsenen. Das Gesicht ist nackt, eher rosa bei Jungtieren und später schwarz. Das Gesicht der Borneo-Variante ist schlanker und kürzer, und die Haare sind dunkler bis schokoladenfarben.

Orang-Utans halten einige Rekorde. Da Männchen wie Weibchen fast immer allein herumziehen, sind sie die unsozialsten Menschenaffen und überdies jene mit dem extremsten Baumleben – bis zu 95 Prozent der Zeit bei Weibchen und Jungtieren. Gewichte von 60–90 kg bei Männchen und 35–50 kg bei Weibchen weisen sie zudem als schwerste Baumbewohner überhaupt aus. Schließlich sind Orang-Utans die sich am langsamsten fortpflanzenden Primaten, denn zwischen Geburten vergehen oft acht bis neun Jahre.

Ähnlich Menschen dauert der Menstruationszyklus um 28 Tage und Schwangerschaften acht Monate. Erst mit 12–15 Jahren bringen sie ihr erstes Kind zur Welt. Drei Jahre lang klammern sich Babys an ihre Mütter, die sie bis ins fünfte Jahr stillen. Selbst Entwöhnte halten beim Klettern Mamas Hand und teilen ihr Nachtnest, das jeder Orang-Utan jeden Abend neu durch Umbiegen belaubter Zweige im Geäst konstruiert.

Orang-Utans bevorzugen Dschungel des Tieflands, während Mangroven und Bergwälder nur dünn besiedelt werden. Zwischen 300–800 Meter zieht jeder Erwachsene täglich durch ein eigenes Wohngebiet, das bei Männchen 5–25 und bei Weibchen 1–10 Quadratkilometer umfasst.

Warum wandern Orang-Utans als Eremiten durch den Urwald – abgesehen von seltenen sexuellen Begegnungen und permanenten Mutter-Kind-Paaren? Eigentlich ist die Frage falsch gestellt. Denn sie geht davon aus, dass Primaten von ihrer Grundeinstellung her sozial angelegt sind. Besonders für Weibchen ist ein Leben in der Gruppe jedoch problematisch. Sie brauchen gewichtige Anteile Körperfett für die energieaufwendige Schwangerschaft und Stillzeit. Andere Weibchen sind darum in erster Linie Konkurrentinnen um Nahrung, denen frau besser aus dem Wege geht. Überdies werden Parasiten und Krankheitserreger im Gemeinschaftsleben leichter übertragen. Schließlich stellen Todesstürze, bei Menschenaffen ohnehin nicht selten, eine echte Gefahr dar. Äste mit zehn Orang-Utans darauf, die eine halbe Tonne wiegen, würden umso eher brechen.

Somit sollten Weibchen sich nur zusammenschließen, wenn das Gruppenleben solche Nachteile aufwiegt. Ein Vorteil wäre das deutlich kleinere Risiko, gefressen zu werden. Verglichen mit einem Singledasein beträgt es in einer beispielsweise zehnköpfigen Gruppe lediglich ein Zehntel. Zudem sind mehr Augen wachsamer, und gemeinsam lässt sich ein Raubtier überdies oft in die Flucht schlagen.

Die großwüchsigen Orang-Utans haben allerdings kaum natürliche Feinde. Nebelparder können auf Borneo wie Sumatra Babys gefährlich werden. Auf Sumatra sind zusätzlich Rothunde, Leoparden und Tiger zu fürchten – doch in den Baumkronen sind die Menschenaffen vor ihnen praktisch sicher. Wirkliche Gefahr besteht nur für erwachsene Männchen, wenn sie wegen ihrer Schwere über den Boden hinweg den Baum wechseln.

Sozialleben kann theoretisch auch von Vorteil sein, um Nahrung gegen Nachbargruppen zu verteidigen. Effektiv monopolisieren lassen sich jedoch nur „geklumpte" Essvorräte, etwa einzeln stehende große Fruchtbäume oder räumlich klar abgegrenzte Haine. Im Dschungel der Orang-Utans scheint es jedoch viele kleine und zerstreute Nahrungsquellen zu geben, an denen sich bestenfalls Einzeltiere sättigen können.

Somit ist es eigentlich logisch, dass die Wald-Menschen das Eremitentum bevorzugen. In Zoos sind die Nachteile des Gruppenlebens nicht relevant, da sie mit genügend Nahrung versorgt werden und Tierärzte Infektionen kontrollieren. Hier wird offenbar, dass es sich nicht um eingefleischte Einzelgänger handelt. Vielmehr verwandeln Orang-Utans sich in solchen Situationen in regelrechte Party-Animals, die sich tagtäglich am Miteinander freuen.

In der Wildnis versuchen dominante Männchen, möglichst viele der kleinen und sich oft überlappenden Wohngebiete von Weibchen unter Kontrolle zu bringen. Da wegen Schwangerschaft und Kinderaufzucht gewöhnlich Jahre zwischen ihren fruchtbaren Phasen liegen, können Männchen trotz der räumlichen Vereinzelung der Weibchen praktisch eine Haremssituation herstellen. Denn sie müssen nur jene Dame genauer bewachen, bei der eine erneute Befruchtung gerade möglich ist.

Manche Männchen besitzen ausladende Backenwülste. Diese Anhängsel verstärken jene Rufe, die Orang-Utan-Männer mittels enormer Kehlsäcke produzieren. Andere reagieren deutlich auf die lautstarken Vokalisationen: Fruchtbare Weibchen nähern sich den potentesten Krachmachern und geben sich ihnen willig hin – während weniger bemittelte Geschlechtsgenossen sich fern halten.

Nur wenige erwachsene Männchen entwickeln die auffälligen Charakteristika. Die meisten sehen aus, als seien sie Adoleszente. Doch täuscht der Schein, denn die Halbstarken sind zumindest vom Alter her bereits erwachsen. Weil ihre Konstitution für direkte Konkurrenz nicht gut genug ist, verharren sie in einem jüngeren Stadium, was zudem weniger Aggression der Dominanten provoziert.

Das hält die Halbstarken freilich nicht von einer alternativen Strategie der Fortpflanzung ab: der sexuellen Nötigung. Regelmäßig nämlich zwingen sie Weibchen zum Sex, was sich an deren Gegenwehr ablesen lässt. Von keiner anderen Primatenart außer Menschen sind Vergewaltigungen bekannt. Dies mag damit zu tun haben, dass sowohl Weibchen von *Pongo pygmaeus* wie von *Homo sapiens* oft ohne Begleitung allein umherziehen. Die Übergriffe haben zumindest manchmal reproduktive Konsequenzen, denn genetische Tests belegen, dass auch halbstarke Orang-Utans Kinder zeugen.

Ein dominanter Mann hat seinen Zenit überschritten, wenn seine Backenwülste matt und runzelig sind, von Parasiten befallen und mit Narben übersät. Nun schlägt die Stunde derer, die oft länger als ein Jahrzehnt als Heranwachsende „verkleidet" auf ihre Chance gewartet haben. Es mag nur Wochen dauern, bis Hormonstöße einem Neuling genug Selbstvertrauen einflößen, und er selbst Kehlsäcke und Backenwülste bildet.

Warum lassen Außenstehende sich eigentlich von an sich nutzlosen Merkmalen wie Körperanhängseln und Fernrufen beeindrucken? Zum einen lässt sich – ähnlich wie beim Brüllen von Hirschbullen – über die Lautstärke und Tiefe des Tons auf die Körpergröße schließen. Zum anderen kostet die Produktion von Backenwülsten und Gesängen Kraft – etwa Suchzeit, um die nötige hochqualitative Nahrung zu finden, und aggressive Energie, um sie zu verteidigen. Rufe verraten Raubtieren zudem den eigenen Standort, und das schwergewichtige Gewebe um den Hals macht Verteidigung oder Flucht schwieriger. Ähnlich wie ein Pfauenschwanz sind derlei Merkmale also unter dem Gesichtspunkt des reinen Überlebens eher hinderlich, weshalb man vom evolutionsbiologischen „Handikap-Prinzip" spricht. Die extravaganten Merkmale zeigen jedoch „innere Werte" an. Denn derlei Luxus kann sich nur leisten, wer gesund ist und mit gutem Erbgut ausgestattet – Eigenschaften also, die den Träger als Fortpflanzungspartner begehrlich machen.

Strategien der Reproduktion entfalten sich mithin in einem Wechselspiel von Erbgut und Umwelt. Nicht nur in dieser Hinsicht können Studien an Orang-Utans uns trefflich belehren.

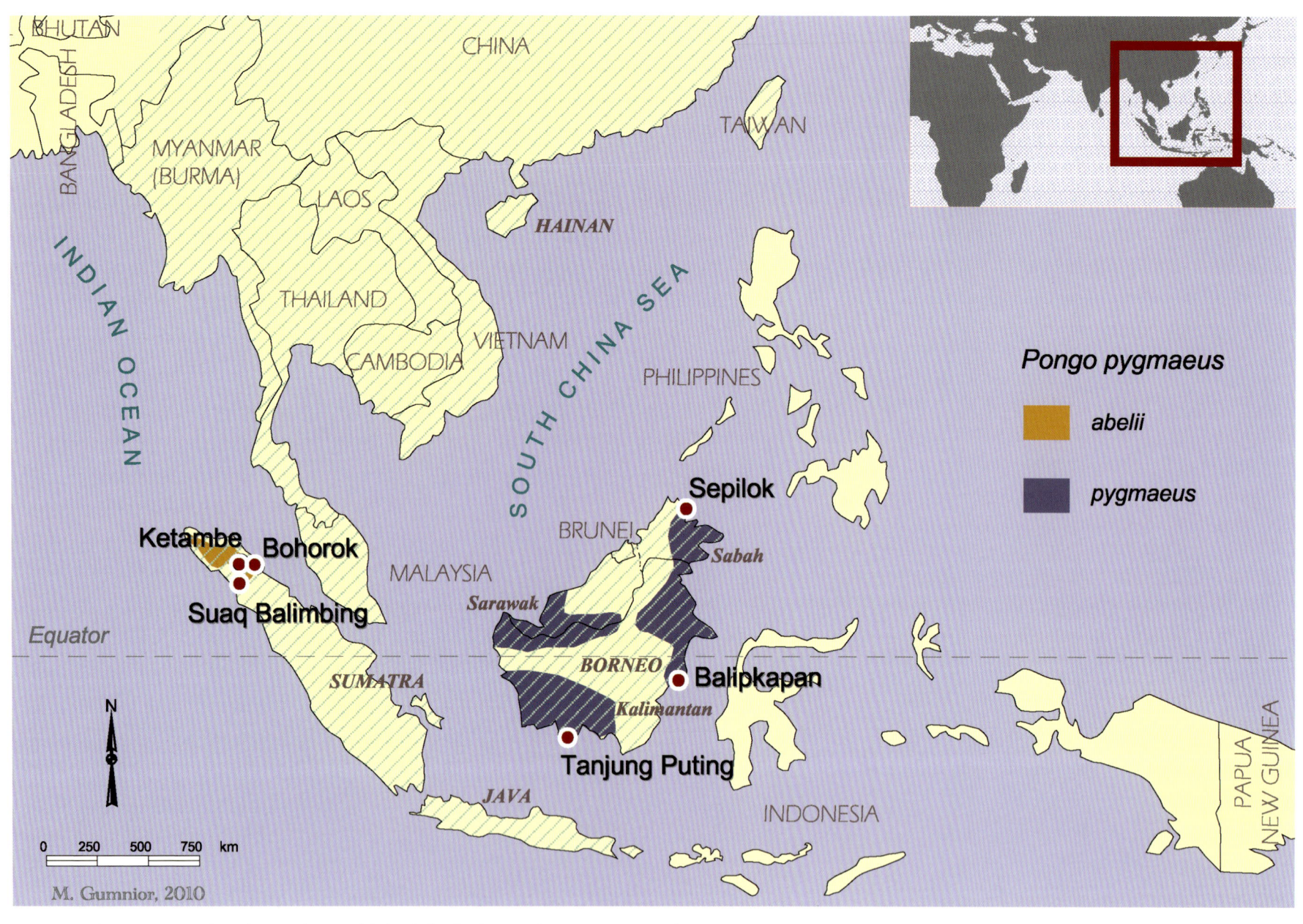

Orang-Utan (Pongo pygmaeus). Verbreitung heute und früher (schraffiert), mit wichtigen Forschungsstationen. Unterarten: P. p. abelii (Sumatra Orang-Utan); P. p. pygmaeus (Borneo Orang-Utan)

Orangutan (Pongo pygmaeus). Current vs. historical (hatched) distribution and important research stations. Subspecies: P. p. abelii (Sumatran orangutan); P. p. pygmaeus (Bornean orangutan)

Orang-Utan / *orangutan*

4. Orangutans

Hermits in the Jungle

Their appearance wasn't always advantageous for the red-haired "forest people", that being the Malay translation of their name. This is because the Dayak, the headhunters of Borneo, would also accept the skull of an orangutan as a trophy. This species is Asia's only great ape. Even a thousand years ago, they were widespread in Southeast Asia and China, as evidenced by bone finds and regional folklore. Sometimes walking upright, these large-bodied primates even make an acceptable prototype for the legendary Yeti. Orangutans are the only apes that habitually roam alone, and related fossils have indeed been dug up in the Himalayas. With increasing density of human settlements, orangutans disappeared from the Asian mainland. Today they survive only in Sumatra and Borneo, but deforestation and plantations are on the brink of destroying whatever little remains of their natural habitat.

A "Strange Sort of Monkey, Named Orang-outang, from the Isle of Borneo" was first described in 1778 as part of the menagerie of the Dutch Prince of Orange. The subsequent scientific name for the genus *Pongo* may derive from "M'Pungu", Congolese for "monster", and originally coined for the gorilla. The species name *pygmaeus,* however, denotes a "dwarf-like tribe" in Greek. The subspecies *Pongo pygmaeus abelii* occurs in the north of the Indonesian island Sumatra. The subspecies *Pongo pygmaeus pygmaeus* lives on Borneo, in the Indonesian part of Kalimantan and the Malaysian states of Sabah and Sarawak. Some scientists classify the forms as a different species. The Sumatran type has long, although sparse and coarse, reddish hair that is bright orange in youngsters and maroon in adults. The face is naked – rather pink when young, and later black. The face of the Borneo variant is slimmer and shorter, and the hair is darker, nearly chocolate-coloured.

Orangutans hold some records. Since males and females almost always travel alone, they are the least social of the great apes. They are likewise those with the most extreme degree of arboreality – as females and juveniles spend up to 95 percent of the time in trees. With weights of 60–90 kg for males and 35–50 kg for females, orangutans are also the heaviest tree dwellers that exist. Finally, they are the slowest-reproducing primates, as the interval between successive offspring is often 8–9 years.

Similarly to humans, the menstrual cycle lasts 28 days and a pregnancy 8 months. Not before 12–15 years will females first give birth. For the first 3 years of their life, babies will cling to their mothers, and they are nursed until they turn five. Even weaned offspring will hold Mum's hand while climbing. They also share her night nest, which each orangutan constructs each evening anew, by bending leafy branches together.

Orangutans prefer lowland jungles, while mangroves and mountain forests are sparsely populated. Each adult occupies its own home range, through which it will roam for an average of 300–800 m per day. Males range over 5–25 and females over 1–10 km^2.

Why do orangutans – apart from rare sexual encounters and permanent mother-child pairs – roam the jungle as hermits? Actually, the question is wrongly put. For it assumes that sociality is the default setting for primates. However, group living is especially problematic for females. They need to build up enough body fat to maintain an energy-expensive pregnancy and lactation. Other females are therefore primarily rivals for food, and are better shunned. Moreover, group life comes with an increased transmission of parasites and pathogens. Finally, fatal crashes, not rare in apes anyway, constitute a real risk. Branches carrying ten orangutans with a combined weight of half a ton would break even more easily.

This being the case, females should therefore only seek each other's company, if group living will outweigh such disadvantages. One benefit would be a significantly smaller risk of falling victim to a predator. Compared to living alone, chances to be eaten are only a tenth in a ten-member group. In addition, more eyes are more watchful, and by working together a predator can also often be put to flight.

However, because of their size, orangutans have hardly any natural enemies. On Borneo and Sumatra, it's possible that a clouded leopard could threaten orangutan babies. On Sumatra alone, wild dogs, leopards and tigers might pose an additional danger – although the canopy provides a very safe haven for the apes. Real danger exists only for adult males, who, because of their weight, will often choose to change from one tree to the next by climbing to the ground.

Social life can also be beneficial in terms of defending food against neighbouring groups. However, only "clumped" resources can effectively be monopolised in this way, for example, single large fruit trees or groves. Orangutan habitat, however, typically harbours many small and scattered food sources, which can at best satisfy individual animals.

Thus, it seems only logical that the "forest-people" prefer to live as hermits. In zoo settings, the disadvantages of group living are not relevant, as the animals are supplied with enough food, and infections are controlled by veterinarians. Here it becomes obvious that the red apes are not dedicated loners. Instead, such situations turn orangutans into real party animals, who seem to enjoy their close coexistence day in and day out.

In the wild, dominant males try to bring as many of the small and often overlapping ranges of females under their control. Because of pregnancy and lactation, years may pass between their fertile phases. Males can thus, despite the spatial separation, practically maintain a harem situation. This is because they only have to pay close attention to a particular lady when re-fertilisation is a possibility.

Impressive cheek-flanges characterise some males. Such appendages may amplify the long-distance calls that orangutan males produce with their huge throat pouches. Others respond clearly to such virile displays: fertile females will approach the most potent noisemakers and willingly mate with them; while competitors that are less well endowed keep their distance.

Only a few males develop the conspicuous cheek-pads and throat sacs. Most others have the appearance of adolescents. But the impression is deceptive, because the smaller males are, at least age-wise, already grown-ups. Nevertheless, as they are not in the physical shape to risk direct competition, they remain "arrested" within a youthful disguise, thus also provoking less aggression from the dominants.

This doesn't deter the arrested males to try an alternative strategy of reproduction: sexual coercion. Regularly, they force females to have sex them, as can be deduced from the resistance females put up. No other primate except humans are known to rape. This may have to do with the fact that females of both *Pongo pygmaeus* and *Homo sapiens* often wander unaccompanied. Such attacks occasionally reap reproductive benefits, as genetic tests demonstrate that orangutans who engage in coercive sex will indeed sire offspring at times.

A dominant male has passed its zenith if his cheek-flanges become dull and wrinkled, infested with parasites and covered with scars. Now the hour of those has come who, as disguised adolescents, often had to wait more than a decade for their chance. It may now only take weeks until a surge of hormones installs enough self-confidence in one of the rising stars to develop his own signature cheek-pads and throat sacs.

But why is it anyway that an audience of competitors and potential mates can be impressed by rather impractical features such as facial appendices and coarse vocalisations? On the one hand, similar to the roars of a deer, listeners can infer the caller's body size from the volume and depth of the sound. On the other hand, the physiological production of cheek-pads and songs comes at considerable cost – in terms of search time and the aggressive energy needed to defend the necessary high-quality food against competitors. At the same time, loud vocalisations alert predators to the location of the caller, and heavy tissue around the neck renders a defense or escape more difficult. Like a peacock's tail, such features are therefore more of a hindrance in terms of pure survival, which is why one speaks of the evolutionary "handicap" principle. The extravagant characteristics show, however, "inner values". Because such luxury items can only be afforded by somebody who is healthy and equipped with good genes – exactly those properties that render the carriers of such traits as sought-after partners for reproduction.

Strategies of procreation will thus unfold through an interplay of genes and environment. This is but one respect in which studies of orangutans can provide us with valuable lessons.

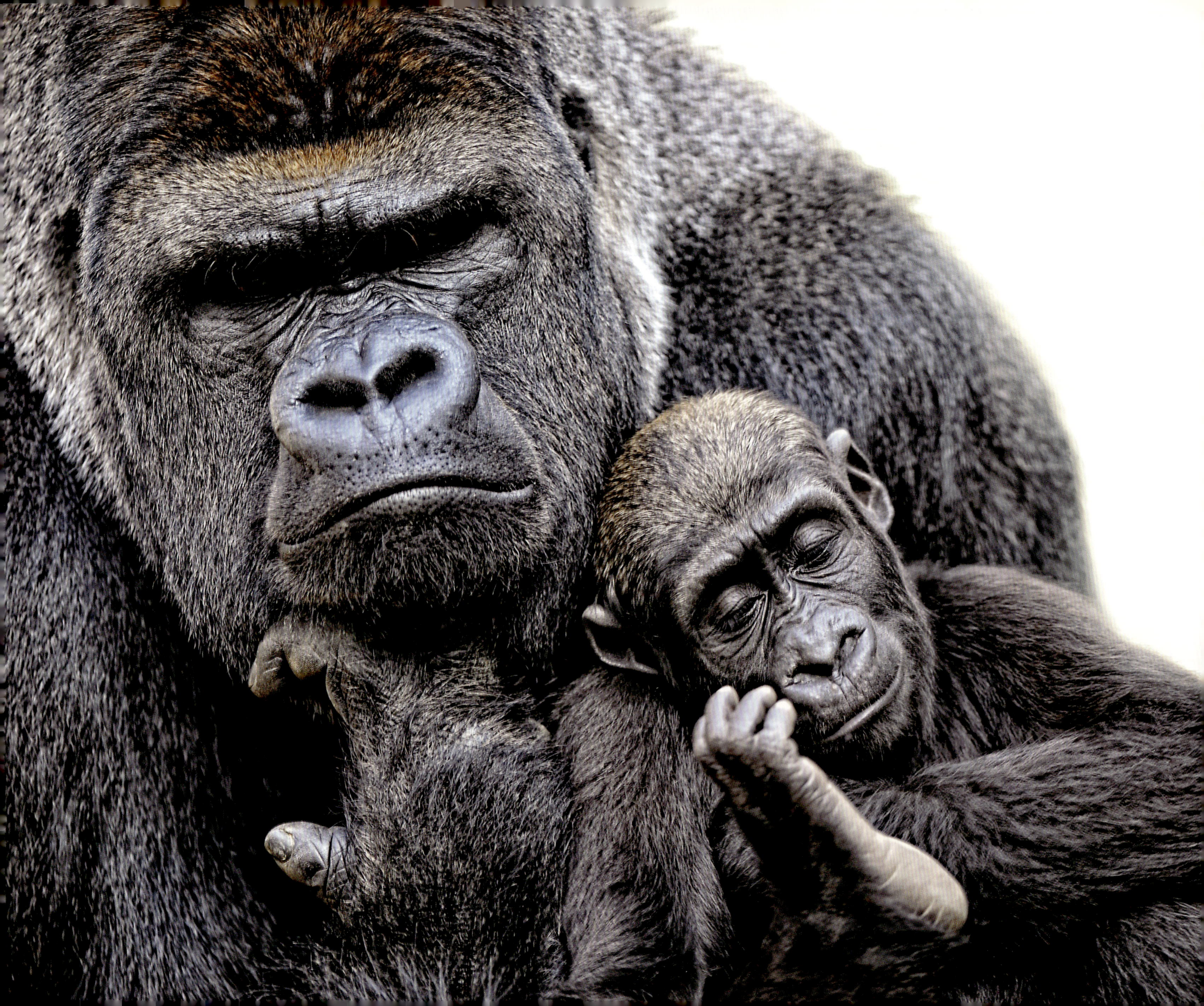

Gorillas

Gorillas

Gorilla / gorilla

Gorilla / *gorilla*

Gorilla / *gorilla*

5. Gorillas

Milde und wilde Riesen

Dokumentarfilme porträtieren Gorillas gerne als „milde Riesen", die gleichermaßen Zerstörungskraft und Beschützerinstinkt verkörpern. Die Fabel von *King Kong* setzte dieses Image überdimensional in Szene – nicht ohne ein Fünkchen Wahrheit.

Gorillas sind die größten lebenden Primaten. Ausgewachsene „Silberrücken" wiegen oft das Mehrfache von Weibchen und anderen Menschenaffen. Trotz mächtiger Muskeln und Eckzähne sind Männchen in der eigenen Gruppe oft ausgeglichen und zärtlich, und die Jüngsten dürfen ungeniert auf den Kolossen herumtollen. Gleichwohl töten Männchen wie Weibchen gelegentlich Babys – ohne mit der Wimper zu zucken.

Was wir über Gorillas wissen, basiert großteils auf jahrzehntelangen Studien an den Berggorillas der ostafrikanischen Virunga-Vulkane, während die Flachlandgorillas wenig erforscht sind. So wird erst allmählich klar, wie ihr Lebensstil von den jeweiligen Umwelten abhängt.

Ihr Name leitet sich vielleicht vom griechischen *gorillai* her. Der karthagische Seefahrer Hanno soll so „behaarte Frauen" bezeichnet haben, denen er um 470 v. Chr. im heutigen Sierra Leone begegnete. Die Erstbeschreibung von 1847 als *Troglodytes gorilla* geht auf den amerikanischen Missionar und Freizeitjäger Thomas Savage zurück, der einen Anatomen der Harvard Universität, Jeffries Wyman, mit Fellen und Knochen belieferte.

Heute werden vier Unterarten unterschieden: *Gorilla gorilla gorilla*, Flachlandgorilla, auch Westlicher Flachland- oder Tieflandgorilla; *Gorilla g. diehli*, Cross River Gorilla; *Gorilla g. graueri*, Grauergorilla, auch Östlicher Flachland- oder Tieflandgorilla; *Gorilla g. beringei*, Berggorilla. Manche Systematiker bevorzugen eine Trennung in zwei Arten: Westlicher Gorilla (*Gorilla gorilla*), mit Unterarten Westlicher Flachlandgorilla (*Gorilla g. gorilla*) und Cross River gorilla (*Gorilla g. diehli*), sowie Östlicher Gorilla (*Gorilla beringei*) mit Unterarten Östlicher Flachlandgorilla (*Gorilla b. graueri*) und Berggorilla (*Gorilla b. beringei*).

Gorillas leben bis zu 500 km nördlich und südlich des Äquators in Zentral- und Ost-Afrika. Dazwischen liegt ein 1.000 km breiter Korridor, in dem sie vor längerer Zeit ausgestorben sein müssen. Allerdings sind sicher nicht alle Bevölkerungen entdeckt. So wurden erst kürzlich, noch dazu im von Menschen dicht besiedelten Kamerun, in üppig bewachsenen, steilen Rückzugsgebieten neue Gruppen gefunden.

Weibchen bringen 60–100 kg auf die Waage, während bei Männchen 130–267 kg gemessen wurden. Korpulente Zooexemplare mögen gar 350 kg wiegen. Das schwärzliche Haar der Gorillas ist oft schütter oder teilweise fehlend. Bei ausgewachsenen Männchen färben sich Rückensattel und zuweilen Oberschenkel Silbergrau, was zu dem treffenden Namen „Silberrücken" inspirierte. Regionale Varianten sind braune Schädelkappen bei westlichen Formen, glänzende Brustpartien bei östlichen Flachlandgorillas und ein zotteliges Fell bei Berggorillas.

Westliche Gorillas besiedeln Wälder in Bergen und Flachland, wo sie in sumpfigen Lichtungen, den „Bhais", einigermaßen gut zu beobachten sind. Im Osten steigen Flachlandgorillas bis auf Wiesen in 2.600 Meter Höhe hinauf, und Berggorillas bis auf alpine Zonen in 4.300 m. Die Größe der Wohngebiete – 2–35 Quadratkilometer – hängt von der verfügbaren Nahrung ab.

Außer Leoparden haben Gorillas keine natürlichen Feinde. Jäger dezimieren sie wegen ihrer Fleischmassen und verwenden andere Körperteile als Trophäen, Fetische und Medizin.

Gorillas sind Pflanzenesser. Sie klettern relativ wenig im Geäst, weshalb der Fruchtanteil ihrer Nahrung mit maximal 40 Prozent deutlich geringer als bei anderen Menschenaffen ist. Bei Berggorillas machen Bodenkräuter gar bis zu 86 Prozent aus. Nur mancherorts beuten sie halbwegs regelmäßig Ameisenkolonien aus. Manchmal essen Gorillas Erde, vermutlich, um Pflanzennahrung zu entgiften. Die Aufnahme des eigenen Kots mag helfen, den Darm mit verdauungsfördernden Bakterien zu besiedeln. Ein Einzelfall von Kannibalismus, bei dem Weibchen ein fremdes Baby verzehrten, hatte wohl weniger mit Ernährung als mit dem Beseitigen von Konkurrenz zu tun. Aus der Wildnis ist lediglich ein Fall von Werkzeugbenutzung bekannt, bei dem ein Weibchen mit einem Stab einen Sumpf auslotete. Zum Nahrungserwerb scheinen Gorillas keine Werkzeuge zu brauchen. Mangelnde Intelligenz ist nicht die Ursache, denn in Gefangenschaft richten Gorillas spontan Stöcke her, um Süßigkeiten aus engen Röhren zu fischen.

Gorillas sind tagaktive Knöchelgänger. Berggorillas verbringen nur fünf Prozent ihrer Zeit auf Bäumen, Flachlandgorillas immerhin 35 Prozent. Wie andere Große Menschenaffen bauen sie jeden Abend ein Schlafnest aus Vegetation. Wohl wegen ihres Gewichts nächtigen sie häufiger auf dem Boden als im Geäst.

Weibchen werden mit etwa zehn Jahren schwanger, in Gefangenschaft jedoch schon drei Jahre früher. Babys kommen nach 8,5 Monaten zur Welt, und zwischen Geburten vergehen vier Jahre. In der Wildnis können Gorillas bis 45 Jahre leben, in Gefangenschaft über 50 Jahre.

Gruppengrößen betragen bei Westlichen Gorillas 10–32 Tiere, bei Östlichen Flachlandgorillas 13–42 und bei Berggorillas 11–47. Die Gemeinschaften sind umso kleiner, je mehr Fruchtanteil die Nahrung hat. Eine große reife Frucht ist ein nährstoffreicher Leckerbissen, den ein Einzelner mit Kraft oder Raffinesse für sich allein beanspruchen kann. Diese Monopolisierung dulden andere bestenfalls zähneknirschend. Wenn also in fruchtenden Bäumen durchschnittlich zehn Tiere ein Auskommen finden, tun die Überzähligen gut daran, eine eigene Clique zu gründen.

Gorillas bilden oft Gruppen von durchschnittlich elf Mitgliedern, in denen ein Mann mit etlichen Weibchen plus Kindern zusammenlebt – ein sogenannter „Harem". Junggesellen, denen ein Silberrücken Zugang zu Weibchen verwehrt, werden Einzelgänger oder schließen sich zu Banden zusammen. Da Männchen manchmal ein Jahrzehnt warten müssen, bis sie selbst Haremshalter werden, ist das Sozialleben unter Männern entsprechend wichtig – homosexuelle Beziehungen eingeschlossen. Besonders Berggorillas bilden Junggesellenbanden, weil Harems dort ziemlich stabil und langlebig sind. Oft sprengt weibliche Konkurrenz Gruppen auf. Im Schatten der Vulkane ist der Wettbewerb jedoch abgemildert, weil hier vornehmlich Kräuter konsumiert werden. Wo Wälder mehr Frucht produzieren, braucht ein Silberrücken nicht selten die Assistenz eines zweiten Mannes, um seinen Harem zusammenzuhalten und gegen Nachbarn zu verteidigen. Jedenfalls leben dort in bis zu 40 Prozent der Gruppen zwei Männchen. Der zweite Mann, nicht selten Sohn des Silberrückens, hält sich meist jahrelang im Hintergrund, bevor er seinem Vater die Paarungsrechte streitig macht.

Konkurrenz unter Männchen kann tödlich enden. Massive Muskeln und Gebiss spiegeln deshalb die Wirkmächtigkeit der „sexuellen Selektion" wider, den Prozess der geschlechtlichen Auslese, in dem die Wehrhafteren mehr Nachkommen hinterlassen. Eine grausame Konsequenz ist das Töten von Babys durch neue Haremshalter, was zumindest bei Berggorillas regelmäßig vorkommt. Bei stillenden Müttern ist der Eisprung gehemmt, und wenn ein Neuer vom Vorgänger gezeugte Säuglinge tötet, werden Weibchen rascher fruchtbar, als wenn sie ihr vormaliges Kind erst entwöhnen. Das Männchen kann seine begrenzte Residenzdauer entsprechend effektiver für eigene Fortpflanzung nutzen.

Männchen sind somit zwar prädestinierte Killer – aber auch geborene Väter. Zu eigenen Kindern sind sie nämlich nicht nur freundlich und fürsorglich, sondern opfern ohne Zögern ihr Leben, wenn ein Jäger sie bedroht. Überdies sind Weibchen zumindest implizit Komplizinnen bei den infantiziden Gewaltakten, da sie sich bereitwillig mit den Tötern ihrer Kinder paaren. Das verschafft vielleicht den Vorteil, selbst einen späteren Kindestöter zu gebären, der mehr Enkelkinder beschert als ein Pazifist es täte.

Weibchen sind außerdem keineswegs passive Handlungsware in Scharmützeln potentieller Haremshalter. Speziell jene mit abhängigen Kindern halten ihrem alten Partner zuweilen durchaus die Treue, selbst wenn er besiegt wurde. Andere Weibchen laufen zum Sieger über und die nächsten suchen sich einen komplett neuen Harem. Wegen dieser Wanderfreude kommen Gorilladamen schlecht miteinander aus, denn ein Harem ist aus Weibchen verschiedener Geburtsgruppen zusammengewürfelt, die keine verwandtschaftliche Bande haben.

Das Risiko der Kindestötung ist denn auch der eigentliche Grund zur Gruppenbildung, und nicht die gegenseitige Zuneigung der Gorilladamen. Vielmehr sucht jedes Weibchen für sich allein die Nähe eines starken Mannes, der ihr Baby vor Außenseitern beschützt. Egoistische Ängste addieren sich mithin zur Sozialgemeinschaft einer Ein-Männchen-viel-Weibchen-Gruppe.

Einmal siegreich, hat ein Haremshalter jedenfalls alleinigen Zugang zu den fruchtbaren Weibchen – mit einer auf den ersten Blick paradoxen Konsequenz.

Denn der Sex ist unspektakulär, was nicht zuletzt daran liegt, dass die Männchen, verglichen mit anderen Primaten und relativ zum Körper, extrem kleine Genitalien besitzen. Selbst erigiert ist der Penis lediglich zwei Zentimeter lang und die Hoden machen gerade 0,2 Tausendstel der Körpermasse aus.

Wie kann das sein? Hierzu muss man sich klarmachen, dass umso weniger Konkurrenz beim Kopulieren besteht, je idealer die Vielweiberei verwirklicht ist. Trotz alleiniger Kontrolle eines Harems sind dann die Genitalien entsprechend sparsam ausgestattet. Denn die Auslese reduziert, was nicht gebraucht wird.

Das Prinzip bestätigt sich im Vergleich mit der sexuellen Freizügigkeit bei Schimpansen und Bonobos. Hier mischen sich regelmäßig verschiedene Ejakulate im Genitaltrakt der Weibchen. Männchen, die mehr Spermien deponieren, haben eine bessere Chance, die Befruchtungslotterie zu gewinnen. Diese Verhältnisse züchten Hoden heraus, die mit 2,7 Promille 14 mal so groß sind wie bei Gorillas. Außerdem ist der Penis bei Schimpansen und Bonobos über zehn Zentimeter lang und läuft spitz zu, was die Notwendigkeit widerspiegelt, konkurrierenden Samen zu durchdringen und den eigenen möglichst nahe am Eingang zur Gebärmutter abzusetzen.

Zudem schwellen bei ovulierenden Schimpansen-Weibchen Genitalien und Analregion an. In Situationen mit mehreren Männchen können Schwellungen die Konkurrenz anstacheln, was den bestmöglichen Paarungspartner beschert. Dementsprechend fehlen Schwellungen bei Gorillas, wo sich Weibchen nur mit einem Mann verpaaren. Schwellungen testen wohl auch die Tauglichkeit des Penis, weil längere und potentere Exemplare das zusätzliche räumliche Hindernis einer Befruchtung leichter passieren können. Schließlich illustriert die Dauer des Koitus, wie stark der Wettbewerb ist. Die stets von anderen bedrängten Schimpansen und Bonobos perfektionierten den Quickie, weil von Intromission bis Ejakulation nur sieben Sekunden vergehen, während ein einzelner Gorillamann sich zehnmal mehr Zeit lassen kann.

Die Verhältnisse bei anderen Menschenaffen liegen dazwischen. Verglichen mit Gorillas können Orang-Utans ihre Weibchen nicht ganz so erfolgreich monopolisieren; ihre Hoden wiegen 0,5 Promille des Körpers. Gibbons, die Kleinen Menschenaffen Asiens, leben oft in Einehe. Ihre Hoden sind jedoch mit ein Promille Gewicht größer als bei vollkommener sexueller Treue zu erwarten wäre. In der Tat haben Gibbonmänner Seitensprünge und damit Doppelbesamung zu fürchten, was zu Samenspendern führt, die wenigstens leichten Konkurrenzdruck aushalten können. Derlei sexualbiologische Prinzipien sprechen übrigens gegen eine ursprünglich einehige Fortpflanzung bei *Homo sapiens*. Denn Hoden um 0,6 Promille Gewicht deuten eher auf Vielweiberei hin, wofür fehlende Genitalschwellungen bei Frauen ebenfalls sprechen.

Gleichwohl beschreiben die Faustregeln zur Sexualbiologie lediglich die wahrscheinlichste Form des Zusammenlebens. Dass bei Gorillas zwar 60 Prozent der Gruppen strikte Harems sind, ein großer Rest jedoch zwei Männchen einschließt, belegt den Einfluss von Umweltbedingungen. Ganz ähnlich variiert bei Menschen die Zahl von Ehepartnern von Kultur zu Kultur. Von 849 im *Ethnographischen Atlas* aufgelisteten Gesellschaften erlauben 83 Prozent die Vielweiberei, während 16 Prozent vom Gesetz her monogam sind und ein winziger Rest Vielmännerei praktiziert.

Die klassische Verhaltensforschung um ihre Gründungsväter Konrad Lorenz und Nikolaas Tinbergen fahndete nach „arterhaltenden" Mechanismen im Verhalten, denn das Individuum wurde begriffen als dem übergeordneten Ziel der Arterhaltung zuarbeitend. Für das regelmäßige und vorhersagbare Töten von Artgenossen war in einer solche Theorie kein Platz – ebensowenig wie für Varianten im Sexualverhalten. Was vom „Arttypischen" abwich, wurde entsprechend als „Pathologie" klassifiziert, als krankhaft. Das statische Bild wich einem dynamischeren, als mit dem Aufkommen der Soziobiologie die Einsicht wuchs, dass die Auslese nicht bei der Art oder Gruppe angreift, sondern am Einzelorganismus. Dadurch ließen sich Varianten als „alternative Strategien" verstehen. Denn was immer zu reproduktivem Erfolg führt, wird von der Selektion begünstigt – ganz gleich, ob die Eigenschaft Artgenossen nützt oder schadet.

In den für Männchen und Weibchen unterschiedlichen Problemen bei der Fortpflanzung wurzeln also Konflikte mit Geschlechtsgenossen ebenso wie jene, die Männer mit Männern und Frauen untereinander austragen. Es mag trösten, dass es sich dabei um uraltes Affentheater handelt – wie nicht nur das Beispiel der Gorillas lehrt.

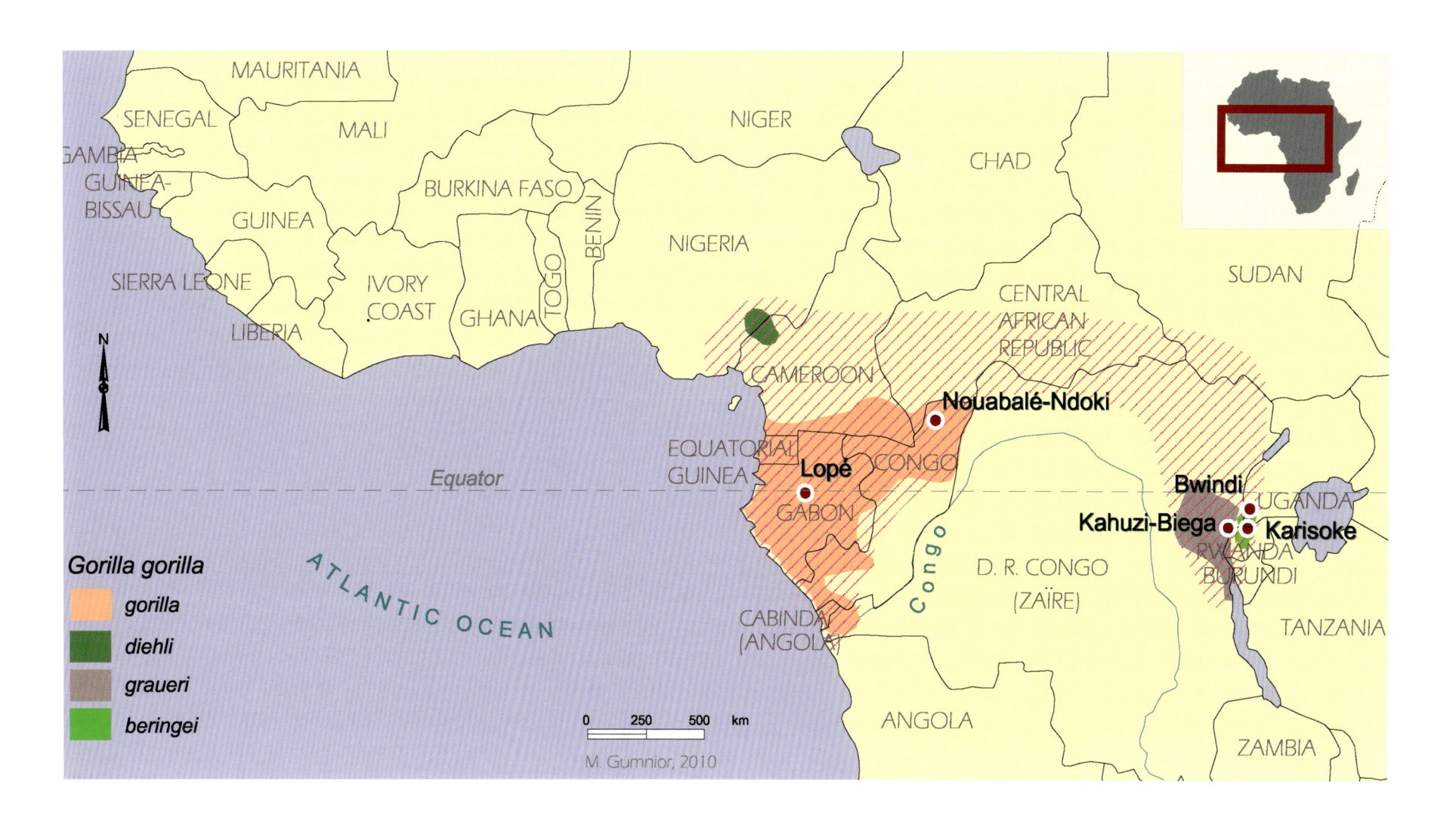

Gorilla (Gorilla gorilla). Verbreitung heute und früher (schraffiert), mit wichtigen Forschungsstationen. Unterarten: G. g. gorilla (Westlicher Flach- oder Tieflandgorilla, Flachlandgorilla); G. g. diehli (Cross River Gorilla); G. g. graueri (Grauergorilla, Östlicher Flach- oder Tieflandgorilla); G. g. beringei (Berggorilla)

Gorilla (Gorilla gorilla). Current vs. historical (hatched) distribution and important research stations. Subspecies: G. g. gorilla (Western lowland gorilla); G. g. diehli (Cross River gorilla); G. g. graueri (Eastern lowland gorilla, Grauer's gorilla); G. g. beringei (mountain gorilla)

Gorilla / *gorilla*

5. Gorillas

Mild and Wild Giants

Documentaries like to portray gorillas as "gentle giants" who simultaneously embody destructive powers and protective instincts. The fable of *King Kong* capitalises on a supersized concept of this scenario – although not without a grain of truth.

Gorillas are the largest living primates. Fully grown "silverbacks" often weigh many times that of females or, for that matter, any other primate. Despite mighty muscle and being armed to the teeth, these males will often come across as composed and tender when in the midst of their own group; youngsters use the colossi fearlessly as living playgrounds. Sometimes, however, males – and also females – will slaughter the innocents without so much as flinching.

What we know about these giants is largely based on decades of research on mountain gorillas in East Africa's Virunga Volcanoes, while lowland gorillas have been much less explored. Thus, we are only gradually learning how the gorilla lifestyle is shaped by particular environments.

The name itself originates perhaps from the Greek *gorillai*. The Carthaginian navigator Hanno supposedly used this word to describe "hairy women" whom he met around 470 BC in what is now Sierra Leone. The first scientific description as *Troglodytes gorilla* from 1847 dates back to the American missionary and recreational hunter Thomas Savage, who supplied an anatomist of Harvard University, Jeffries Wyman, with skins and bones.

Today, four subspecies are distinguished: *Gorilla gorilla gorilla,* lowland gorilla, aka western lowland or lowland gorilla; *Gorilla g. diehli,* Cross River gorilla; *Gorilla g. graueri,* Grauergorilla, aka eastern lowland or lowland gorilla; and *Gorilla g. beringei,* mountain gorilla. Some taxonomists prefer a separation into two species: Western gorilla (*Gorilla gorilla*), with subspecies western lowland gorilla (*Gorilla g. gorilla*) and Cross River gorilla (*Gorilla g. diehli*); and Eastern gorilla (*Gorilla beringei*) with subspecies eastern lowland gorilla (*Gorilla b. graueri*) and mountain gorilla (*Gorilla b. beringei*).

Gorillas are distributed up to 500 km north and south of the equator in Central and East Africa. In between is a 1,000 km-wide corridor where they must have gone extinct some time ago. However, certainly not all populations have been discovered. Thus, on lush, steep slopes new groups were only recently found – and this was in densely populated Cameroon.

Females measure 60–100 and males 130–267 kg. Obese zoo specimen may reach 350 kg. The blackish hair of gorillas is often sparse or partially absent. In adult males, the hair on the rump and sometimes upper thighs will turn into a silvery grey, which inspired the apt term "silverback". Western forms develop brown skull caps; the shiny chests of eastern lowland gorillas are another regional variant, as is the shaggy fur of mountain gorillas.

Western gorillas inhabit forests in mountains and plains, where swampy clearings, so-called "bhais", provide reasonably good opportunities to observe them. Eastern lowland gorillas may forage in meadows in altitudes of up to 2,600 m, whereas mountain gorillas climb up to alpine zones of 4,300 m. Home range sizes of 2–35 km² depend on the quality and availability of food.

Except for leopards, gorillas have no natural enemies. Hunters decimate them because they provide plenty of meat, and relish other body parts as trophies, fetishes and medicine.

Gorillas are plant eaters. They don't climb much around in the canopy, so fruits constitute only up to 40 percent of their diet, considerably less than in other apes. Mountain gorillas may munch for up to 86 percent of the time on terrestrial herbs. Only in some places do gorillas exploit ant colonies with any regularity. Sometimes gorillas ingest soil, presumably to detoxify plant food. They may also swallow their own faeces, perhaps to repopulate the gut with bacteria that aid digestion. A case of cannibalism, in which females consumed the baby of a troop mate, has probably less to do with diet than with the elimination of competition.

Only a single instance of tool use has so far been reported from the wild, when a female used a stick to gauge the depth of a swamp. Gorillas do not seem to require tools as a foraging aid. A deficiency of intelligence is not behind this lack, because in captivity gorillas will spontaneously insert sticks into tubes laced with honey.

Gorillas are day-active knuckle-walkers. Mountain gorillas spend only 5 percent of their time in trees, whereas lowland gorillas do this for 35 percent. Like other great apes, they build a sleeping nest every night from fresh vegetation. Probably because of their weight, they sleep more often on the ground than in the canopy.

Females become pregnant at approximately 10 years, but 3 years earlier in captivity. Babies are born after a gestation of 8.5 months, and births are spaced by about 4 years. In the wild, gorillas can live up to 45 years, and in captivity more than 50.

Groups of western gorillas have 10–32 animals, those of eastern lowland 13–42 and those of mountain gorillas 11–47. Groups are smaller if the diet contains more fruits. This is because a large ripe fruit is a nutritious delicacy that can be monopolised by a single individual through force or cleverness. Others will tolerate this at best grudgingly. Thus, if fruit trees can satisfy an average of, let's say, 10 animals, then supernumeraries are better off starting their own clique.

The average gorilla group is made up of 11 members, in which a single male lives together with several females plus their offspring – a so-called "harem". Bachelors, denied access to females by a silverback, will roam on their own or form all-male bands. Males may sometimes have to wait for a decade until they can establish themselves as a harem resident. Correspondingly, social life among males is important – including homosexual relationships. Mountain gorillas in particular form bachelor bands, because their harems are quite stable and durable. Often, it is competition amongst females that causes groups to disintegrate. However, in the shadow of the Virunga volcanoes, rivalry is less pronounced because herbs are the most important food stuff. In forests where sought-after fruits grow, silverbacks will often need the assistance of a second male to hold their harem together and to defend it against ambitious neighbours. In such areas, up to 40 percent of all groups contain two males. The second macho-man, often the son of the silverback, may remain in the background for years, before disputing his father's mating privileges.

Competition among males can be lethal. Massive muscles and dentition therefore reflect the forces of sexual selection, by which more powerful males will leave more offspring. A consequence is the gruesome killing of babies by new harem holders, a regular occurrence at least in mountain gorillas. Lactating females tend to not ovulate. If a new male kills a predecessor's baby, females will resume their fertility faster than if they first wean their offspring. In this way, a male can use his limited residence time more effectively to enhance his own reproduction.

Males are therefore predestined killers – but also born fathers. To their own children they are not only kind and caring, but males will sacrifice their lives without hesitation if a hunter threatens their progeny. Moreover, females are at least implicit accomplices in the violent incidents of infanticide, as they will readily mate with the killer of their children. This provides them perhaps with an advantage of their own. Because, if they give birth to an infant-killer themselves, he may bestow more grandchildren upon them then a pacifist would.

Females are also not passive victims in skirmishes between potential harem holders. Especially those with dependent children will at times remain loyal to their old partners even if he is defeated. Other females will desert to the winner, and again others will scout for a completely new harem. Because of this tendency to wander off, females don't get along with one another, because harems constitute a patchwork of members from different natal groups without ties of kinship.

The risk of infanticide, rather than mutual affection of females, is therefore the true reason for the formation of groups. Basically, each female on her own seeks to be close to a strong male who can protect her baby against outsiders. Selfish fears thus add up to the complexities of the gorilla society.

Once victorious, a harem holder gains exclusive access to fertile females – with at first glance paradoxical consequences. Because sex is a rather unspectacular affair. Gorilla males possess extremely small genitals, relative to their giant body and also compared to other primates. Even when erect, the penis is a mere 2 cm long, and testes weigh only 0.2 promille – thousandths – of the body mass.

Why is this? Well, the less competition for copulation exists, the more perfect is the one-male-multi-female system of polygyny. Accordingly, despite him controlling a harem, the genitals of a gorilla male can be less endowed, as unnecessary features will be weeded out by the processes of selection – reflecting the principle of "use it or lose it".

A comparison with the sexually promiscuous social systems of chimpanzees and bonobos illustrates this point. Here, females mate with multiple males in short succession, and various ejaculates get mixed up in their genital tracts. Males who deposit more sperm cells will have a better chance of winning the lottery of fertilisation. Such multi-male-multi-female societies select for testicles which, with 2.7 promille, are 14 times as large as those of gorillas. In addition, a chimpanzee or bonobo penis is more than 10 cm long and tapers, reflecting the need to penetrate competing ejaculates and deposit its own sperm as close to the entrance of the uterus as possible.

In addition, the vaginal and anal region of chimpanzees will develop swellings around the time of ovulation. Such rounded shapes are suitable to incite competition if multiple males are present, thus increasing the chance of copulation with the best suitable mate. Accordingly, swellings are absent in gorillas, where females mate with only with a single male. In addition, swellings probably select for a lengthy penis, because longer and more potent specimen can more easily penetrate this additional spatial obstacle for fertilisation. Finally, the degree of competition is also echoed in the duration of the coitus. Chimpanzees and bonobos are always hard-pressed by others and have thus perfected the quickie. They need a mere seven seconds from intromission to ejaculation, while a gorilla, unbothered by rivals, can afford to take ten times as long.

The state of affairs in other apes is intermediary. Compared to gorillas, orangutans cannot monopolise females quite as successfully, and their testes thus measure 0.5 promille of their body weight. Gibbons, the small apes of Asia, will often live in monogamy. However, their testicles, with 1 promille, are larger, as one would expect under conditions of perfect sexual fidelity. In fact, gibbon males have to fear extra-pair copulations and thus double-matings of their females. This selects for organs that can withstand at least mild degrees of sperm competition. Such basics of sexual biology, by the way, speak against the assumption that monogamy was the ancestral mating system of *Homo sapiens*. For testes of 0.6 promille – and also the lack of genital swellings in women – indicate an original tendency to form polygynous societies.

Nevertheless, these are only rules of thumb, which merely predict the most likely forms of interaction between the sexes. The fact that gorillas form strict harems in 60 percent of cases, but that the great remainder includes two males, demonstrates the influence of environmental conditions. Similarly, the number of spouses varies between human cultures. Of 849 societies listed in the *Ethnographic Atlas,* 83 percent allow polygyny, while 16 percent are monogamous by law, and a small minority practices polyandry.

Classic comparative ethology as developed by its founding fathers, Konrad Lorenz and Nikolas Tinbergen, postulated that animals aimed to "preserve the species". Individuals were seen as serving the overarching goal of what is good for the group. This theory could neither accommodate a behaviour such as the regular and predictable killing of conspecifics nor variability in sexual behaviour. Whatever didn't fit the template of "species-typical" behaviour, was classified as dysfunctional – as a "pathology". This static picture gave way to a more dynamic interpretation, when, with the advent of sociobiology, the realisation grew that selection doesn't target the species or group, but the individual organism. Consequently, variants can be understood as "alternative strategies". Thus whatever trait leads to reproductive success will be selected for – independent from whether it harms or benefits others.

Conflicts between members of the same sex as well as discord between males and females are therefore rooted in the fact that the sexes are confronted with different sets of problems while trying to reproduce. Perhaps some comfort can be found in the realisation that such fracases are part of what it means to be a primate – as not only the example of the gorilla illustrates.

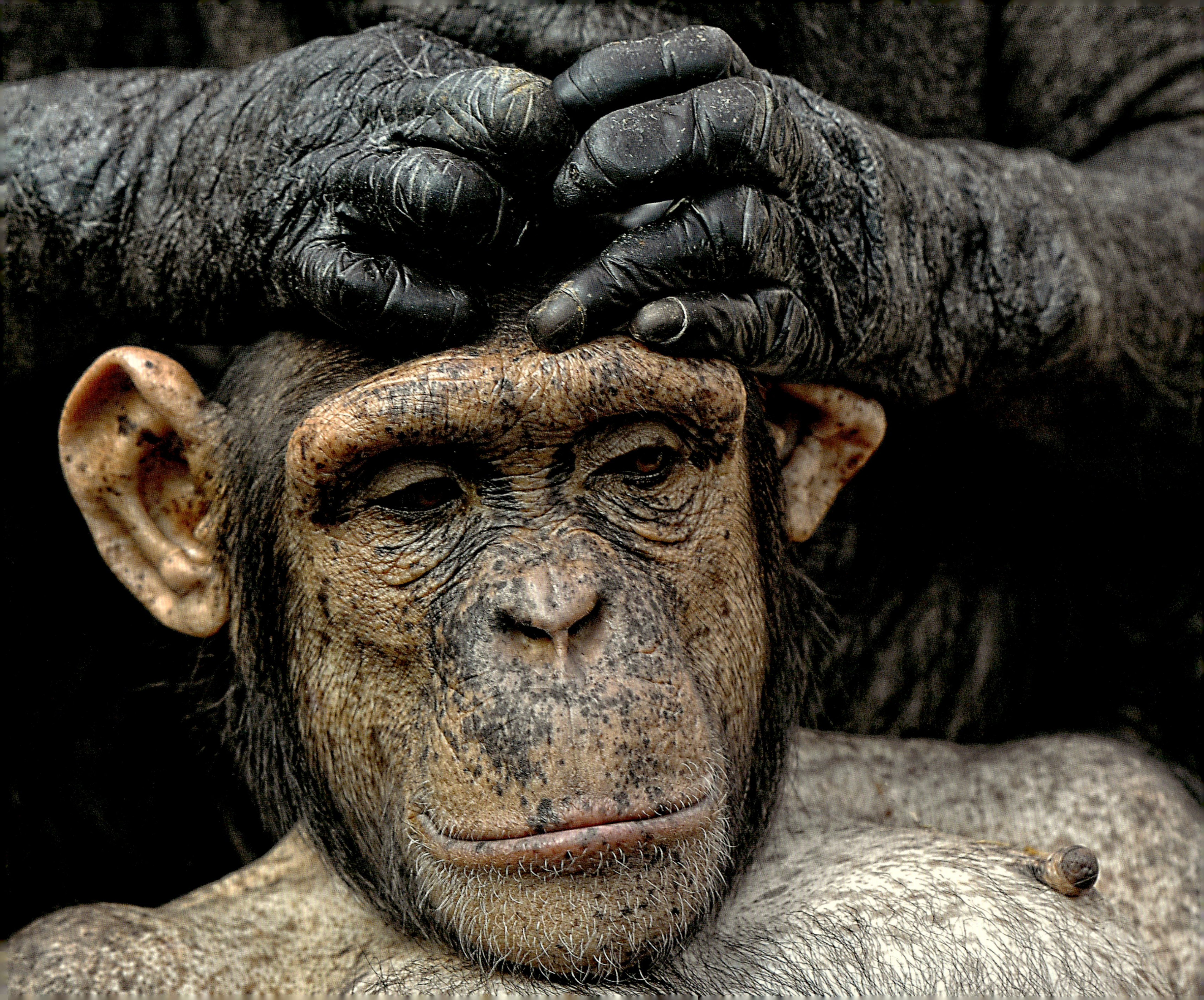

Schimpansen
Chimpanzees

Schimpanse / *chimpanzee*

Schimpanse / *chimpanzee*

6. Schimpansen

Keine besseren Menschen

Weil sie die am besten und am längsten erforschten Menschenaffen sind, wurden manche erstaunlichen Fähigkeiten nicht-menschlicher Tiere zum ersten Mal bei Schimpansen beobachtet. Etwa, dass sie geschickt Werkzeuge verwenden, dass ihre Gesellschaften unterschiedliche Sitten pflegen oder dass sie sich als gewiefte Politiker erweisen können. Untersuchungen an Schimpansen waren aber ebenfalls bahnbrechend hinsichtlich der Erkenntnis, dass tierische Intelligenz auch dunkle Seiten haben kann – etwa wenn diese Menschenaffen rivalisierende Nachbarn ausrotten oder systematischem Kannibalismus frönen.

Eine Doppelgesichtigkeit haftet Schimpansen schon vom Namen her an. *Pan troglodytes* – „höhlenbewohnender Pan" – verweist auf jene griechische Gottheit, halb Mensch, halb Tiergestalt, deren plötzliches Erscheinen Terror auslöste, den „panischen" Schrecken. Ähnlich beschrieb Nicolaes Tulpius einen 1641 in die Niederlande gelangten Schimpansen als „Indischen Satyr". Der Zwiespalt von Wissenschaftlern, die die Menschenähnlichkeit von Schimpansen erkannten, aber gleichwohl unsere Einzigartigkeit retten wollten, spiegelt sich im Wandel des Namens wider – vom usprünglichen *Homo* über *Simia* bis *Pan*.

Heutzutage werden vier Unterarten unterschieden: *Pan troglodytes verus*, Westafrikanischer oder Echtschimpanse; *Pan t. vellerosus* (neuerdings auch *Pan t. ellioti* genannt), Nigerianisch-Kamerunscher Schimpanse; *Pan t. troglodytes*, Zentralafrikanischer Schimpanse oder Tschego; *Pan t. schweinfurthii*, Ostafrikanischer oder Langhaarschimpanse.

Im Zoo bringen fette Schimpansen bis 90 kg auf die Waage. Das männliche Normalgewicht beträgt zwischen 37–60 kg, das weibliche 30–47 kg. Wie bei anderen Menschenaffen ist in etwa monatlichem Abstand eine Menstruationsblutung sichtbar. Anders als bei Orang-Utans, Gorillas und Menschen zeigt eine rosafarbene Schwellung der Ano-Genital-Region die ungefähre Zeit des Eisprungs an. Mit etwa zwölf Jahren bringen Weibchen ihr erstes Kind zur Welt, und weitere Geburten folgen alle vier bis sechs Jahre. Viele wilde Schimpansen überleben mehr als 40 Jahre, gefangen gehaltene mehr als 60 Jahre.

Schimpansen sind tagaktive Knöchelgänger, die sich aufrichten können, um Nahrung zu erlangen oder bei aggressiven Zurschaustellungen. Männchen verbringen um 40 Prozent ihrer Tageszeit auf Bäumen, Weibchen 60 Prozent. Je nach verfügbarer Nahrung durchstreifen Schimpansen Gebiete von 5–500 Quadratkilometer. Jeden Abend baut jeder Schimpanse eine Schlafstätte im Gezweig und manchmal tagsüber für die Siesta. Bodennester, zwar selten, gibt es auch – verblüffenderweise gerade in Gegenden, wo ihre wichtigsten Raubfeinde lauern könnten: Leoparden.

Schimpansen leben in geschlossenem Regenwald wie in Mosaik-Biotopen aus Ufer- und Tieflandwäldern und Savanne. Diese bemerkenswerte ökologische Flexibilität hat zur Konsequenz, dass Schimpansen als am weitesten verbreitete Menschenaffen in 21 afrikanischen Ländern vorkommen. Sicherlich drückt sich hierin auch Intelligenz aus, denn Schimpansen ergattern schwer zugängliche Nahrung mittels verschiedener Geräte. Hierzu zählen Hämmer und Ambosse aus Holz oder Stein, um Nüsse zu zerschlagen; kurze Lanzen, um Halbaffen in ihren Höhlen zu erdolchen; Blattschwämme, um Wasser aus Vertiefungen aufzunehmen; lange Stöcke, um aggressive Ameisen zu erangeln; aufgefächerte Stäbchen, um Honig zu erlöffeln. Werkzeuge werden auch im sozialen Kontext eingesetzt, darunter Knüppel zum Bedrohen und Steine als Wurfgeschosse – wobei genaues Zielen nicht Sache der Schimpansen ist.

Mancherorts unternehmen Schimpansen Jagdzüge mit oft klarer Rollenverteilung zwischen Treibern und Fängern. Doch werden Stummelaffen, Waldantilopen, Buschschweine, Paviane und Nagetiere auch opportunistisch ergriffen und erlegt. Der Raubtier-Charakter von Schimpansen macht übrigens auch vor Menschen nicht halt, denn mehrfach haben sie Säuglinge von Dorfbewohnern oder Wildhütern aufgegriffen und verzehrt. Schimpansen wurden überdies beim Töten eines kleinen Leoparden beobachtet, in dem sie vielleicht eine zukünftige Gefahr heranwachsen sahen.

Obwohl sich Weibchen nicht an der Jagd beteiligen, erhalten sie dennoch nicht selten Brocken der Beute, oft im Tausch mit Sex. Während Männchen vornehmlich jagen, ist Sammeln von Kleintieren eher Frauensache. Kolonien von Termiten, Bienen und Ameisen werden oft systematisch ausgebeutet, mit Brut und Honig als Leckerbissen. Der Geschlechtsunterschied entspricht in gewisser Hinsicht jener Arbeitsteilung, wie sie in Jäger-Sammler-Völkern zu finden ist.

Auch bei Schimpansen ist es die Not, die erfinderisch macht. Denn mancherorts jagen sie weder noch setzen sie Werkzeug ein, um schwer zugängliche Nahrung zu extrahieren – vielleicht, weil ihr Wohngebiet üppig genug ist. In solchen Schlaraffenländern beschränken sie sich auf ihre Hauptspeise, Früchte, die 56–71 Prozent ihres Menüs ausmachen. Ergänzend essen sie Blätter und andere Pflanzenteile wie Blüten und Kräuter.

Schmackhafte Früchte wachsen nicht auf vielen Bäumen. Da Kommunitäten von Schimpansen durchschnittlich 41 Mitglieder umfassen und zuweilen um die 100, sind gemeinsame Tageswanderungen unökonomisch. Permanenter Streit um die besten Leckerbissen wäre unvermeidbar. Speziell Mütter mit Kleintieren halten sich deshalb am besten abseits. So entwickelte sich ein Sozialsystem, bei dem die Kommunität in Grüppchen aufgeteilt ist. Im Mittel gehen sechs Schimpansen gemeinsam auf Nahrungssuche, wobei sie sich periodisch mit anderen Grüppchen vereinen (*fusion*), um in wechselnder Zusammensetzung wieder auseinanderzugehen (*fission*).

Gemeinsam versuchen die Männchen, ein möglichst reichhaltiges Gebiet gegen Nachbarmänner abzuschotten. Je größer das Territorium, desto mehr Fortplanzungspartnerinnen kann es beherbergen. Die Zusammenarbeit der Männchen beruht stark auf ihrer genetischen Verwandtschaft. Sie verbleiben lebenslang in ihrer Geburtsgruppe und sind deshalb oft Halbbrüder. Weibchen hingegen wandern aus verschiedenen Nachbarschaften ein. Entsprechend gespannt sind die Verhältnisse der Damen untereinander. Aber auch Männchen kennen Konflikte, denn einzelne versuchen, sich durch Körperkraft und sozialtaktisches Koalieren als Alpha-Affe zu etablieren, was mit einer erhöhten Chance einhergeht, Kinder zu zeugen.

Jane Goodall begann um 1960, Schimpansen in der Wildnis zu erforschen. Die Engländerin zeichnete zunächst ein paradiesisches Bild, demzufolge Schimpansen-Gesellschaften auf Kooperation gründen und friedlichem Einsatz von Intelligenz. Botschaft: Schimpansen sind die besseren Menschen. Goodall stand damit in der Tradition der 200 Jahre alten Naturromantik von Jean-Jacques Rousseau. Darauf aufbauende Theorien des Kulturpessimismus suggerierten, dass Feindschaft in menschlichen Urgesellschaften unbekannt war und sittlicher Niedergang erst mit Perversionen von Technologie und Wissenschaft begann.

Gesellschaften von Schimpansen – wie die von Menschen – entbehren allerdings nicht „historischer" Dimensionen. Eine Anthropologin vom Mars, die im Westeuropa des letzten Jahrzehnts lebte, würde Friedfertigkeit herausstreichen, hätte bei einem Besuch ab 1939 aber ein entgegengesetztes Urteil gefällt. Ähnlich ging es Jane Goodall: Von 1960–1970 waren ihre Gombe-Schimpansen friedlich – aber danach entpuppten sich viele als Killer. Es schockte Goodall, als ihre geliebten Schimpansen um 1974 begannen, einander zu töten: Männliche Allianzen rotteten Nachbargruppen aus und entführten junge Weibchen. Die Primatologen-Pionierin war ehrlich genug, die Grausamkeiten detailgetreu zu dokumentieren – bis hin zur schockierenden Praxis, Blut von Besiegten zu schlürfen.

Auch Forscher andernorts berichteten alsbald von letalen Übergriffen inklusive Verzehr von Säuglingen. Männchen scheinen Babys vor allem dann zu töten, wenn wahrscheinlich ist, dass sie in einer Nachbargruppe gezeugt wurden. Weibchen wiederum bringen, vermutlich aus Konkurrenz, gelegentlich Babys nichtverwandter Gruppengenossinnen um und essen sie dann auf. Schimpansen-Männchen erweisen sich zudem als gnadenlose Frauenunterdrücker, die stets die besten Brocken für sich beanspruchen – ganz gleich, ob schattige Plätzchen oder schmackhafte Frucht.

Derlei Aggressionen sind Wasser auf die Mühlen der Anhänger der Philosophie von Thomas Hobbes. Als Antipode von Rousseau hatte Hobbes den Krieg aller gegen alle für den Naturzustand gehalten und einen starken Staat gefordert, um, quasi im Tausch gegen Autonomie, ein gesichertes Zusammenleben zu ermöglichen.

Als Galionsfigur einer „Zurück-zur-Natur"-Bewegung taugt der Schimpanse mithin nicht. Die intellektuellen Erben von Hippie-Happenings und Studentenrevolte freilich wollen lieber Gutes als Schlechtes über unsere natürlichen Neigungen hören. Da bietet es sich an, die Rolle der Friedensbotschafter auf die Bonobos zu übertragen. Denn was diese anderen Mitglieder der Gattung *Pan* tun – und was sie *nicht* tun –, ist geeignet, Naturromantiker zu versöhnen.

Bonobos pflegen nämlich ein variantenreiches Sexualleben, ohne sich kriegerisch zu bekämpfen. Das erlaubt, nunmehr *sie* zu besseren Menschen zu stilisieren. Diese Wahrnehmung ist allerdings ebenfalls verzerrt, und zwar ziemlich hoffnungslos. Denn auch bei diesen Menschenaffen sind harte Auseinandersetzungen nicht unbekannt. So können Bonobos noch nicht einmal als „bessere Schimpansen" durchgehen; bei ihnen ist blutige Aggression jedoch eine weibliche Domäne.

In der Natur ist also vieles möglich. Eben deshalb liegen Naturromantiker falsch. Denn nicht alles „Natürliche" ist automatisch gutzuheißen – wie das Vorkommen von Kannibalismus, Kindestötung, Ausrottung von Nachbarn und Vergewaltigung bei unseren nächsten Verwandten belegt. Die simpel genug klingende Forderung, dass wir Gutes tun und Böses lassen sollen, ist deshalb gar nicht so einfach in die Tat umzusetzen. Denn unser natürliches Erbe beschert uns die Fähigkeit zu Eigennutz und gnadenloser Konkurrenz ebenso wie die zu Mitleid und fruchtbarer Kooperation – setzt also Grenzen und beinhaltet Chancen. Deshalb kann es gewiss nicht schaden, wenn wir unseren inneren Affen umso eifriger erforschen.

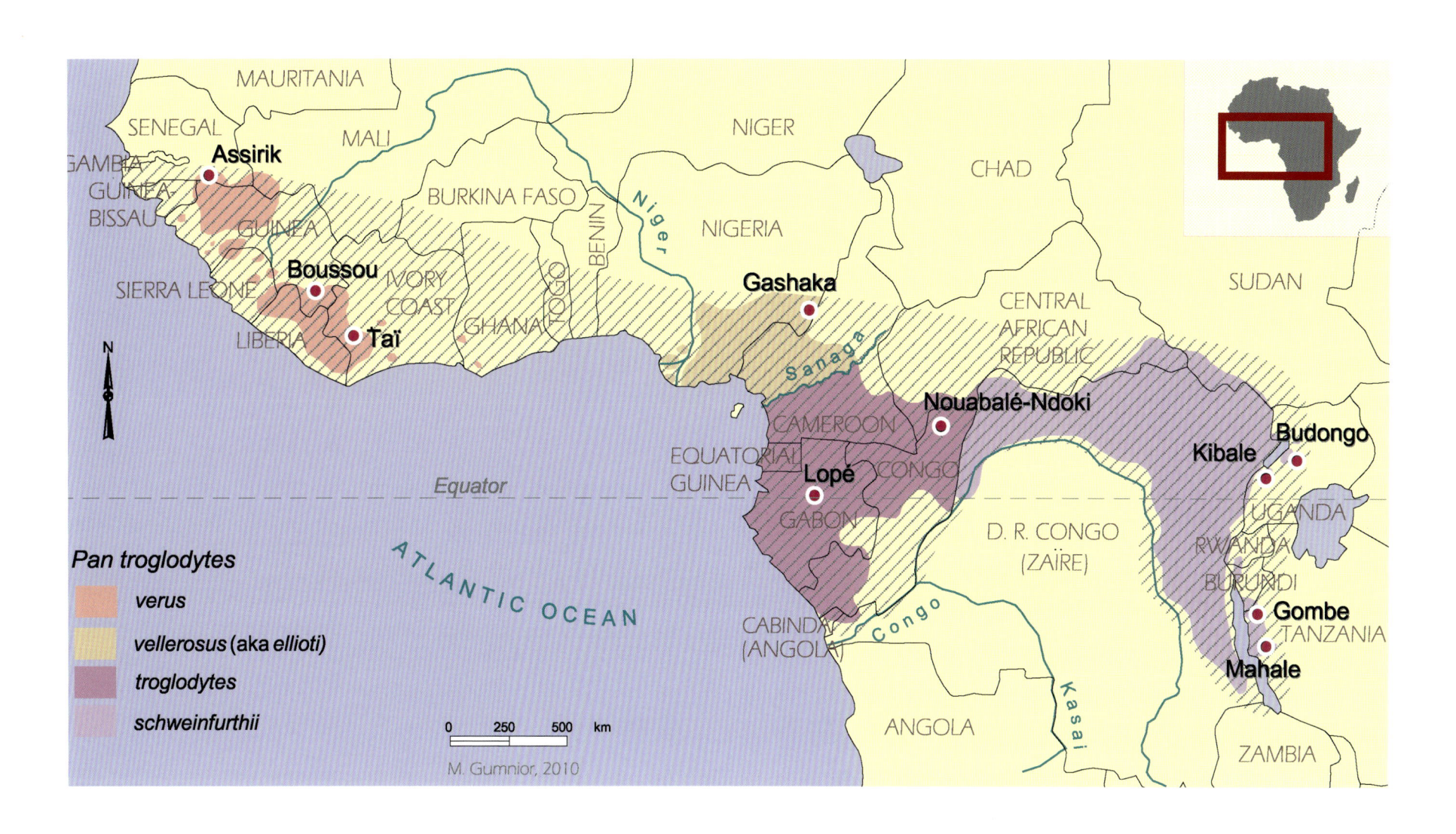

Schimpanse (Pan troglodytes). Verbreitung heute und früher (schraffiert), mit wichtigen Forschungsstationen. Unterarten: P. t. verus (Westafrikanischer Schimpanse); P. t. vellerosus oder ellioti (Nigerianisch-Kamerunscher Schimpanse); P. t. troglodytes (Zentralafrikanischer S.); P. t. schweinfurthii (Ostafrikanischer Schimpanse)

Chimpanzee (Pan troglodytes). Current vs. historical (hatched) distribution and important research stations. Subspecies: P. t. verus (West African chimpanzee); P. t. vellerosus aka ellioti (Nigeria-Cameroon chimpanzee); P. t. troglodytes (Central African chimpanzee); P. t. schweinfurthii (East African chimpanzee)

6. Chimpanzees

Not Better People

Some of the amazing capabilities of non-human animals were first discovered in chimpanzees, the best- and longest- studied apes. For example, they skilfully employ tools, their communities adhere to local customs, and they can prove to be slick politicians. Studies of chimpanzees were also the first to reveal that animal intelligence can have a dark side – for example, when they exterminate rival neighbours, or indulge in systematic cannibalism.

A certain two-facedness is already implied in their name. *Pan troglodytes* – "cave-dwelling Pan" – refers to that Greek god, half human, half animal, whose sudden appearance caused terror – i.e., "panic". Similarly, the anatomist Nicolaes Tulpius described a chimpanzee that arrived in 1641 in the Netherlands as an "Indian Satyr". The inner conflict of scientists who acknowledged the human-like qualities of chimpanzees, but nevertheless wanted to hang on to our uniqueness, is reflected in a succession of name changes – from the initial *Homo* via *Simia* to *Pan*.

Today, four subspecies are recognised: *Pan troglodytes verus,* the West African chimpanzee; *Pan t. vellerosus* (now also known as *Pan t. ellioti*), the Nigeria-Cameroon chimpanzee; *Pan t. troglodytes,* the Central African chimpanzee or Tschego; and *Pan t. schweinfurthii,* the East African chimpanzee.

A fat zoo chimpanzee may topple the scales at 90 kg. Normally, males weigh between 37–60 and females 30–47 kg. As in other apes, menstrual bleeding is visible in roughly monthly intervals. Unlike orangutans, gorillas and humans, the approximate time of ovulation is indicated in chimpanzees by a pink swelling of the ano-genital region. At about 12 years of age, females will give birth to their first child, and further parturitions follow every 4–6 years. Many wild chimpanzees survive for more than 40 years, but those held in captivity for sometimes more than 60 years.

Chimpanzees are day-active knuckle-walkers who may stand up to obtain food or in aggressive display. Males spend 40 percent of the day in trees, females 60 percent. Depending on the available food, chimpanzees range over 5–500 km^2.

Every night, every chimpanzee constructs a sleeping platform in a tree, and sometimes during the day for a siesta. Ground nests, although rare, likewise exist – and remarkably, especially in areas where their main predators could lurk: leopards.

They live in closed rainforests as well as in mosaic habitats of gallery and lowland forests and savannah. This considerable ecological flexibility is reflected in the fact that chimpanzees are found in 21 African countries, which makes them the most widely distributed apes. Certainly, this also points to their intelligence, because chimpanzees are able to access hard-to-obtain food sources through various implements. These include hammers and anvils made of wood or stone to smash nuts; short spears, to stab prosimian primates hidden in tree holes; leaf sponges to reach water accumulated in narrow depressions; long sticks to harvest aggressive ants from a safe distance; and brush-ended sticks to dip into honey. Tools are also used in social contexts, including clubs to threaten and stones as missiles – although precise aim is not a strong suit of chimpanzees.

In some locations, chimpanzees hunt with a clear division of roles between drivers and catchers. But prey such as colobus monkeys, forest antelopes, bush pigs, baboons and rodents is also taken opportunistically. The predatory character of chimpanzees, by the way, doesn't stop there, because on several occasions they have snatched human babies from villagers or rangers and eaten them. Chimpanzees have also been observed killing a young leopard, perhaps perceived as a future danger once grown.

Although females do not participate in hunts, they might still obtain chunks of the prey, often in exchange for sex. While males mostly hunt, the gathering of small animals is mainly a female task. Colonies of termites, bees and ants are often systematically exploited, with brood and honey being favoured treats. The sex difference corresponds in some way to the division of labour typical for human hunter-gatherer societies.

In some locations, chimpanzees neither hunt nor do they use tools to extract hidden food – perhaps because their habitat is lush. Thus it seems that in chimpanzees, as in humans, necessity is the mother of invention. In lands of plenty, they can easily make do with their main food, fruit, which accounts for 56–71 percent of their diet. In addition, they eat leaves and other plant parts such as flowers and herbs.

Tasty fruits do not grow on a lot of trees. As communities of chimpanzees include an average of 41 members, and sometimes around 100, it would be uneconomical if everybody moved around together. Perennial disputes over treasured delicacies would be inevitable. Especially mothers with small babies will therefore often stay on their own. Thus, a social system developed in which the community divides itself into smaller groups. An average of 6 chimpanzees travels together in search of food. They will periodically unite themselves with other parties (fusion), just to disperse again with yet another composition of members (fission).

Jointly, males – and males alone – try to shield off a resourceful territory against neighbouring chimpanzee communities. Because, the larger the area, the more reproductive partners it can accommodate. Male cooperation benefits strongly from their relatively close genetic relatedness. They remain in their natal group for life and therefore are often half-brothers. Females, on the other hand, emigrate from different neighbourhoods into a given community. Relations amongst the ladies are therefore always strained. Nevertheless, males are also well versed in conflict. This is because some attempt to establish themselves through physical force and clever alliances as alpha males, for with this status come increased opportunities to sire offspring.

Jane Goodall began to study wild chimpanzees in 1960. Initially, the Englishwoman painted a paradisiacal scenery, according to which chimpanzee societies embodied cooperation and peaceful use of intelligence. Message: chimpanzees are the better people. Goodall thus embraced viewpoints inspired by Jean-Jacques Rousseau, who, 200 years earlier, had romanticised nature. Cultural pessimists in his tradition maintained that hostility was unknown in primitive societies, and that moral decline began only with the perversions of technology and science.

However, societies of chimpanzees – like those of people – are not free from historical contexts. An anthropologist from Mars, who ventured through Western Europe during the last decade, would emphasise its peacefulness. Would she have visited from 1939 onwards, she would have arrived at the opposite conclusion. Jane Goodall had a similar experience: between 1960–1970, her Gombe-chimpanzees were peaceful – but later, many turned out to be killers. It shocked Goodall when her beloved apes, beginning around 1974, began to slaughter each other. Male alliances massacred neighbouring groups, particularly the males, and kidnapped young females. The pioneering primatologist was honest enough to document such aggression in every detail – including the gruesome practice of sipping the blood of vanquished.

Researchers elsewhere likewise began to report lethal assaults, including the cannibalisation of babies. Males seem to kill especially those youngsters that were likely conceived in a neighbouring group. Occasionally, females also kill and devour babies of unrelated mothers, probably to reduce competition. Moreover, males prove to be merciless subjugators of females, nastily claiming the best resources for themselves, be it shady spots or tasty food.

Such aggression is grist to the mill of supporters of the philosophy of Thomas Hobbes. As an antipode of Rousseau, Hobbes believed that war of all against all was the primordial state of nature. He therefore felt that it was necessary to relinquish some autonomy and instead strengthen the powers of the state to enable a secure coexistence.

Chimpanzees thus do not make a suitable figurehead for a "back-to-nature" movement. Of course, the intellectual heirs of hippie happenings and student revolts would rather hear something good than bad about our natural inclinations. Therefore, the role of the ambassador of a peaceful nature has been handed over to the bonobos. For what these other members of the genus *Pan* do – and what they *don't* do – coincides beautifully with the romantic visions of nature protagonists. This is because bonobos engage in a varied sex life, but not militant conflicts. So, are *they*, after all, the better people? Alas, this perception is also distorted – and quite hopelessly so. For even in these apes, aggression and violent clashes are not unknown. In fact, bonobos cannot even pass as the "better chimpanzees", because in their societies, females are the sex that regularly inflicts blood-drawing injuries.

Ergo: much is possible in nature. Because of this, nature romantics get it wrong. Not everything "natural" is automatically desirable from an ethical point of view – as is testified by the occurrence of cannibalism, infanticide, rape and extermination of neighbours in our closest relatives. The simple-enough sounding prescription that we should do good and refrain from evil is therefore not easily implemented. For our natural heritage may instil selfishness and ruthless competition in us as well as empathy and fruitful cooperation – thus, setting limits and opening up opportunities at the same time. Therefore, it can't harm if we explore our inner ape with even greater zeal.

Schimpanse / *chimpanzee*

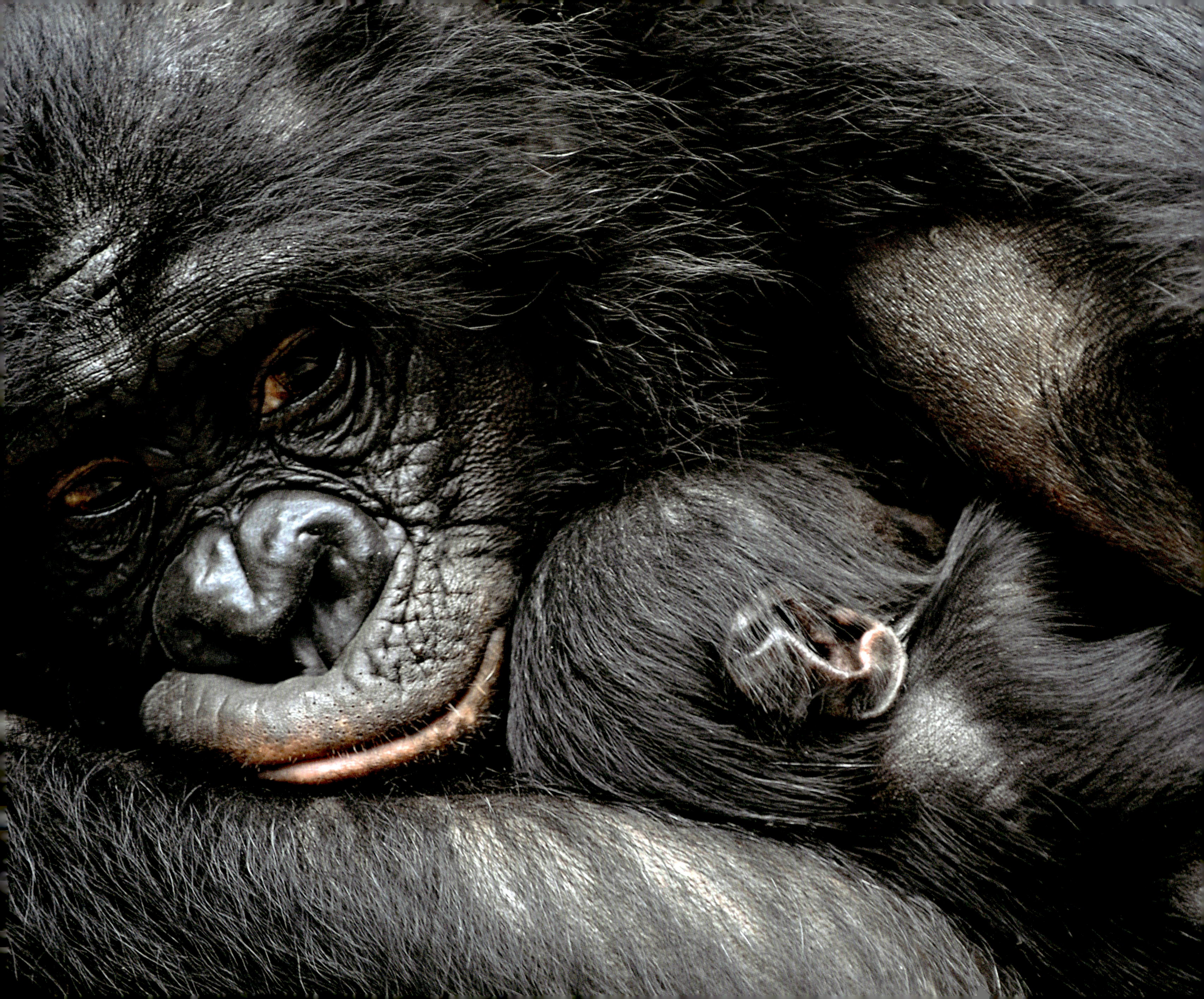

Bonobos

Bonobos

Bonobo / *bonobo*

Bonobo / *bonobo*

7. Bonobos

Im feministischen Utopia?

Wenn es um die nächsten Verwandten der Menschen geht, werden oft nur Schimpansen genannt. Dabei stehen uns Bonobos genauso nahe. Denn die zu uns Menschen führende Abstammungslinie teilte sich von der unserer nächsten Verwandten bereits vor vier bis sechs Millionen Jahren, während Schimpansen und Bonobos erst vor anderthalb Millionen Jahren eigene Wege einschlugen. Bonobos werden auch deshalb seltener erwähnt, weil es tatsächlich weniger zu berichten gibt. Denn die ohnehin seltenen Freilandstudien sind wegen logistischer Schwierigkeiten und Bürgerkriegen oft kurzlebig.

Bonobos stiegen gleichwohl zu Popstars unter den Menschenaffen auf, weil die Medien sich auf einen Ausschnitt ihres Sozialverhaltens konzentrieren: Sex – inklusive homosexueller Kontakte. Da Bonobos überdies als friedfertig gelten, haftet ihnen das Blumenkinder-Image von „make-love-not-war" an. „Böse" Schimpansen mit „netten" Bonobos zu kontrastieren – Affen „vom Mars" mit Affen „von der Venus" – ist allerdings irreführend, denn Bonobos sind keineswegs pazifistisch. Vielmehr sind die bösen Buben bei ihnen die Mädchen. Im Gegensatz zu „gewöhnlichen" Schimpansen leiden bei Bonobos die Männchen unter Aggressionen der Weibchen, was den Spitznamen „ungewöhnlicher Schimpanse" anders als ursprünglich intendiert rechtfertigt.

Dem deutschen Zoologen Ernst Schwarz fielen um 1929 Besonderheiten an einem angeblichen Schimpansen-Schädel auf. Daraufhin beschrieb der amerikanische Anatom Harold Coolidge *Pan paniscus* 1933 als eine eigene Art. Sein wissenschaftlicher Name bedeutet „der kleine Pan", was die Bezeichnung „Zwergschimpanse" ebenfalls suggeriert. Die Tiere sind jedoch weder kleiner noch leichter als Schimpansen, sondern bestenfalls schlanker gebaut. Auch deshalb bürgerte sich der Phantasiename „Bonobo" ein. Der leitet sich vielleicht von der Siedlung Bolobo am Unterlauf des Kongo ab, von wo aus erste Exemplare nach Europa gelangten.

Bonobos leben nur in der Demokratischen Republik des Kongo, dem vormaligen Zaïre, wo sie 350.000 Quadratkilometer am südlichen Ufer des Kongo besiedeln. Soweit bekannt, überschneiden sich Biotope von Schimpansen und Bonobos nirgendwo.

Gleich Gorillas und Schimpansen sind Bonobos tagaktive Knöchelgänger, doch richten sie sich regelmäßig auf. Etwa die Hälfte des Tages verbringen sie in Bäumen, mehr also als andere afrikanische Menschenaffen. Jeden Abend konstruieren sie eine Schlafstatt im Geäst. Schimpansen kommen mit hellem Gesicht zur Welt, das sich bei manchen Erwachsenen schwarz färbt. Bonobos werden hingegen schwarz geboren, und bleiben so ihr Leben lang. Männchen wiegen 33–57 kg, Weibchen 28–49 kg. In Gefangenschaft können sie ein erstes Kind mit acht Jahren zur Welt bringen, im Freiland erst mit zwölf. Zwischen Geburten vergehen etwa fünf Jahre. In Zoos können Bonobos mehr als 60 Jahre alt werden.

Feuchter Regenwald mit geschlossenem Kronendach ist ihr primäres Biotop, doch mancherorts nutzen sie grasige Lichtungen. Leoparden können Bonobos gefährlich werden, doch Jäger sind ihr Hauptfeind. In Wohngebieten von 22–58 Quadratkilometern sind Kommunitäten von 10–58 Mitgliedern zuhause. Wie bei Schimpansen ist die gesamte Gruppe nur selten zusammen. Gemäß dem Muster von „fission-fusion" streifen Bonobos vielmehr in Grüppchen stetig wechselnder Zusammensetzung umher.

Drei Viertel ihrer Nahrung bestehen aus Früchten, ergänzt um Baumblätter und Bodenkräuter. Im Gegensatz zu Schimpansen benutzen wilde Bonobos jedoch keine Werkzeuge und beuten auch keine Insektenkolonien aus. Neuere Beobachtungen zeigen, dass auch Bonobos gemeinsam Affen jagen – wobei, wiederum anders als bei Schimpansen, Weibchen sich ebenfalls beteiligen. Ein seltsamer Fall von Kannibalismus sollte ebenfalls erwähnt werden, bei dem Weibchen, einschließlich der Mutter, ein zuvor gestorbenes Kleinkind verzehrten.

Während die Machtverhältnisse bei Schimpansen auf Männerherrschaft und *Patriarchat* hinauslaufen, haben bei Bonobos die Frauen ein *Matriarchat* etabliert und werden häufig handgreiflich. Männchen sind jedoch auch bei dieser

Spezies größer und körperlich eigentlich überlegen. Frauenpower lässt sich deshalb nur ausüben, weil Bonobo-Weibchen zusammenarbeiten. Gemeinsam weisen sie Männchen in die Schranken und machen ihnen Nahrung streitig. In Zoos, wo wenig Gelegenheit zur Flucht besteht, werden die armen Kerle oft schrecklich von Weibchen zugerichtet. Bisswunden, fehlende Finger und Zehen, Kerben in Ohrmuscheln, ein durchtrennter Penis – alles kommt vor. In der Wildnis sieht es kaum anders aus. Als beispielsweise ein den Alpha-Status anstrebender Bonobo sich aggressiv gegenüber einem Baby verhielt, wurde er von einer Weibchen-Koalition dermaßen zugerichtet, dass er auf Nimmerwiedersehen verschwand.

Allianzen unter Weibchen ließen sich erklären, wären sie miteinander verwandt. Das trifft jedoch weder auf wilde Schimpansen noch auf Bonobos zu, wie DNS-Analysen aus Kot, Haaren und Mundschleimhaut belegen. Heranwachsende Weibchen der Gattung *Pan* verlassen in der Regel ihre Geburtsgemeinschaft – wohl, um Inzucht zu vermeiden, denn Männchen verbleiben in der Gruppe. Weibchen müssen deshalb in Kauf nehmen, als Fortpflanzungsfähige mit einem Sammelsurium unverwandter Geschlechtsgenossinnen konfrontiert zu sein – und diese sind eigentlich erbitterte Konkurrentinnen.

Wie können Bonobo-Damen ihre Bündnisse trotz solcher Widrigkeiten kitten? Im Biotop der Bonobos sind Baumkronen breit und damit nahrungsreich, enthalten Früchte wenig Schadstoffe und wachsen eiweißreiche Kräuter, auf die in mageren Zeiten zurückgegriffen werden kann. In diesem üppigen Lebensraum kann sogar auf den Einsatz von Werkzeugen verzichtet werden. Der Streit um Nahrung ist somit abgemildert, was Frauenfreundschaften erleichtert.

Außerdem bauen Bonobos auf ein einzigartiges System gegenseitiger Belohnung: gleichgeschlechtlichen Sex. Die Partnerinnen liegen dabei Bauch-auf-Bauch und reiben die für die Gattung *Pan* typischen Schwellungen der Ano-Genitalregion aneinander. Bei diesem „gg-rubbing" – dem „genito-genitalen Reiben" – wirkt vor allem die voluminöse Klitoris stimulierend. Homosexuelle Kontakte haben nichts mit Ersatzbefriedigung zu tun. Vielmehr bevorzugen Weibchen oft trotz eindeutiger Angebote der Männchen nicht nur lesbisches Miteinander, sondern brechen sogar Hetero-Sex ab, um sich Homo-Sex zuzuwenden. Dass Weibchen dabei Orgasmen erleben, legen tranceartige Mimik und lustvolle Laute nahe.

Vor allem niederrangige Weibchen initiieren Sex, während ranghohe häufig die Top-Position einnehmen. Subordinierte verschaffen ihren Partnerinnen also Lusterlebnisse, und diese positiven Gefühle erleichtern die Kooperation. Sexualität ist mithin weniger zum Friedenstiften da als ein sozialer Schachzug, mit dem Weibchen Machtverhältnisse zu ihren Gunsten verschieben.

Dank ihrer lustbetonten Bündnispolitik können Weibchen begehrte Nahrungsbrocken gegenüber Männchen monopolisieren. Weibchen teilen untereinander sowohl zufällig gefangene Nagetiere und kleine Waldantilopen wie gemeinsam erjagte Affen und die bis 20 kg schweren *Trecularia*-Früchte.

Derlei Frauenpower zahlt sich auf der Ebene der Fortpflanzung aus. Zum einen sind Kindestötungen bisher unbekannt. Zum anderen bringen Bonobos Babys früher zur Welt als Schimpansinnen, und ziehen – zumindest in Gefangenschaft – 0,7 Nachkommen mehr auf. Bei nur zwei bis drei überlebenden Kindern insgesamt ist das ein erheblicher Gewinn.

Wenn sich Koalitionen reproduktiv dermaßen lohnen, warum lassen sich Schimpansinnen selbst dann von Männern unterdrücken, wenn sie in einem reichhaltigen Biotop leben? Denn in zumindest manchen Schimpansen-Gebieten, wie im ugandischen Budongo, ist die Ernährungslage so unproblematisch, dass auch hier auf den Einsatz von Werkzeug verzichtet wird. Warum verbünden sich Schimpansen-Weibchen nicht wenigstens in Zoos, wo Nahrung ja keineswegs knapp ist? Oder umgekehrt: Warum pochen Bonobo-Damen selbst in Tierparks auf Dominanz, obwohl sie dort gut versorgt werden?

Wahrscheinlich legten die Ausleseprozesse der letzten paar Millionen Jahre die Zweige der Gattung *Pan* allmählich auf bestimmte Sozialsysteme fest. Der üppige Urwald im ökologisch stabilen Herzen Afrikas begünstigte die Ausbildung eines Matriarchats, bis sich weibliche Macht den Bonobos unumkehrbar eingefleischt hatte. Die wechselnden und oft mageren Umwelten weiter im Norden – in denen vielerorts Gorillas die Konkurrenz verschärfen – erlaubten es Weibchen nicht, sich miteinander zu verbünden, und verfestigten so das Patriarchat der Schimpansen.

Wie sollen wir uns die ursprüngliche Situation vorstellen? Lebten die gemeinsamen Vorfahren von Menschen, Schimpansen und Bonobos männerzentriert, wäre die frauenzentrierte Gesellschaft als späterer Sonderweg zu begreifen. Schwangen hingegen ursprünglich Frauen das Zepter, wären patriarchale Verhältnisse erst später entstanden.

Anthropologen und Kulturwissenschaftler sind uneins, ob im Laufe der Menschwerdung jemals matriarchale Verhältnisse herrschten. Im allerletzten Abschnitt unserer Stammesgeschichte setzte sich männliche Dominanz jedenfalls ziemlich flächenmäßig durch. Denn als vor 15.000 Jahren Landwirtschaft aufkam, öffnete sich die soziale Schere zwischen Habenichtsen und Besitzenden. Reichere Männer konnten dadurch oft nicht nur mehrere Frauen an sich binden, sondern schotteten sie auch von ihrem Geburtsclan ab. In 70 Prozent aller Kulturen ziehen Frauen heute zu ihrem Mann – ein patrilokales Wohnen, während der Mann viel seltener zur Frau zieht. Dabei werden Frauen, die in ihrer Ursprungsfamilie bleiben, weniger oft Opfer männlicher Gewalt als wenn sie getrennt von Verwandten leben.

Manches spricht dafür, dass in naturnahen Jäger-Sammler-Gesellschaften die Macht gleichmäßiger verteilt ist. Einerseits haben Frauen mehr Freiheit, weil Männer sie auf Sammelzügen schlecht überwachen können. Andererseits sind die Geschlechter bei der Nahrungsbeschaffung aufeinander angewiesen. Außerdem belegen DNS-Sequenzen, dass Frauen in Jäger-Sammler-Völkern öfter in ihrer Geburtsgruppe bleiben, wo sie mit Schwester, Müttern, Großmüttern und Tanten zusammenleben. Solche Matrilinien sind für Männer einfach schwer zu kontrollieren.

Gemäß einer Ikone des Feminismus, Simone de Beauvoir, scheiterten frühe Emanzipationsbestrebungen, weil Frauen „verteilt unter den Männern leben" statt sich zu verbünden. Frauen in moderneren Gesellschaften liegen damit im Trend anderer Säugetiere, weil Koalitionen unter Nicht-Verwandten generell ungewöhnlich sind.

Ungewöhnlich – aber nicht unmöglich, wie die Bonobos lehren. Deren ideelle Schwesterschaft vermag selbst Artgrenzen zu überbrücken. Als die Primatologin Amy Parish ihren neugeborenen Sohn der Bonobo-Dame Lana des Zoos von San Diego zeigte, schaute diese verblüfft drein, holte dann ihr eigenes Baby und hielt es hoch – offenbar, um mit der Primatologin Mutterfreuden zu teilen. Ein andermal winkte Parish der Alpha-Frau Louise zu, damit diese sich zur Kamera drehen sollte. Louise deutete die Geste als Futterbetteln und warf ihr die Hälfte ihres Sellerie-Bündels zu...

Welcher Affe in uns steckt, ob Schimpanse oder Bonobo, ist etwa hinsichtlich der Frage wichtig, ob und wie wir gerechtere Gesellschaften schaffen können. Westliche Gesellschaften lehnen patriarchale Strukturen aus ethischen Gründen ab. Ist die Mitgift der Evolution jedoch vom Typus der Schimpansen, müssen wir dabei gegen unser ursprüngliches Erbe ankämpfen. Gaben uns die Urahnen hingegen Frauenpower mit auf den Weg, könnten wir im Bemühen um Gleichberechtigung an alte Traditionen anknüpfen.

Zum Glück spricht einiges dafür, dass wir sozial noch flexibler sind als andere Primaten, was vermutlich zum Rezept für unsere umfassendere Ausbreitung gehörte. In keinem Falle allerdings ist Gerechtigkeit einfach zu erreichen. Denn die Erfahrung lehrt, dass Konflikte auch dann bleiben, wenn Frauen regieren.

Bonobo, Zwergschimpanse (Pan paniscus). Verbreitung heute und früher (schraffiert), mit wichtigen Forschungsstationen

Bonobo, pygmy chimpanzee (Pan paniscus). Current vs. historical (hatched) distribution and important research stations

7. Bonobos

In Feminist Utopia?

When it comes to *the* closest relatives of humans, people often refer only to chimpanzees. Still, bonobos are just as near. This is because the lineage leading to humans split from the line of our closest ape relatives already 4–6 million years ago, while bonobos and chimpanzees parted much later, only 1.5 million years ago. Bonobos are also mentioned less frequently because there is actually less to report, as field studies have been cut short due to logistical problems and civil war. Bonobos, nevertheless, have risen to the status of pop stars amongst primates, because the media focus on just a part of their social behaviour: sex – including homosexual contacts. Since bonobos can also be described as relatively peaceful, they got saddled with the flower-power image of "make-love-not-war". However, to contrast "evil" chimpanzees with "nice" bonobos – "apes from Mars" versus "apes from Venus" – is misleading, as bonobos are certainly not pacifists. Because when it comes to bonobos, the "bad guys" are girls. In contrast to "common" chimpanzees, males suffer aggression from females in bonobo societies, a fact that justifies the nickname "uncommon chimpanzee" in other ways than originally intended.

The German zoologist Ernst Schwarz noticed around 1929 some special features in what was allegedly a chimpanzee skull. This lead the American anatomist Harold Coolidge to describe *Pan paniscus* in 1933 as its own, separate species. Its scientific name means "the small Pan", similar to what is suggested by the vernacular "pygmy chimpanzee". Still, the animals are neither smaller nor lighter than chimpanzees; at best, their bodies are slimmer. Not least because of this misnomer, the fancy name „bonobo" caught on. This epithet can perhaps be traced to the settlement Bolobo on the banks of the lower Congo, from where specimens might first have been shipped to Europe.

Bonobos are found only in the Democratic Republic of the Congo, formerly Zaïre, distributed over 350,000 km² on the southern bank of the Congo River. There is no confirmed overlap in habitat between chimpanzees and bonobos anywhere.

Like gorillas and chimpanzees, bonobos are day-active knuckle-walkers, but also regularly stand on two feet. About half of the day is spent in trees, more so than in other African apes. Every evening, they construct a new sleeping platform in trees. Chimpanzees are born with a pale facial colour that turns black in some adults. Bonobos, by contrast, are born black and remain so throughout their lives. Males weigh 33–57 kg, females 28–49. In captivity, females may have their first baby at 8 years of age, but in the wild only at 12 years. The interval between births is about 5 years. In captivity, some bonobos survive for more than 60 years.

Closed-canopy rain forest is their primary habitat, although in some places they also enter grassy clearings. Leopards can be dangerous to them, but hunters constitute their main enemy. Home ranges of 22–58 km² support communities of 10–58 members. As with chimpanzees, the entire group is rarely seen together, and bonobos follow the same "fission-fusion" pattern in that they range in small parties of often-changing composition.

Three-quarters of the time, bonobos champ fruit, supplementing this diet by leaves and terrestrial herbs. Unlike wild chimpanzees, bonobos do not make use of tools, nor do they exploit insect colonies. Recent observations reveal that bonobos do some low-key communal hunting of monkeys – but again, unlike chimpanzees, females participate in these exploits. A strange case of cannibalism should also be mentioned in which an unrelated female and the mother herself ate a baby that had previously died.

In chimpanzees, males hold power over females and thus practice what could be called *patriarchy*. Amongst bonobos, the reverse is true, in that females will often dominate males physically, thus establishing a *matriarchy*. This is odd, as in this species males are likewise larger and heavier than females, which should give them an edge over the "weaker" sex. Girl power is only a reality because females work together. They cooperate to put males in their place and to deprive them of food. In zoos, where there is little opportunity to escape, the poor fellows are often terribly accosted by the females. Bites, missing fingers and toes, nicks in the ear, a severed penis – anything can happen. In the wild, it looks hardly different. As an example, when a male in one bonobo group aspired alpha status and behaved aggressively towards a baby, he was severely attacked by a group of females. And disappeared forever.

Alliances among females could be easily explained, if they were based on kinship. However, this is neither true for wild chimpanzees nor for wild bonobos, as DNA analyses from faeces, hair and saliva indicate. Adolescent females of both species usually leave their natal group, probably to avoid incest, given that males stay put. Adult females therefore live with a hodgepodge of unrelated womenfolk and thus in theory, without kin-based alliances, bitter rivalries should ensue amongst them.

How, in spite of such adversity, do bonobo females cement their alliances? There might be several explanations. Trees in the bonobo biotope grow relatively wide canopies with lots of food; fruits are nutritious and lack substances problematic for digestion; the apes can in lean times resort to protein-rich herbs. Not unexpectedly, such favourable conditions render the use of tools as foraging aids superfluous. As a consequence, conflicts over food are less severe, facilitating friendships between females.

Moreover, bonobos developed a unique system of mutual reward: homosexual sex. Females lie down, belly-on-belly, pressing their ano-genital swellings against each other. This "genito-genital-" or "GG-rubbing" stimulates the voluminous clitoris in particular. Homosexual sex has nothing to do with substitute satisfaction in lieu of heterosexual antics. Instead, females often prefer lesbian contacts, despite unmistakeable offers by males, and may even interrupt hetero-sex to engage in homo-sex. Joyful sounds and trancelike facial expressions strongly suggest that they experience orgasmic feelings.

Low-ranking females, in particular, initiate sex, and the more dominant partner tends to take up the top position. With this offering, subordinates arrange lustful events for their partners, and these positive emotions facilitate cooperation. Sexuality therefore is less peacemaking than a social move, with which females tip the balance of power in their favour.

Thanks to their pleasurable policy of mending alliances, females can monopolise coveted food against males. Females also share food with each other, including rodents and small forest antelopes snatched by chance, monkeys caught during communal hunts as well as heavy *Trecularia* fruits that may weigh up to 20 kg. Such female power pays off at the level of reproduction. On the one hand, infant-killings by males are unknown. On the other hand, bonobos have babies at an earlier age than chimpanzees and they raise – at least in captivity – 0.7 more offspring. With only two or three surviving children overall, this constitutes a significant gain.

If coalitions come with such a substantial benefit, why are chimpanzee females tolerating male suppression even when living under the bonobo-like conditions of lush surroundings? At least in sites such as in Uganda's Budongo forest, food acquisition seems to be so unproblematic that chimpanzees will likewise dispense with tool use. Similarly, why do female chimpanzees not form alliances when kept in a zoo, where food is not scarce at all? Or conversely: why do bonobo ladies, even in captive settings, insist on dominance, although they are well cared for? Probably, selection processes during the last 2 million years constrained the two species gradually into specific social systems. The nourishing jungle that grows in the ecologically stable heart of Africa encouraged the formation of a matriarchy, until this system of female power was irreversibly ingrained in the bonobo psyche. The changing environments and often lean habitats further to the north – where the presence of gorillas will often lead to even fiercer competition for resources – made it impossible for females to unite, and so solidified the patriarchal system of chimpanzees.

How are we to imagine the original situation? If the common ancestor of humans, chimpanzees and bonobos formed male-centred societies, then we would have to understand female-centred groups as a later development. If, however, females ruled in the first place, then patriarchal relations would have emerged only secondarily.

Anthropologists are generally sceptical that matriarchal conditions prevailed any time during the course of human evolution. At the very least, male dominance became rather ubiquitous during the last days of our pre-history. This is because the emergence of agriculture some 15,000 years ago also opened a widening social gap between haves and have-nots. Due to this fact, wealthier men could frequently not only attract more women, but were also able to severe most contacts to their natal kith and kin. Nowadays, in 70 percent of all cultures, wives will move to their husband's homestead – a patrilocal arrangement – while men will only rarely change to their wife's place. Interestingly, women who stay in their family of origin are less often victims of male violence than those living apart from relatives. There is some evidence that power is more evenly distributed in traditional hunter-gatherer societies. Here, women enjoy greater freedom simply because males cannot exert much control when females are out on foraging trips. Moreover, DNA sequences reveal that, indeed, women born into hunter-gatherer societies stay more often within their natal group, residing with sisters, mothers, grandmothers and aunts. Men have a much harder time trying to impose their own will on such matrilines.

According to an icon of feminism, Simone de Beauvoir, early attempts of emancipation failed because women lived "distributed among the men", instead of teaming up. Women in modern societies thus follow the trend of other mammals in that females leave their natal units to join up with non-relatives, which makes the formation of coalitions uncommon.

Uncommon – but not impossible, as bonobos demonstrate. Their idea of sisterhood may even bridge species barriers. When primatologist Amy Parish showed her newborn son to Lana, this bonobo female of San Diego Zoo looked somewhat perplexed, but then went and got her own baby to hold her up – apparently aiming to share the joys of motherhood with the researcher. Another time, Parish beckoned alpha-female Louise to turn around, so that the primatologist might get a better shot with a camera. Louise misunderstood the gesture and thought it was food begging, whereupon she threw half of her celery bundle over…

Whether our inner primate is a monkey, a chimpanzee or a bonobo is relevant with respect to the question how to create more just social systems. Western societies are opposed to patriarchy, for ethical reasons. However, if the chimpanzee type is at the heart of our evolutionary heritage, then we would face an uphill battle against our original inclinations. If our ancestors, however, practiced female power, then we could built on age-old traditions in our efforts to achieve equality.

Fortunately, it seems as if we are socially even more flexible than our primate cousins, a likely ingredient to the recipe that aided our extensive geographical spread. In no case, however, is justice within easy reach – as bonobos exemplify. For conflict remains even when women rule.

Bonobo / *bonobo*

HORIZONTE
HORIZONS

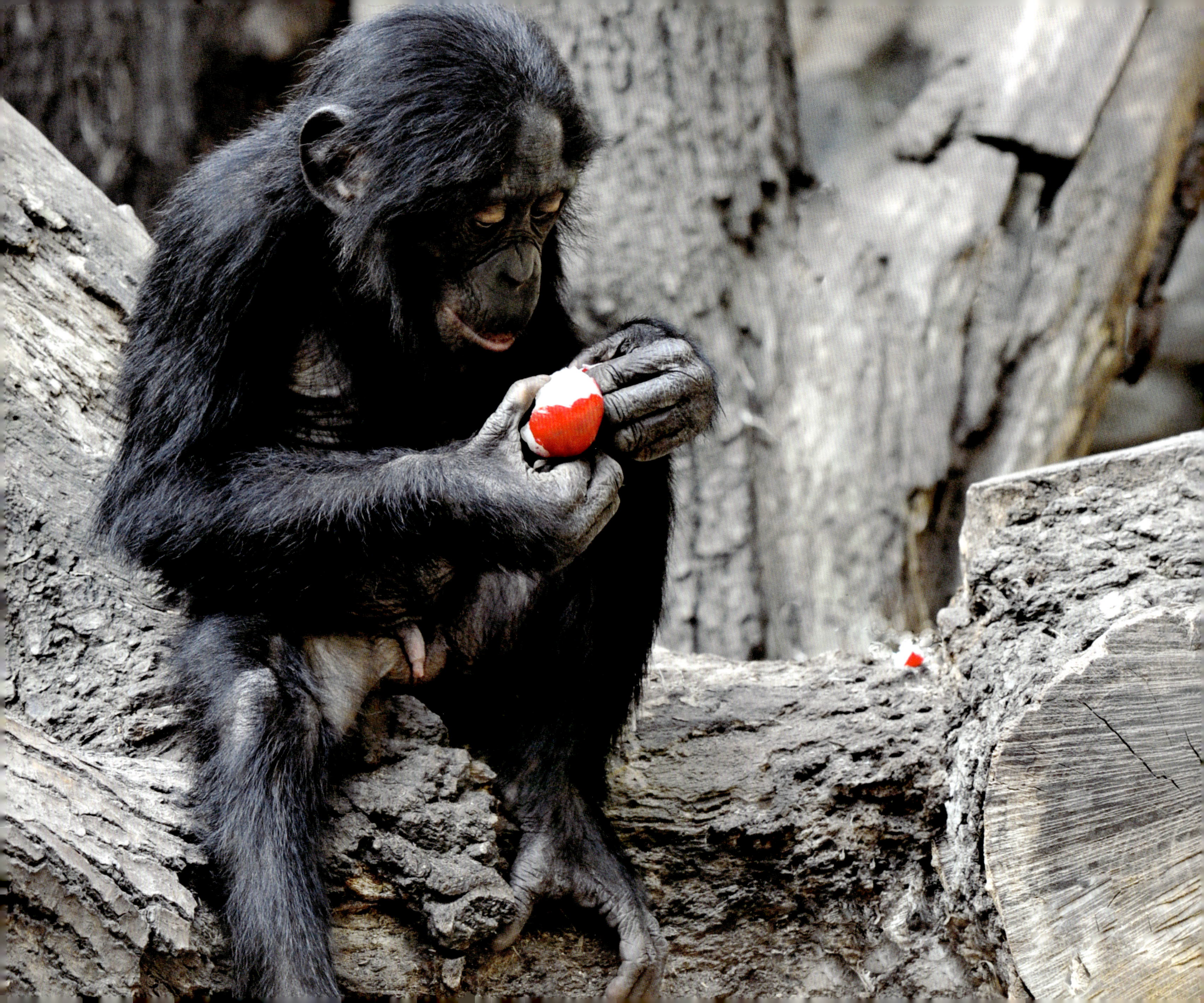

Bonobo / *bonobo*   Schimpanse / *chimpanzee*   Bonobo / *bonobo*   133

134 Bonobo / *bonobo* Bonobo / *bonobo*

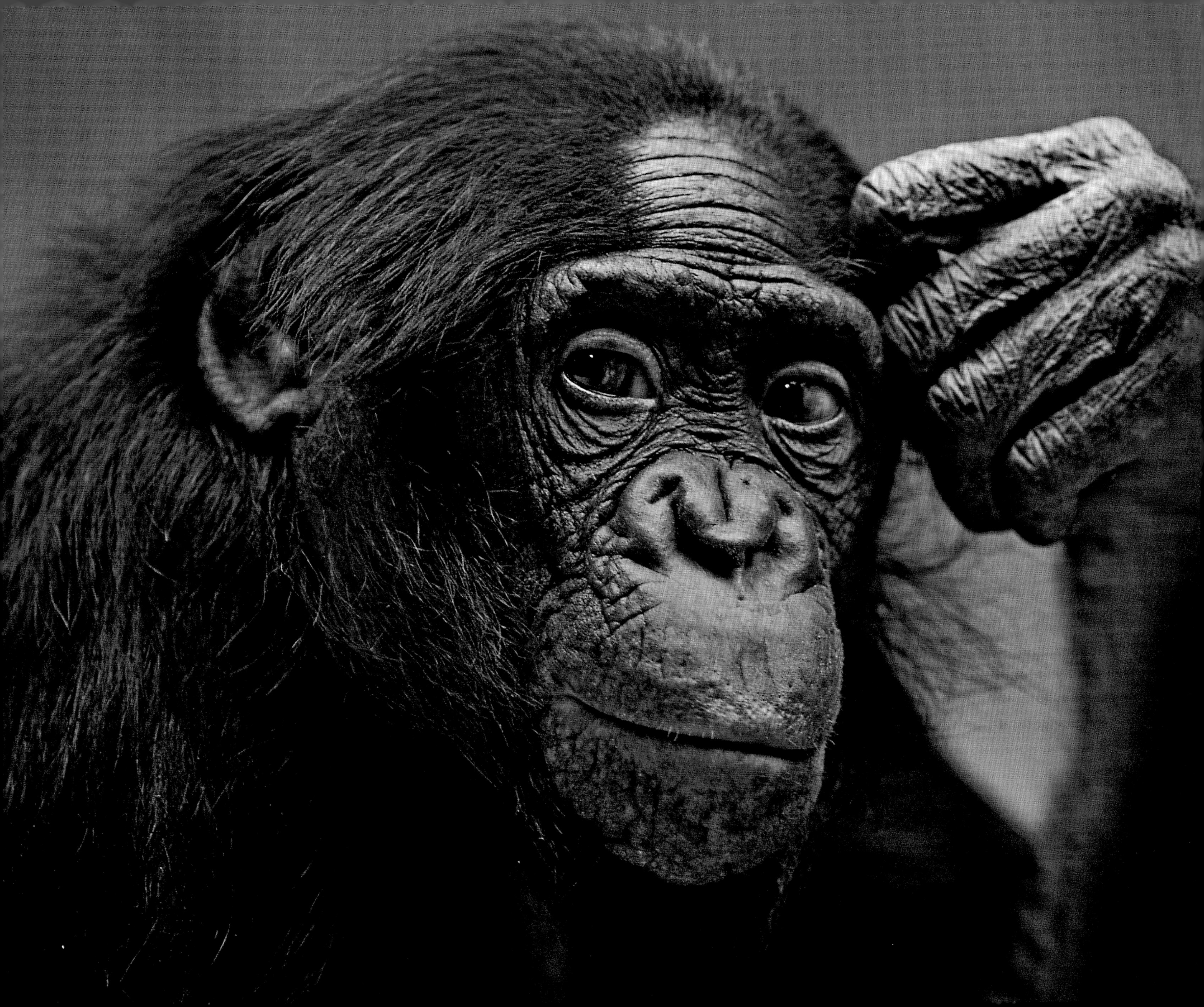

Bonobo / *bonobo*

Bonobo / *bonobo*   137

138   Gorilla / *gorilla*   Bonobo / *bonobo*

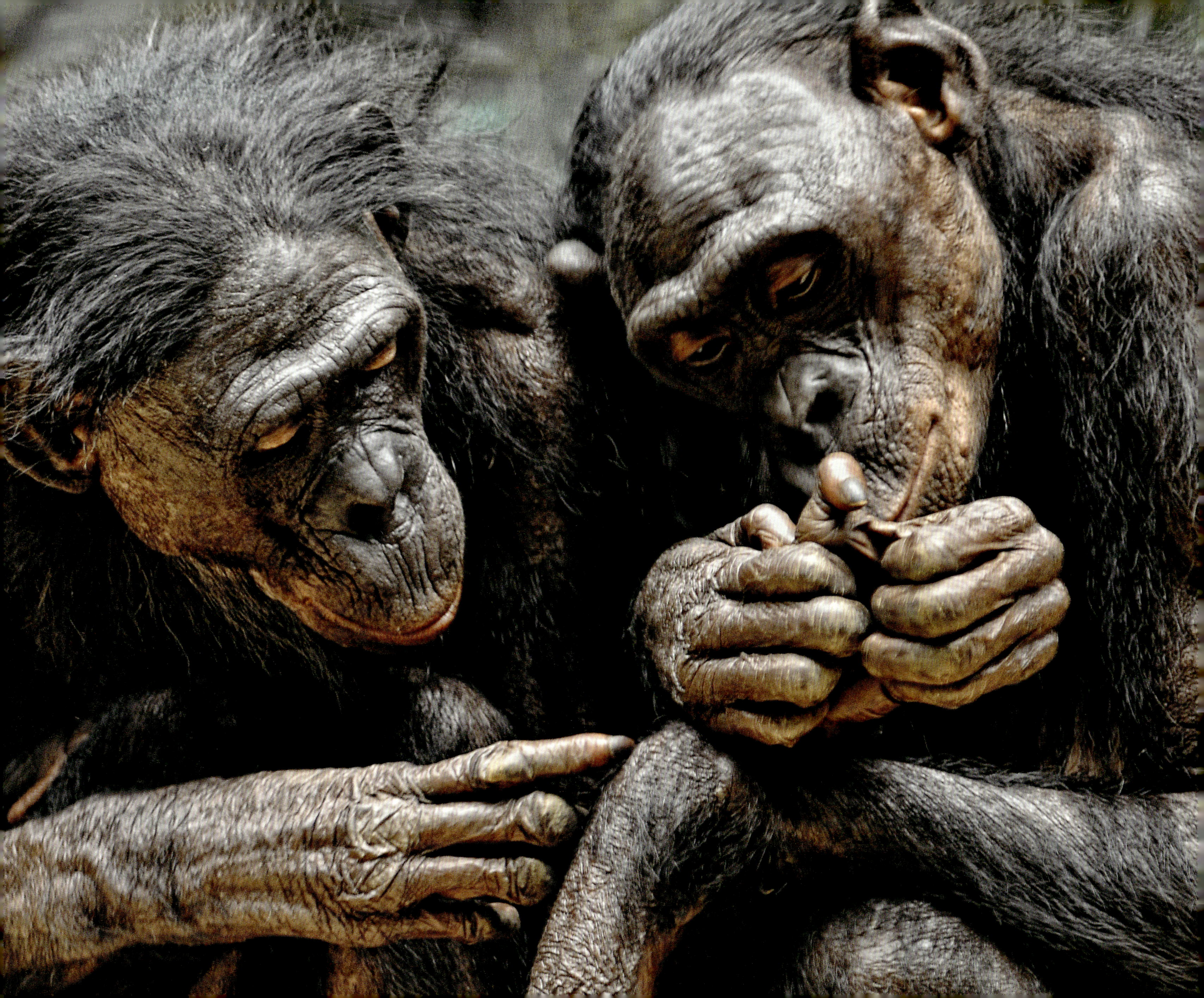

Orang-Utan / *orangutan*

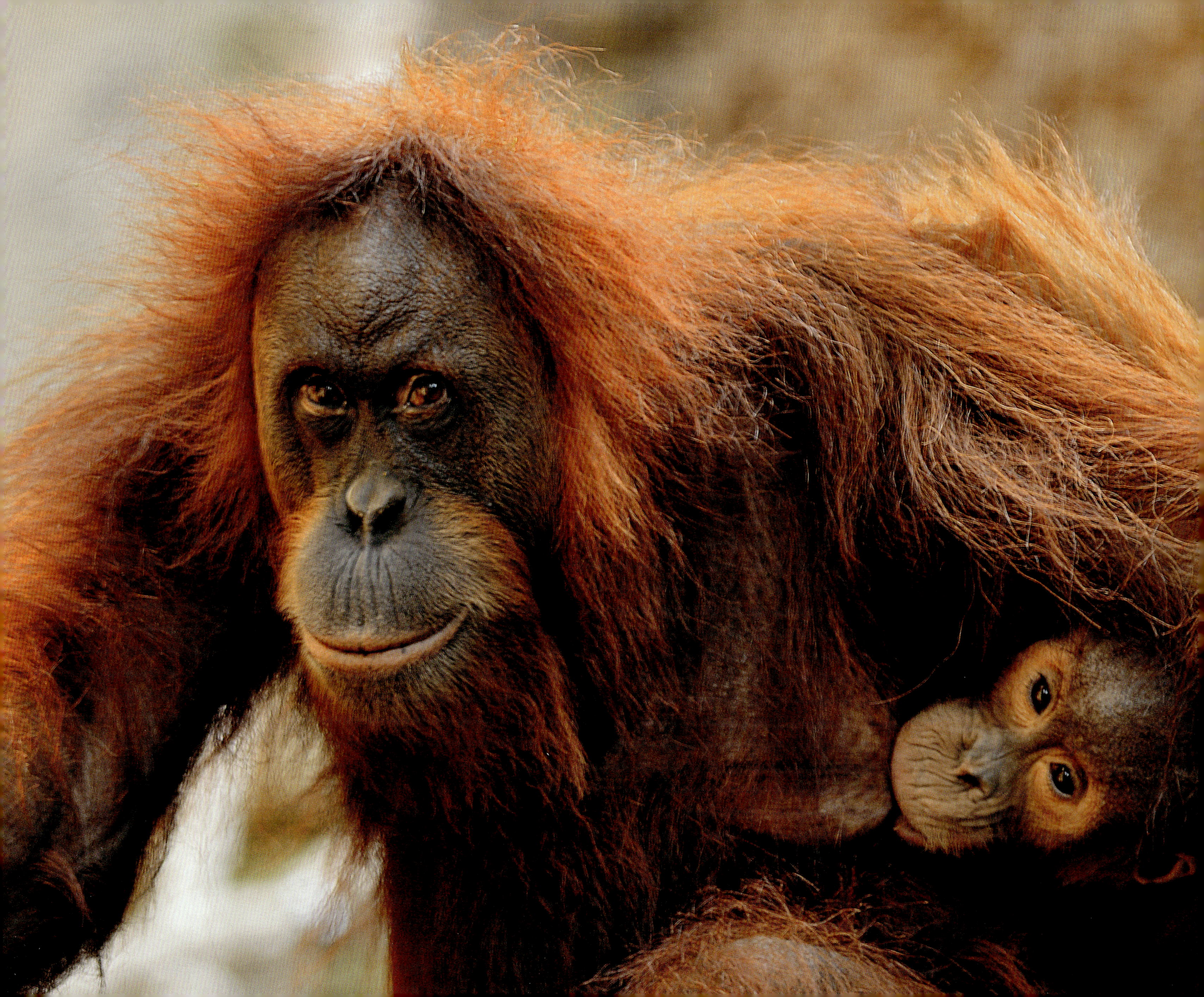

Gorilla / *gorilla*

Bonobo / *bonobo*

Bonobo / *bonobo*   Bonobo / *bonobo*   Bonobo / *bonobo*   Bonobo / *bonobo*

Bonobo / *bonobo*　　Bonobo / *bonobo*　　Gorilla / *gorilla*　　Schimpanse / *chimpanzee*　　　　145

146   Schimpanse / *chimpanzee*   Orang-Utan / *orangutan*

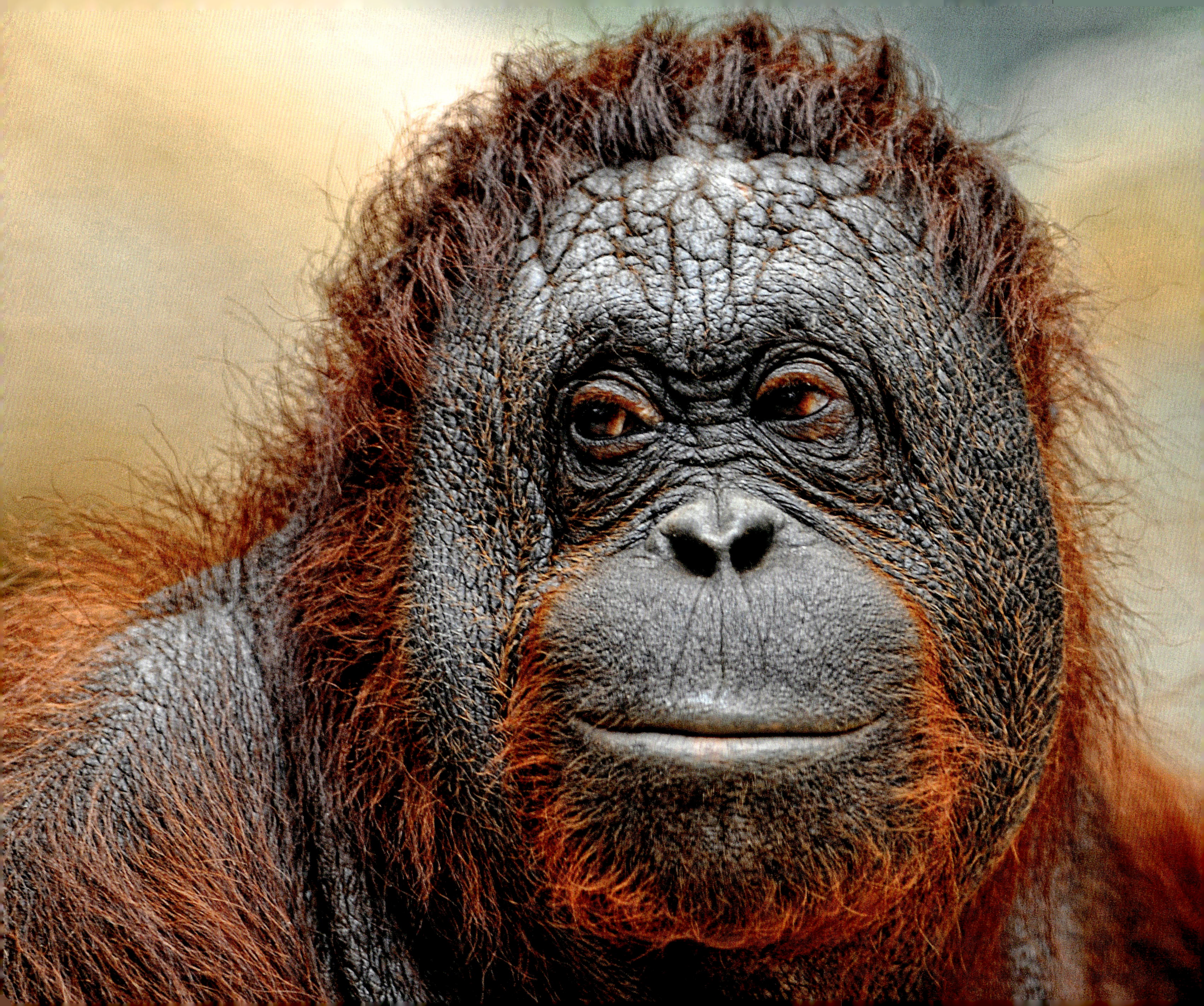

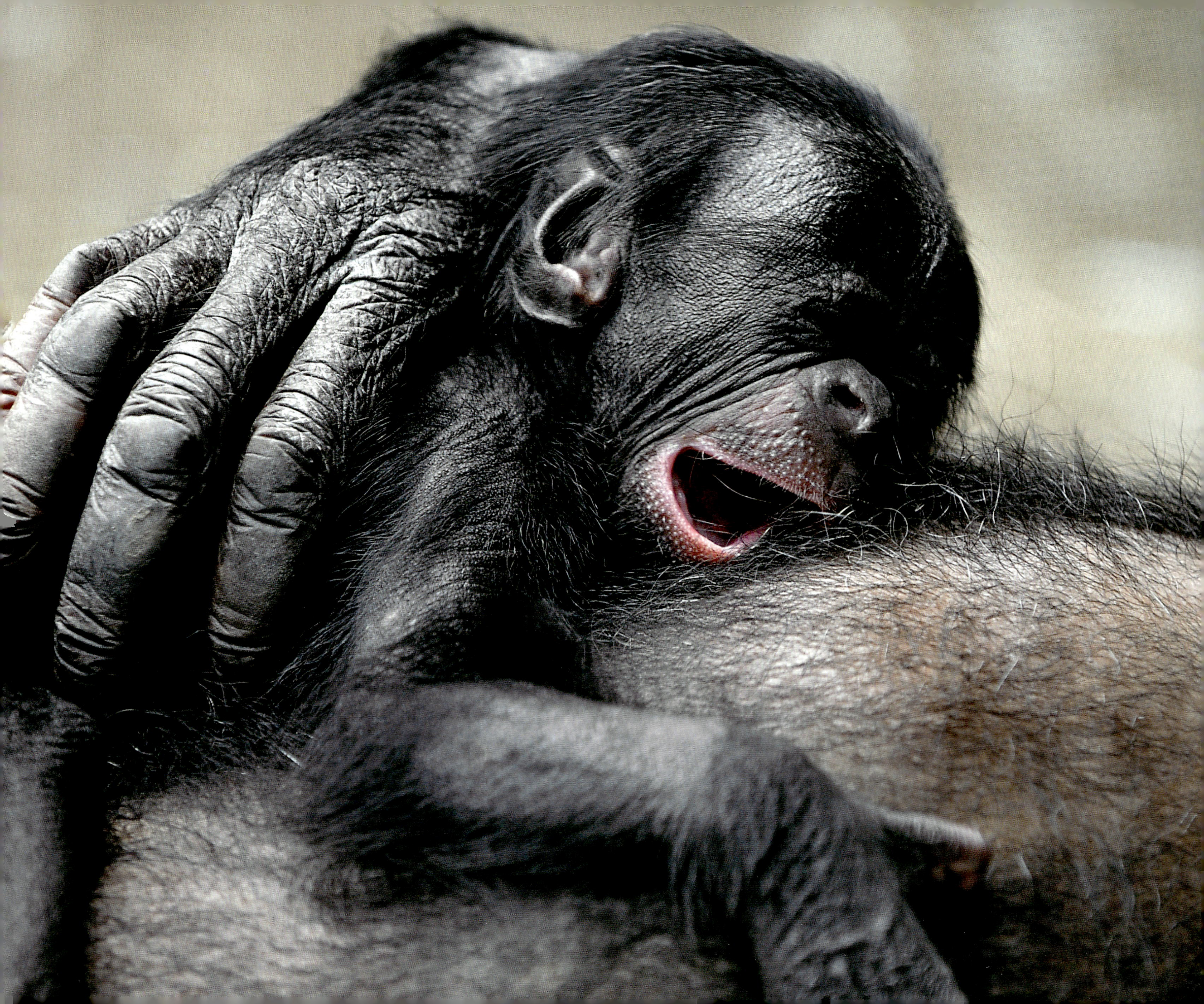

Bonobo / *bonobo*

Bonobo / *bonobo* 149

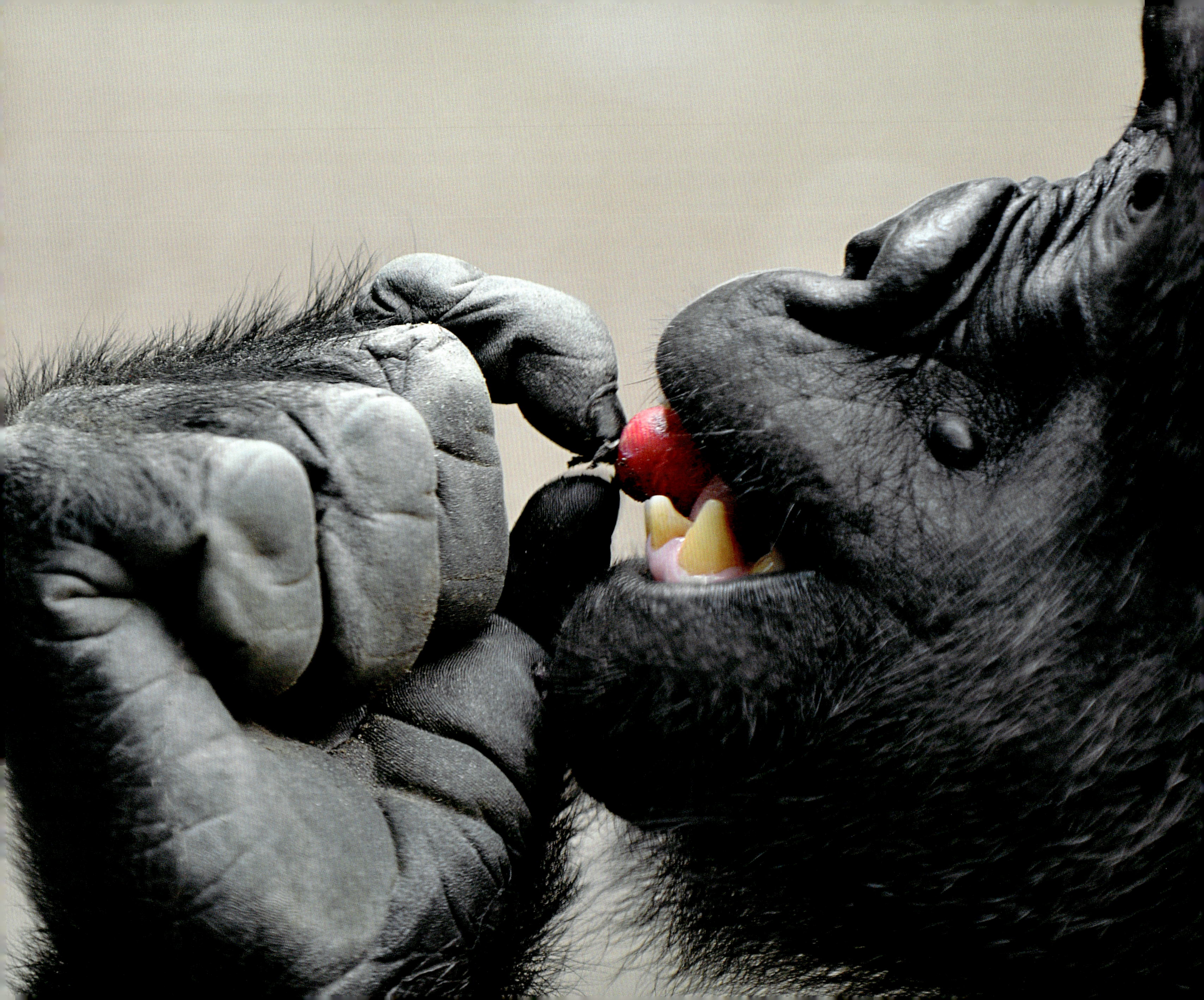

Intelligenz
Intelligence

Bonobo / *bonobo*

Orang-Utan / *orangutan* 153

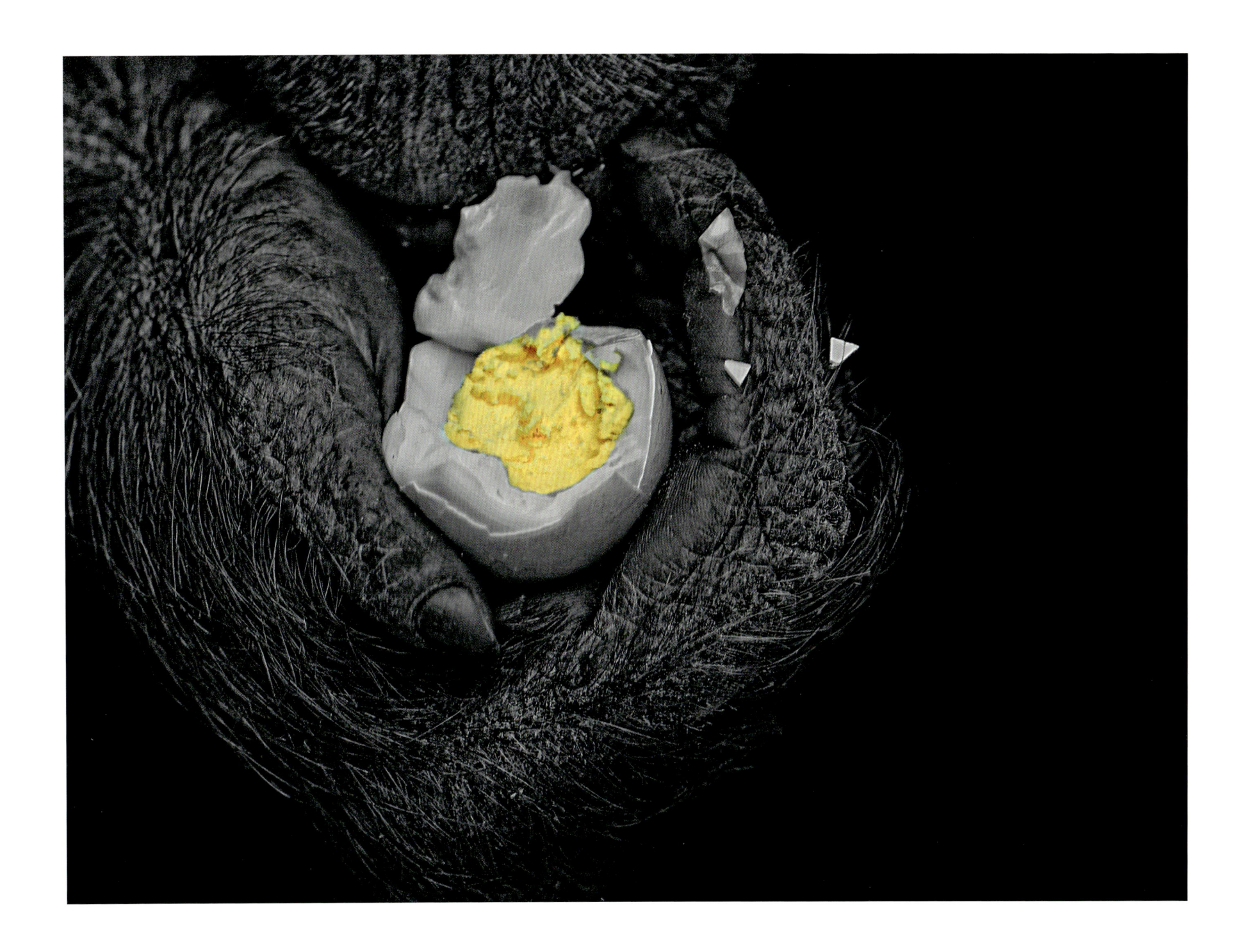

8. Intelligenz

Mentale Landschaften

Dass wir Kinder der Evolution sind, lässt sich an einer Hand ablesen: Weil wir weithin dieselbe Geschichte teilen, sind auch Extremitäten von Affen fünfgliedrig, samt Hautleisten und Plattnägeln. Die gemeinsame Entwicklung, von der vergleichenden Anatomie bereits grob analysiert, wird durch stetig bessere Methoden von Genetik oder Neurobiologie immer feiner rekonstruiert.

Unsere äffische „Hardware" ficht unser Selbstverständnis inzwischen nur noch wenig an. Unbehagen regt sich hingegen, wenn es um die „Software" geht, um das „Geistige". In *dieser* Arena verteidigen wir unseren Einmaligkeitsanspruch gerne auch weiterhin. Allerdings bleiben Definitionen dessen, zu dem allein Menschen fähig sind, nur solange in Mode, bis ein nicht-menschliches Tier entdeckt wird, das genau das kann, was angeblich allein die Krone der Schöpfung auszeichnet.

Nehmen wir eine beliebte Inkarnation des Einmaligen, den *Homo faber*. Demnach machte Werkzeugbenutzung das spezifisch Menschliche aus, bis Jane Goodall erstmals beobachtete, wie wilde Schimpansen Zweige zurichteten, um damit Termiten aus ihren Bauten zu fischen. Ihr Mentor, der Paläoanthropologe Louis Leakey, erklärte darauf: „Nun müssen wir entweder ‚Werkzeug' oder ‚Mensch' neu definieren, oder Schimpansen als Menschen ansehen." Die meisten Wissenschaftler entschieden sich für die erste Möglichkeit, und legten die Latte einfach höher. Zu den revidierten Behauptungen gehörte: Allein Menschen fertigen Geräte vorausschauend und für zukünftigen Gebrauch, bewahren sie für erneute Benutzung auf, und setzen verschiedene Artefakte in logischer Folge ein.

Speziell Forschungen an Schimpansen belegen, wie müßig auch solch neuerliche Abgrenzungsversuche sind. So wählen die Menschenaffen bestimmte Pflanzenarten, je nachdem, ob sie hartes oder biegsames Rohmaterial benötigen, und transportieren die Zweige über teils erhebliche Distanz zum späteren Einsatzort. Wollen sie etwa Termiten fischen oder Bienenhonig erlöffeln, fächern sie die Zweigenden bürstenartig auf. Das vergrößert die Oberfläche und damit die Ausbeute. Bienen nisten gern in Baumhöhlen. Die Schimpansen zeigen zuweilen extreme Geduld, um diese Behausungen aufzubrechen, sind doch mehr als tausend Schläge mit einem Knüppel nötig. Zeitweilig beginnen sie die Arbeit am Morgen, legen das Holz in der Baumkrone ab, pausieren über Mittag, und fahren dann fort.

Wilde Schimpansen spüren überdies metertief im Boden verborgene Ressourcen durch Probebohrungen auf. Im Umkreis von Termitenbauten gilt es etwa, dicht bevölkerte Kammern zu finden. Dazu drücken die Menschenaffen einen harten Stock in die Erde, ziehen ihn heraus und beriechen das Ende. Das wiederholen sie vielfach, bis sie über Geruch und Erdwiderstand eine lohnende Quelle lokalisieren. Dann führen sie ein zweites, biegsames Werkzeug ein. Um Erdhöhlen stacheloser Bienen zu finden und auszubeuten, setzen Schimpansen gar fünf, sechs verschieden gestaltete Grabstöcke und Höniglöffel ein – so, wie wir unseren Werkzeugkästen diverse Schlüssel entnehmen.

Auch Beobachtungen in Gefangenschaft können aufschlussreich sein, etwa jene an einem Schimpansenmann eines schwedischen Zoos, der kaltblütig für die Zukunft plante. Dies entkräftet den Einwand, Menschenaffen könnten Gegenwart und Zukunft nicht kognitiv trennen, da ihre Beutezüge von einem unmittelbaren Nahrungsbedürfnis motiviert seien. Der Zooschimpanse sammelte jedenfalls Steine auf und klopfte Gehegemauern auf Brocken hin ab, die er handlich zerschlug. Das Material versteckte er strategisch beim Wassergraben. Erst Stunden oder Tage später erschreckte er mit diesen Wurfgeschossen das Zoopublikum – was er offenbar unterhaltsam fand.

Seine Munitionssammlungen ähneln 2,6 Millionen Jahre alten Anhäufungen von Steinwerkzeugen in Ostafrika, die wie selbstverständlich frühen Hominiden zugeschrieben werden, also Angehörigen einer jener Linien, die schließlich zu uns Menschen führte. Aber wurden diese Artefakte wirklich immer von „Früh-Menschen" bevorratet? Oder sitzen wir nicht dem Kardinalfehler auf, Belege für „Fortschritt", wenn schon nicht für uns Heutige, so doch für Urmenschen zu reservieren? Das darf man hinterfragen – zumal Ausgrabungen nachweisen, dass westafrikanische Schimpansen seit mindestens Jahrtausenden steinerne Hämmer und Ambosse zum Nüssezerschlagen einsetzen.

Erst seit wenigen Jahrzehnten ist das Benutzen lithischer Artefakte durch Schimpansen genauer dokumentiert. Und erst seit ein paar Jahren wissen wir, dass andere nicht-menschliche Primaten ebenfalls Steinwerkzeuge zum Extrahieren von Nahrung einsetzen, darunter Kapuzineraffen in Südamerika und Makakenaffen in Thailand. Oft sammeln sich die Steine mit ihren deutlichen Abnutzungsspuren an bestimmten Lokalitäten an – als wären es urmenschliche Werkstätten.

Zu behaupten, wir hätten die Bandbreite technologischer Fähigkeiten anderer Tiere bereits ausgelotet, ist also ziemlich voreilig. Denn viele angebliche Belege für archaische menschliche Erfindungskraft mögen in Wirklichkeit demonstrieren, dass auch Menschenaffen – und andere Spezies – in ihrem Denken nicht auf das Hier und Jetzt beschränkt sind.

Ein neueres Beispiel ist die Entdeckung, dass Primaten wie Gorillas und Schimpansen Selbstmedikation anwenden. Speziell wenn sie an Durchfall leiden, pflücken sie rauhe, pricklige Blätter ausgewählter Pflanzen, falten sie und schlucken sie unzerkaut, was den Darm reizt und Wurmparasiten ausscheidet. Offenbar werden Blätter bewusst in Gänze konsumiert – denn zerkaut bliebe die Darmreinigung aus. Wie solche Selbstbehandlung ensteht, und wie die Naturheilkunde über Generationen weitergegeben wird, ist noch unbekannt. Aber Menschenaffen scheinen zu wissen, dass Medizin nichts für Kinder ist. Denn als eine kränkliche Schimpansin das medizinale Mark des Bitterkrauts extrahierte, wollte ihr Kind davon probieren – was die Mutter nicht zuließ…

Gradualisten, also jene Biologen, die in Übergängen statt in Sprüngen denken, argumentieren gerne primatozentrisch. Allerdings scheinen menschenähnliche mentale Fähigkeiten in paralleler Evolution auch in anderen zoologischen Ordnungen entstanden zu sein. Diese Konvergenz der Denklandschaften wurde durch komplexe soziale Umwelten begünstigt, wie sie nicht nur bei Primaten zum Alltag gehören, sondern ebenfalls bei Elefanten, Ratten, Walen, Papageien oder Raben. Ein kompliziertes Miteinander stellt offenbar harte Anforderungen an Gehirne. Denn Sozialleben bietet nicht nur Vorteile, etwa Schutz vor Raubfeinden oder Möglichkeiten der Zusammenarbeit, sondern Gruppengenossen sind vor allem auch Konkurrenten, die den eigenen Vorteil suchen. Sie scheuen sich dabei nicht, Täuschung und Falschinformation einzusetzen, was ein entsprechendes mentales Wettrüsten in Gang setzte und jenen Typ von Intelligenz produzierte, der auch uns auszeichnet.

Zu den zäheren Versuchen, das Einzigartige der *conditio humana* zu belegen, zählt die Berufung auf unsere Kulturfähigkeit. Doch dieser Graben erodiert ebenfalls, wenn wir eine undogmatische Definition vornehmen und Kultur als „sozial weitergegebenes Verhalten" verstehen – auch wenn diese simplifizierende Perspektive gewiss nicht von allen Kulturwissenschaftlern geteilt wird. Bei Menschen jedenfalls zeigt sich kulturelle Vielfalt darin, dass wir je nach Wohnort anderen Sitten folgen, und die sind in der Regel nicht angeboren, sondern im sozialen Kontext erlernt. Verhaltensbiologen arbeiten immer deutlicher heraus, dass sich die Gebräuche von Tieren gleichfalls je nach Lebensraum unterscheiden können, weil an unterschiedlichen Orten unterschiedlich gelernt wird. Obwohl also zur selben Art zählend, differieren ihre Populationen hinsichtlich sozialer Gepflogenheiten, Subsistenztechniken oder Nahrungsgewohnheiten.

Als in dieser Hinsicht „kulturfähig" können beispielsweise Kapuzineraffen in Costa Rica gelten. Bei diesen Primaten kommen periodisch bizarre Spiele in Mode. Ausgewählten Partnern lutschen die Affen dann an den Zehen, schieben ihnen Finger in die Nase oder gar unter die Augäpfel. Dies dürfte kaum angenehm sein und erfordert einiges Vertrauen. Genau das ist wohl die Funktion der Intimitäten: Wer sie teilt, signalisiert Bereitschaft zu Allianz in anderen, meist aggressiven Situationen. Außergewöhnlich geht es ebenfalls unter Japanmakaken zu. Dort klopfen die Affen mancherorts Kiesel klackernd aneinander – eine nutzlose Tätigkeit, die vielleicht eine Gefühl lokaler Zusammengehörigkeit kreiert.

Auf Sumatra wiederum wurden Lokaltraditionen von Orang-Utans entdeckt. Dazu zählen ein kurioses Lippenplustern zur Begrüßung sowie das Abschirmen des Körpers mit Vegetation wenn es regnet. Aus den stacheligen Riesenfrüchten des Neesia-Baumes wiederum extrahieren die rothaarigen Menschenaffen mittels im Mund gehaltener Stöckchen fetthaltige Samen. Neesias und Orang-Utans gibt es beiderseits des Alas-Flusses. Am einen Ufer, im Singkil-Sumpf, ist der Boden mit benutzten Werkzeugen übersät, während Orang-Utans des gegenüberliegenden Batu-Batu Sumpfes keine Geräte benutzen. Die nützliche Erfindung muss mithin auf der Singkil-Seite gemacht worden sein, doch die Fluss-Barriere verhinderte, dass sich die Technik auch in Batu-Batu etablierte.

Musterschüler in Sachen Kultur sind erneut Schimpansen – was diesbezüglicher Forschung an der Gattung *Pan* den treffenden Spitznamen *Panthropologie* eintrug. Die bestuntersuchten Bevölkerungen von Schimpansen leben in Bossou in Guinea, Taï in der Elfenbeinküste, Mahale und Gombe in Tansania sowie Kibale und Budongo in Uganda. Eine sorgfältige Synopse ihres Verhaltens ergab, dass sie sich dutzendfach hinsichtlich Körperpflege, Werkzeugen oder sozialem Miteinander unterscheiden. Nur manche Verhaltensweisen machen Schule, während die meisten Neuerungen wohl Eintagsfliegen bleiben. Keine Nachahmer fand beispielsweise jene wilde Schimpansin, die einen Streifen aus dem Fell eines erbeuteten Stummelaffen verknotete und in offensichtlicher Selbstdekoration um den Hals hängte.

So verfügt jede Gemeinschaft über einen unverwechselbaren Cluster an Gewohnheiten. Ähnlich wie bei Menschen von einem „japanischen" oder „französischen" Kulturkreis gesprochen wird, ordnen Primatologen Schimpansen anhand ihres spezifischen Straußes an Verhaltensmustern etwa der ostafrikanischen „Gombe-Kultur" oder der westafrikanischen „Taï-Kultur" zu – in bewusster Analogie zu kulturwissenschaftlichem Vokabular.

Ähnlich den bizarren Ritualen des Augeneindrückens und Kieselklackerns bei Affen scheint auch bei Schimpansen soziale Identität speziell über „irrationale" Traditionen zu entstehen. So planschen die des Senegal in flachen Teichen, während beispielsweise ostafrikanische Gruppen das Nasse meiden wie der Teufel das Weihwasser. Im nigerianischen Gashaka wiederum isst jeder Schimpanse jeden Tag Ameisen, rührt aber nie die weitaus nährreicheren Termiten an.

Wären Schimpansen Menschen, würden sie – so darf man spekulieren – aufgrund des Wasser- oder Termiten-„Tabus" vermutlich als Anhänger einer magisch-religiösen Weltanschauung gelten. Die Psychologie der Menschenaffen dürfte jedenfalls jener ähnlich sein, über die sich Ethnien definieren: „Du willst ein Gashaka-Schimpanse sein? Dann iss Ameisen soviel du willst. Aber komm' bloß nicht auf die Idee, je eine Termite anzurühren. Oder die Wassergeister zu stören. Bei uns macht man so etwas nicht…"

Der Katalog an Merkmalen, mit denen sich eine menschliche Sonderstellung gerade *nicht* belegen lässt, ist mittlerweile umfangreich. Jene, die unbeirrt an der Dichotomie Tier-Mensch festhalten, werden zuweilen mit eigenen Waffen geschlagen. Etwa, wenn in einem in Japan durchgeführten Experiment an Bildschirmen geschulte Schimpansen zufällig erscheinende Zahlenfolgen durch Drücken entsprechender Felder schneller und genauer rekapitulieren können als – noch dazu japanische – Studenten.

Doch wie Menschenaffen auch mit Leistungen verblüffen – Skeptiker werden ihre Vorbehalte haben. Und weitere Einwände auflisten: Kein Menschenaffe hat je Selbstmord begangen; Orang-Utans hängen keiner Religion an; Gorillas wissen nicht um ihre eigene Sterblichkeit; Bonobos geht der Kunstsinn ab; Menschenaffen führen keine Diskussionen über Evolutionstheorie…

Menschengesellschaften werden seit Jahrtausenden dokumentiert, während systematische Beobachtungen wilder Menschenaffen erst vor 50 Jahren begannen und auf wenige Bevölkerungen beschränkt sind. Darum ist auf jeden Fall richtig, dass wir – auf welcher Seite des Disputs man stehen mag – eigentlich noch immer recht wenig über das Leben und Treiben unserer Verwandten wissen.

Bonobo / *bonobo* 157

8. Intelligence

Mental Landscapes

That we are children of evolution is obvious with a glance at our hands. Because of a shared history, monkeys and apes likewise have five fingers and toes, equipped with epidermal ridges and flat nails. This communal phylogeny, already grossly analysed by comparative anatomy, sees finer reconstructions through the constantly improving methods of genetics and neurobiology.

That we possess a basically primate "hardware" hardly challenges our self-esteem. However, we become slightly uneasy when our "software" is at stake: our mind. In this arena, we tend to hang on to claims of uniqueness. Still, definitions of what humans alone can do remain in fashion only until a non-human animal does exactly what is supposedly reserved for the crown of creation.

Take a popular incarnation of the unique, *Homo faber*. This paradigm of "man the toolmaker" understood the wielding of devices as something specific to humans – until Jane Goodall witnessed how wild chimpanzees modify sticks to fish in termite mounds. Upon which her mentor, palaeoanthropologist Louis Leakey famously responded, "Now we must redefine 'tool', redefine 'man' or accept chimpanzees as humans." Most scientists chose the first option. They simply raised the bar, assuming that apes wouldn't be able to master new criteria: only humans create tools with foresight and for future utilisation; only humans keep utensils for re-use; only humans employ a variety of artefacts in a logical sequence.

Research on chimpanzees demonstrates that such recent attempts to reinstate a solid animal/human divide are likewise futile. Thus, apes often select very particular plant species as tool sources, depending on whether they need hard or pliable raw material, and then transport the vegetation parts over sometimes considerable distance to the location of their intended use. They may carefully fray the tool-tips before harvesting termites or honey. This procedure enlarges the surface area and thus the yield. Chimpanzees can also display extreme patience in breaking into bee hives in tree cavities, wearing the trunk down with more than a thousand strokes from a club. At times, they start this work in the morning, then pause for a siesta – not without leaving the bludgeon in the tree top – before continuing.

Wild chimpanzees also drill up to a metre into the soil to find resources hidden underground. In the vicinity of termite mounds, they aim, for example, to locate densely populated chambers. For this, they insert a sturdy probe into the ground, pull it out again and smell the end. They repeat this many times until, guided by resistance and scent, they identify a suitable location. The apes then insert a second, flexible tool into the chamber to harvest the insects. To locate and exploit the underground nest cavities of stingless bees, chimpanzees may even employ up to five or six differently shaped digging sticks and spoon-like honey probes – similar to how we make use of various keys in a tool box.

Observations in captivity can also be revealing, such as those of a chimpanzee in a Swedish zoo who coldly calculated for the future. This undermines the argument that apes cannot mentally separate the present and the future, because their actions are always motivated by an immediate need, such as for food. Said chimpanzee collected stones and also removed pieces out of the walls of his enclosure, which he broke down into handy scraps. He hid the material strategically, near the moat. Only hours or even days later would he deploy these missiles against startled visitors – something he might very well have found amusing.

His collections of ammunition were similar to 2.6-million-year-old accumulations of stone tools discovered in East Africa. Naturally, these were attributed to early hominids, thus members of the human lineages. But were these artefacts really always stocked by "early man"? Or do we not commit the cardinal sin of ascribing evidence of "progress", if not to modern humans, then at least to the inner circle of our forebears? Such assumptions can be questioned – especially since excavations have proven that West African chimpanzees used stone hammers and anvils to smash nuts since certainly thousands of years.

Only in the last decades has the use of stone tools by chimpanzees been documented in some detail. And only in most recent years have we known that other non-human primates likewise handle stones to extract food, including capuchin monkeys in South America and macaques in Thailand. Often, these tools with their unmistakable traces of wear accumulate at specific locations – as if they were the abandoned workshops of "primitive man".

Clearly, the range of technological abilities of other animals is not yet sufficiently explored. Possibly, much of the evidence attesting to the ingenuity of archaic humans may in fact demonstrate that the thoughts of apes – or even other species – are likewise not limited to the here-and-now.

Another recent example is the discovery that primates such as gorillas and chimpanzees can resort to self-medication. When suffering from diarrhoea, they will pluck rough-bladed leaves from selected plants, fold them and swallow without chewing. This irritates the gut and induces the excretion of parasitic worms. The leaves are deliberately not chewed, as this would disable the desired effect of intestinal cleansing. How this self-treatment originated and how the techniques were passed on through generations is still unknown. But apes seem to know that medicine is not for children. A sickly chimpanzee mother was once observed extracting the bitter pith of a medicinal herb. Her offspring wanted to sample the herb as well – but the mother didn't allow it.

Gradualists, those biologists who imagine transitions instead of jumps, often have a "primatocentric" mindset. However, through parallel evolution, human-like mental abilities might have also emerged in other zoological orders. This convergence of mental landscapes was favoured by complex social environments that are not only part and parcel of everyday life in primates, but also experienced by elephants, rats, whales, parrots and ravens. A complicated group life apparently places heavy demands on the brain. This is because sociality not only provides benefits, such as protection against predators, or potential for cooperation – but one's companions are also chief competitors who seek their own advantage. Thus, our fellow travellers will not refrain from deception and misinformation, which sets a corresponding mental arms race in motion and produces those modes of intelligence that characterise us.

One of the more resilient attempts to ascertain the uniqueness of the human condition focuses on our cultural capacity. But this divide erodes likewise when we employ a non-dogmatic definition of culture as "socially transmitted behaviour". To be sure, this simplistic perspective will certainly not be adopted by all who study "culture". In any case, cultural diversity in humans is embodied by the fact that we stick to different customs, depending on where we grow up. These rules are not genetically determined, but are learned in a social context. Behavioural ecologists are working out ever more clearly that non-human animals, too, may follow varying traditions, because different conventions develop in different habitats. Thus, populations of the same species may exhibit a diversity of social codes, techniques of subsistence or eating habits.

Such cultural propensities can, for example, be ascribed to the capuchin monkeys of Costa Rica. Periodically, these primates will invent bizarre games. In certain pairs, they will suck on each other's toes, push fingers up their noses or partially dislodge their eyeballs through poking. This can hardly be pleasant and definitely requires mutual trust. Exactly herein lies the probable function of these intimacies: whoever shares them indicates the willingness to be a reliable ally in other, typically aggressive, situations. Extraordinary behaviours are also displayed by Japanese macaques. In some localities, monkeys will handle pebbles, roll and pile them or clack them together – a "useless" pastime that might well contribute to a local group identity.

Local traditions of orangutans have been discovered on Sumatra. They may blow a raspberry for a greeting or shield their body with vegetation when it rains. Some orangutans, with sticks skilfully lodged between their teeth, extract fatty seeds from the enormous but very prickly fruit of the Neesia tree. Neesias and orangutans are found on both sides of the Alas River. On one bank, in the Singkil-swamp, the ground is littered with discarded tools, while orangutans dwelling in the opposite Batu-Batu swamp do not use any implements. The practical invention must therefore have been devised on the Singkil side, but the natural barrier prevented the technique to spread to Batu-Batu.

Advanced pupils when it comes to the subject of culture are once again chimpanzees. This facility earned *Pan*-related research into this topic the fitting nickname *Panthropology*. The best studied populations of chimpanzees live in Bossou in Guinea, Taï in the Ivory Coast, and Gombe and Mahale in Tanzania, as well as Kibale and Budongo in Uganda. A detailed synopsis shows how these populations differ in dozens of behavioural patterns related to hygiene, tool use, foraging and social interaction. Only some fads will spread, whereas most innovations probably remain short-lived. For example, nobody imitated the wild chimpanzee female who knotted a strip of skin from a colobus monkey prey into a simple necklace and hung it in an obvious attempt of self-decoration around her neck.

Each chimpanzee community is therefore characterised by a unique cluster of habits. In a human context, we might speak about "Japanese" or "French" culture. Similarly, primatologists will assign chimpanzees according to their specific bouquet of behavioural patterns to, for example, the East African "Gombe culture" or the West African "Taï culture" – in deliberate analogy to the vocabulary of cultural anthropologists or sociologists.

As with the bizarre rituals of the eye-gouging or pebble-piling monkeys, social identity in chimpanzees may likewise be tied to preferentially "irrational" traditions. Thus, Senegalese apes splash in shallow ponds, while East African apes avoid even the smallest creek as the devil would holy water. In Nigeria's Gashaka site again, each chimpanzee will eat ants daily – but will never touch a termite, although they are available and far more nutritious.

If these chimpanzees were humans, they would be classified as followers of a magico-religious belief system, devotees who observe a water or termite "taboo". In any case, the psychology of apes is likely similar to mind-sets with which ethnic groups define themselves: "You want to be a Gashaka-chimpanzee? Then eat ants as much as you want. But don't even think about touching a termite. Or disturbing the spirits in the water. This is not the way we do things here…"

The catalogue of features *not* suitable to justify human uniqueness has become extensive. What is more, those who cling steadfastly to the animal-human dichotomy are sometimes defeated with their own weapons. For instance, an experiment conducted in Japan had chimpanzees trained on touch-screens recapitulate randomly appearing numbers. The apes performed faster and more accurately than human students – even Japanese ones.

But with whatever skills apes may amaze us – sceptics will retain their reservations. And come up with further objections: no ape has ever committed suicide; orangutans do not practice religion; gorillas are not aware that they are mortal; bonobos have no artistic sense; apes do not discuss evolutionary theory…

Human societies have been documented over millennia, whereas systematic observations of wild apes first started 50 years ago and are still limited to a few populations. Thus, whatever side of the dispute we might be on, it is certainly true that we actually still know little about the life and travails of our relatives.

Bonobo / *bonobo*

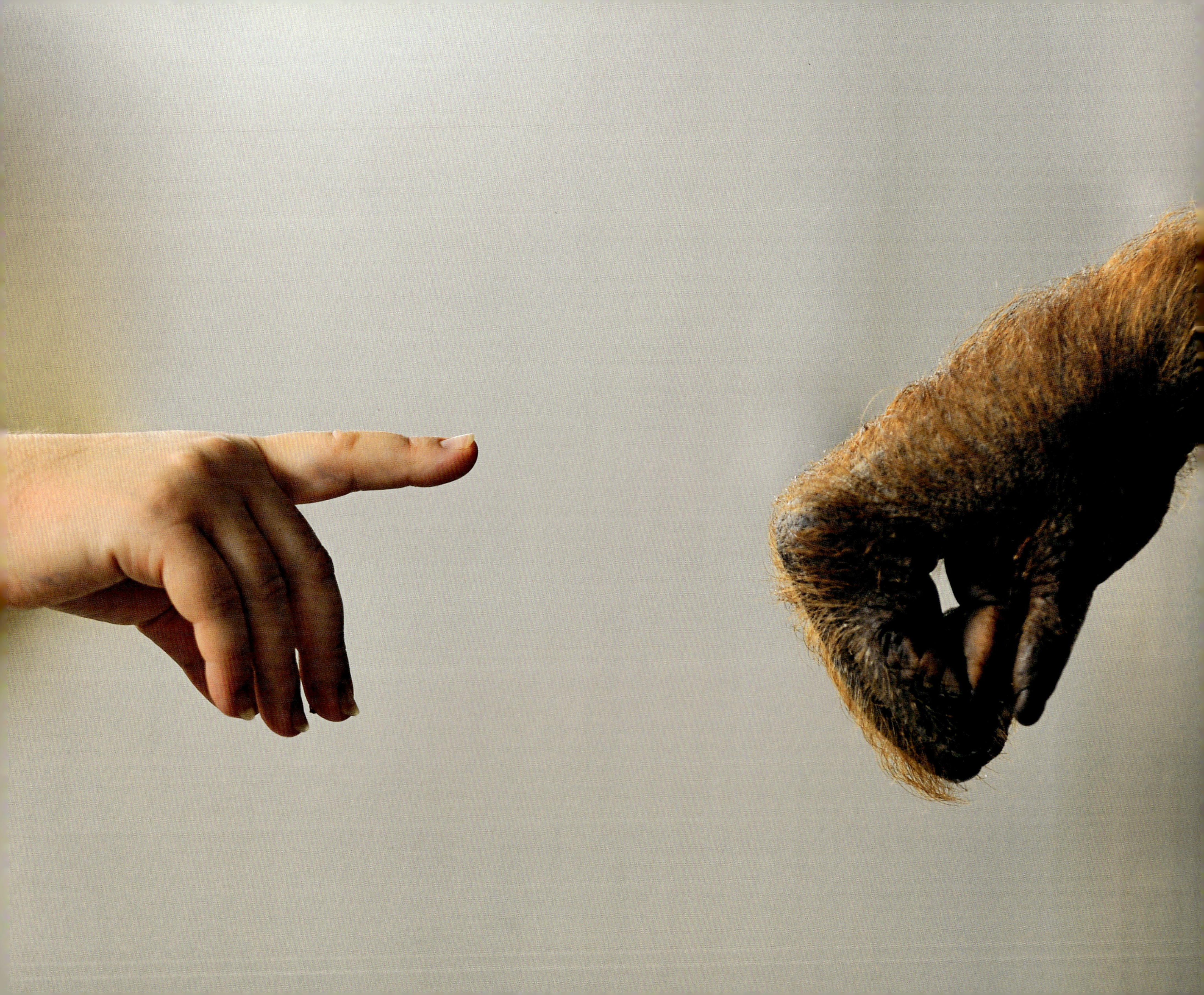

Philosophisches
Philosophising

Orang-Utan / *orangutan*

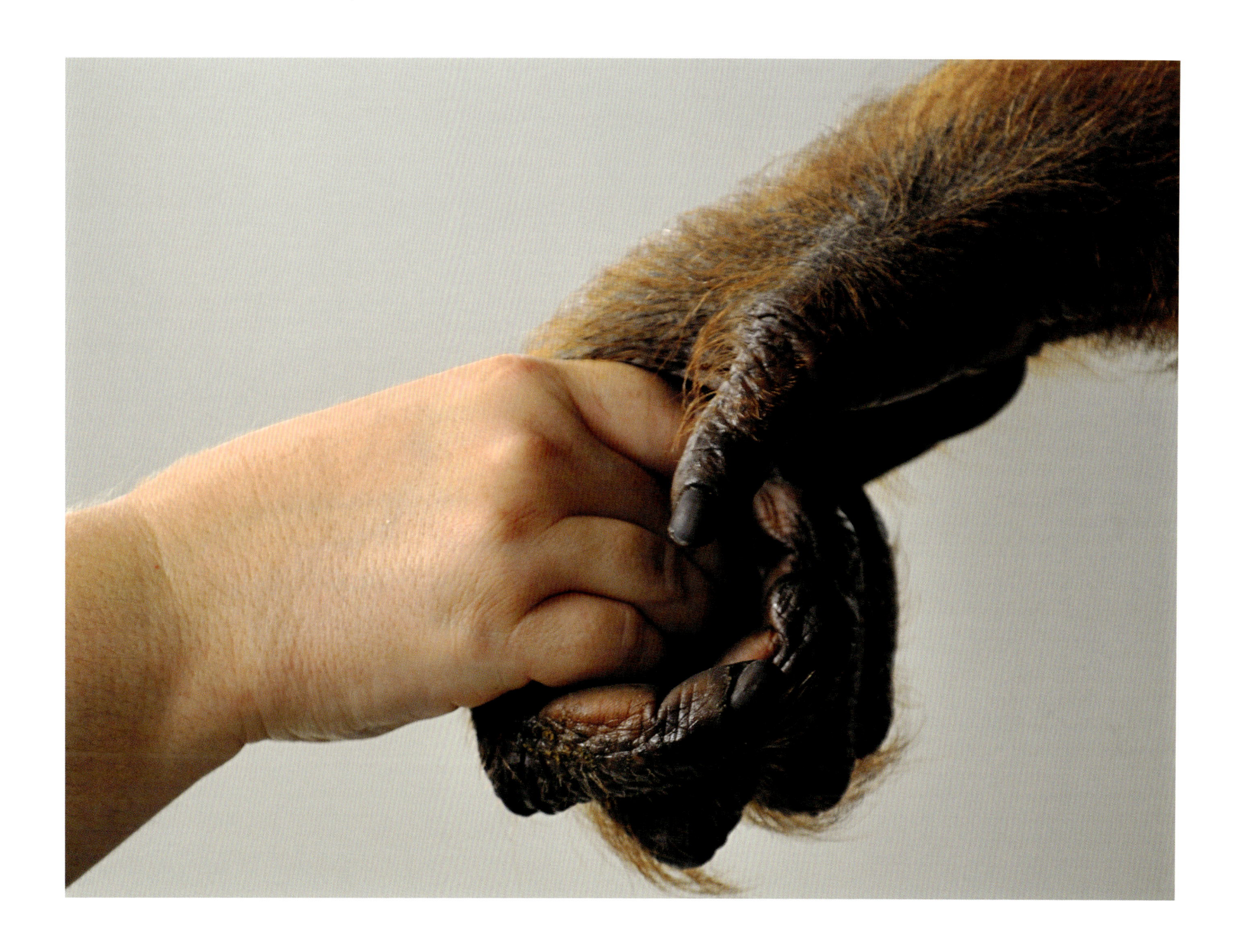

Orang-Utan / *orangutan*

9. Philosophisches

Die Provokation des Monismus

Unsere Alltagssprache trennt „Mensch" und „Tier". Diese beliebte Abgrenzung wurzelt vielleicht in einem Verlangen nach Selbstfindung. Denn die Frage „Wer bin ich?" ist leichter zu beantworten, wenn ich „das Andere" benennen kann. Sigmund Freud meinte überdies, das Eingeständnis, selbst dem Tierreich zu entstammen, würde unseren Stolz und unser Selbstwertgefühl verletzen. In der Tat: Könnte der Orang-Utan denken, verfügte der Gorilla über einen freien Willen und hätte der Bonobo ein Bewusstsein: Würde das nicht unseren überlegenen Geist aus metaphysischen Höhen zu Boden ziehen? Und eine Seele gar für Schimpansen? Plötzlich säße sie schief, die Krone der Schöpfung…

In der westlichen Denktradition ist die Tier/Mensch-Polarität mit dem Philosophen René Descartes verbunden. Der leitete im 17. Jahrhundert die Moderne ein, indem er das kritische und denkende Ich zum Anker seiner Überlegungen machte. Descartes Philosophie unterscheidet streng zwischen einer denkenden Sache (*res cogitans*) – dem Geist – und einer ausgedehnten Sache (*res extensa*) – der Materie. Der Geist – mehr oder weniger identisch mit der Seele – ist immateriell, nicht an irgendeinem Ort lokalisiert und unterliegt deshalb nicht den Naturgesetzen. Nur Menschen besitzen echten Geist und Seele, die Tieren hingegen fehlen.

Descartes konnte somit behaupten, dass Tiere keinen wirklichen Schmerz fühlen. Er propagierte deshalb die Vivisektion – die operative Zerlegung lebender Tiere – um menschliche Gesundheit und Krankheit besser verstehen zu können.

Doch wie konnte Descartes Versuche am Tier zum Wohle des Menschen für sinnvoll halten, wo sie doch so unterschiedlich hinsichtlich der geistigen Sphäre sind? Er argumentierte, dass alle Lebewesen sehr wohl den gleichen natürlichen Regeln folgen, wenn es um ihre Körper geht, die ja stets aus Materie bestehen. Unter anderem davon inspiriert, dass Uhren seinerzeit der Höhepunkt mechanischen Handwerks waren, versteht Descartes Lebewesen deshalb als Maschinen: Die Körper von Tieren wie von Menschen sind Automaten, die das feine Räderwerk der Naturgesetze illustrieren.

Descartes war einer der ersten Denker, der biologische Vorgänge unter dem Gesichtspunkt der Mechanik analysierte. Er postulierte ununterbrochene Sequenzen von Ursache und Wirkung – ähnlich eben den Wechselwirkungen zwischen den genau eingestellten Teilen eines Uhrwerks. Descartes Denkansatz ist von kaum zu überschätzender Bedeutung für die Fortschritte der westlichen Wissenschaft und ihrer praktischen Erfolge in Technologie, Physiologie oder Medizin. Der Tier-Mensch-Dualismus bezüglich des Geistigen befeuerte aber zugleich jene Philosophie, die eine menschliche Sonderstellung aufgrund angeblich einmaliger Charakteristika wie Technologie, Kultur, Sprache oder Sozialverhalten behauptet. Die Suche nach dem Einmaligen mit seiner trennenden Perspektive des Alles-oder-Nichts intensivierte sich deshalb paradoxerweise trotz des Siegeszugs der Evolutionstheorie, obwohl diese ja eigentlich eine vereinigende Perspektive des Mehr-oder-Weniger einnimmt.

Detaillierte Forschungen des letzten halben Jahrhunderts und speziell Studien an Menschenaffen ließen es allerdings stetig zweifelhafter erscheinen, dass die sogenannten „Humana" wirklich ein menschliches Privileg sind – von Werkzeugherstellung über Empathie bis hin zu Zukunftsplanung. Diese neuerlichen Erkenntnisse, obwohl nicht unumstritten, sind nicht nur wissenschaftlich bedeutsam, sondern haben auch Konsequenzen für „große Fragen" in ethischer und existenzieller Hinsicht. Unter dem Stichwort *evolutionärer Humanismus* gewinnen entsprechende Debatten zunehmend an Fahrt.

Diskussionsbedarf besteht beispielsweise hinsichtlich des rechtlichen Status von Menschenaffen. Das von den Philosophen Peter Singer und Paola Cavalieri initiierte *Great Ape Project* fordert für Orang-Utans, Gorillas, Bonobos und Schimpansen einige jener Privilegien, die bisher nur für Menschen gelten. Dazu zählt das Recht auf Leben, Freiheit und ein Verbot von Folter. Augenmaß ist dabei durchaus gewahrt, denn niemand fordert ein Recht auf Bildung für Bonobos, Wahlrecht für Gorillas, Datenschutz für Schimpansen oder ein Mindestalter für Sex unter Orang-Utans. Unterstützt von Dutzenden der renommiertesten

Primatologen macht sich die Initiative seit 1993 dafür stark, die „community of equals" – die „Gemeinschaft der Gleichen" – in gewisser Hinsicht zu erweitern. Es würde damit als Unrecht gelten, Große Menschenaffen in medizinischen Experimenten zu schädigen, zu Tode zu richten oder ihren Lebensraum zu zerstören. Weil die Leidensfähigkeit von Menschenaffen der unseren entsprechen dürfte, weil sie sich in andere Wesen hineinversetzen und in die Zukunft denken können, sollen sie überdies als „Personen" gelten.

Die Forderung nach elementarer Gleichstellung der Menschenaffen ist im Grunde eine zeitgenössische Fortsetzung vormaliger Erörterungen – etwa der, ob Frauen das Wahlrecht besitzen sollen, ob dunkelhäutige Afrikaner oder australische Aborigines Menschen sind oder ob Homosexuelle heiraten dürfen. Vielerorts wurde die Gemeinschaft der Gleichen nach oft leidenschaftlichen Diskussionen und Auseinandersetzungen entsprechend erweitert. Manche Philosophen und Primatologen halten den historischen Moment für gekommen, erneut inklusiver zu werden. Aufzuheben wäre nunmehr die Schranke des „Speziesismus", der die Ungleichbehandlung von Lebewesen allein aufgrund ihrer Artzugehörigkeit rechtfertigt. In weiterer Konsequenz bedeutet dies selbstverständlich, dass auch die willkürliche Grenze zwischen Menschen und Menschenaffen im Unterschied zu anderen Tieren hinterfragt werden kann. Interessanterweise formiert sich eine entsprechende Lobby gegenwärtig gerade für Wale und Delfine. Praktische Einschränkungen sprechen nicht gegen den Grundsatz. Denn obwohl ihnen körperliche Unversehrtheit zusteht, dürfen beispielsweise viele Menschen – Kinder, Komakranke – nicht wählen, und ihnen wird auch keine Verantwortung abverlangt. Wie für solche „unmündigen" Menschen könnten die grundsätzlichen rechtlichen Belange von Menschenaffen durch einen Vormund vertreten werden. In Neuseeland und Spanien wurden bereits entsprechende Gesetzentwürfe erarbeitet.

Die neuen Erkenntnisse zu Menschenaffen liefern zudem sicherlich neue Argumente gegen den Leib-Seele-Dualismus des Descartes. Der wird zwar von der zeitgenössischen Philosophie praktisch nicht mehr vertreten, spielt aber weiterhin eine prominente Rolle in populären Vorstellungen. Katholische Christen beispielsweise glauben an die Existenz einer immateriellen und unsterblichen Seele. Manche Tierforscher sympathisieren durchaus mit solchen Vorstellungen, wollen aber den Grenzstein zwischen „beseelter Menschheit" und „unbeseelter Natur" verschieben und schreiben deshalb Tieren gleichfalls eine Seele zu. Die prominente Primatenforscherin Jane Goodall bekennt sich öffentlich zu solchem Glauben, einschließlich eines Lebens nach dem Tode – und ihrer Überzeugung, dass Unsterblichkeit auch auf Schimpansen wartet.

Wem der Dualismus von Mensch und Tier suspekt ist, kann aber auch radikaler vorgehen und die Unterscheidung von Geist und Materie grundsätzlich anzweifeln. Das Resultat wäre ein neuer *Monismus* – eine Weltanschauung, die nichtmaterielle Dimensionen gänzlich aufgibt und psychisch-„geistige" Vorgänge ebenfalls komplett auf physikalisch-chemische Prozesse im Gehirn zurückführen will. Es entbehrt nicht gewisser Ironie, dass dies eine Konsequenz des Descartschen Programmes einer Mechanisierung der Natur ist, das nun genau jene Sphäre einholt, die davon explizit ausgenommen war: eben das Geistig-Seelische. Denn Disziplinen wie Paläontologie, Medizin, Genetik oder Neurobiologie haben ja nicht nur Tiere, sondern zugleich uns Menschen Stück um Stück in Einzelteile zerlegt und Lebensvorgänge entsprechenden Ketten von Ursache und Wirkung zugeordnet. Im Lichte dieser Weltanschauung stünden wir mit einem Male als Automaten da, deren begabtes Gehirn sich sowohl den Geist selbst erfand als auch die Seele schuf. Kann aber alles auf Materie zurückgeführt werden, sind wir mit einem Male aufs Innigste mit den Tieren wiedervereint.

Ob man diesen Monismus vertreten will oder nicht – auf jeden Fall beseitigt er ein Paradoxon des klassisch-dualistischen Denkens: Wie konnte eine ihrerseits unbeseelte Urmutter irgendwann ein beseeltes Kind zur Welt bringen? Monisten müssen sich nicht an solchen Mirakeln abarbeiten und können sich stattdessen an säkularen Wundern freuen – den Wundern der Natur und dem so genährten Gefühl, anderen Lebewesen nahe zu stehen. Damit wäre auch Sigmund Freuds psychoanalytische Deutung der emotionalen Unterscheidung von Mensch und Tier passé. Denn jene, die die Evolutionsbiologie ernst nehmen, empfinden es nicht als Kränkung, sondern als Bereicherung, sich als Tier zu begreifen – als Säugetier im Allgemeinen und als Menschenaffe im Besonderen.

9. Philosophising

The Provocation of Monism

Our everyday language separates "human" and "animal". This popular definition is perhaps rooted in a desire for self-discovery. For the question "Who am I?" is easier to answer if I can designate "the other".

Sigmund Freud had another take on this. He theorised that the admission that humans derive from the animal kingdom would hurt our pride and self-esteem. Indeed, if the orangutan could think, if the gorilla commanded a free-will and the bonobo possessed consciousness, would this not drag our superior minds from metaphysical heights down to rather earthly abodes? And chimpanzees permeated by a soul? Suddenly, the pinnacle of creation would fall flat…

In Western intellectual history, the animal/human polarity is tightly connected with the philosopher René Descartes. His 17th-century ideas signal the beginnings of modernity. The critical and thinking self became the hinge for Descartes' dualism of body and soul. Within this philosophy, there is a strict distinction between entities of thought (*res cogitans*) and matter (*res extensa*). The mind – more or less identical with the soul – belongs to the former category. It is nonmaterial, does not occupy space and therefore does not follow the laws of nature. Only humans possess a true mind or soul, whereas animals do not.

This led Descartes to say that animals did not feel real pain. He thus advocated the practice of vivisection – the dissection of live animals – to better understand human health and disease. Descartes maintained that animal testing for the benefit of humans made sense, given how dissimilar they were with respect to the soul. But he argued that all living beings were subject to the laws of nature when it came to their bodies, as they all consisted of matter. Descartes was inspired by clocks, at the time the peak of mechanical craftsmanship, and therefore suggested that bodies, whether those of animals or humans, resembled machines and functioned like a clockwork.

Descartes was one of the first thinkers who looked at biological processes as if they were mechanic. He thus postulated unbroken sequences of cause and effect – similar to the interactions amongst the precisely tuned parts of a watch. This approach is at the core of scientific progress and its practical achievements in technology, physiology and medicine. Nevertheless, Descartes' animal/human dualism with respect to the mind and soul fuelled the very philosophy that claims a special position for humans because of purportedly unique characteristics such as technology, culture, language and social behaviour. The quest for "the unique" with its dividing perspective of all-or-nothing would thus intensify, despite the rise of evolutionary theory with its unifying perspective of a more-or-less.

However, detailed research over the last half century and studies of apes in particular have raised more and more doubts that certain traits are the human privilege we once thought they were – be it tool manufacturing, empathy or planning for the future. This revised state of knowledge, while not undisputed, is not only important in a scientific sense, but has also implications for "big questions" in ethical and existential perspectives. Under the heading of *evolutionary humanism,* such debates are gaining momentum.

Discussion is needed, for example, concerning the legal status of great apes. Initiated by philosophers Peter Singer and Paola Cavalieri, the *Great Ape Project* demands that some privileges that currently apply only to humans should be extended. This includes a right to life, liberty and the prohibition of torture for great apes. Common sense still applies, as nobody calls for granting bonobos a right to education, a right to vote for gorillas, a data protection act for chimpanzees or a legal age for sex between orangutans. Supported since 1993 by dozens of renowned primatologists, the initiative aims for an expansion of the "community of equals". This would render it always unlawful to injure or kill great apes in biomedical experiments or to destroy their habitat. Moreover, great apes should be considered to be "persons", given their human-like psyche that allows them to empathise with the joys and miseries of others, to think into the future and to suffer in the ways we do.

Demanding basic equality for great apes is a contemporary continuation of former debates – for example, if women should have a right to vote, whether dark-skinned Africans or Australian aborigines are human, or whether gay people can marry. In many places, after often heated discussions, the community of equals has been extended accordingly. Some primatologists and philosophers are convinced that the historic moment has arrived to again be more inclusive. This time, we would have to remove the barrier of "speciesism" that justifies inequality amongst living beings solely based on assignment to a particular species. Of course, the arbitrary line between humans and great apes on the one hand and the rest of the animal species on the other could likewise be questioned at any time in the future; interestingly, such a lobby is currently forming for whales and dolphins.

Practical limitations do not contradict the principle. Although many humans such as toddlers and comatose patients are neither eligible to vote nor held responsible for their actions, they are still entitled to physical integrity. As is done for wards incapable of caring for his or her own interests, a guardian could be assigned to individual great apes. Respective legal bills have already been drafted in New Zealand and Spain.

What we now know about apes also certainly provides new arguments against the mind-body dualism of Descartes. To be sure, contemporary philosophy engages with his positions at best for historical reasons. But Cartesian dualism still plays a prominent role in popular conceptions. Roman Catholics, for example, trust in the existence of an immaterial and immortal soul. Some animal researchers are likewise sympathetic to such lines of thought, but they would want to shift the boundary between "soulful humans" and "inanimate animals" and thus ascribe souls also to animals. The prominent ape researcher Jane Goodall publicly confesses such beliefs, which include a life after death – and her conviction that chimpanzees, too, can expect immortality.

However, those sceptical about the conventional human-animal dualism can also be more radical, and question the distinction between mind and matter on principle. The result would be a new *monism* – a world view that renounces non-material interpretations altogether, and maintains that psychological phenomena can be fully explained by physical-chemical processes in the brain. It is not without irony that this is a late consequence of the Cartesian programme of the mechanisation of nature. This train of thought is now catching up with the very dimension that was originally explicitly excluded: the soul. For disciplines such as palaeontology, medicine, genetics and neurobiology have not only dissected animals into finer and finer parts and corresponding chains of cause and effect, but also we humans. Thus, we suddenly find ourselves to be machines – an apparatus that commands a gifted brain which itself created the soul. But if everything can indeed be attributed to materialistic processes, then we are finally reunited with all other animals.

Whether one wants to defend this monism or not, it eliminates a paradox of classic dualistic thinking: how could it happen that an archaic mother who lacked a soul gave birth to a child with a soul? A monist does not have to ponder such a miracle but can enjoy secular wonders – the wonders of nature, and how they instill a feeling of being close to other living things. With this, Sigmund Freud's psychoanalytic interpretation of the stubborn persistence of the mental animal/human divide would likewise be passé. Because those who take evolutionary theory seriously would not find it insulting but empowering and enriching to understand themselves to be an animal – a mammal in general and an ape in particular.

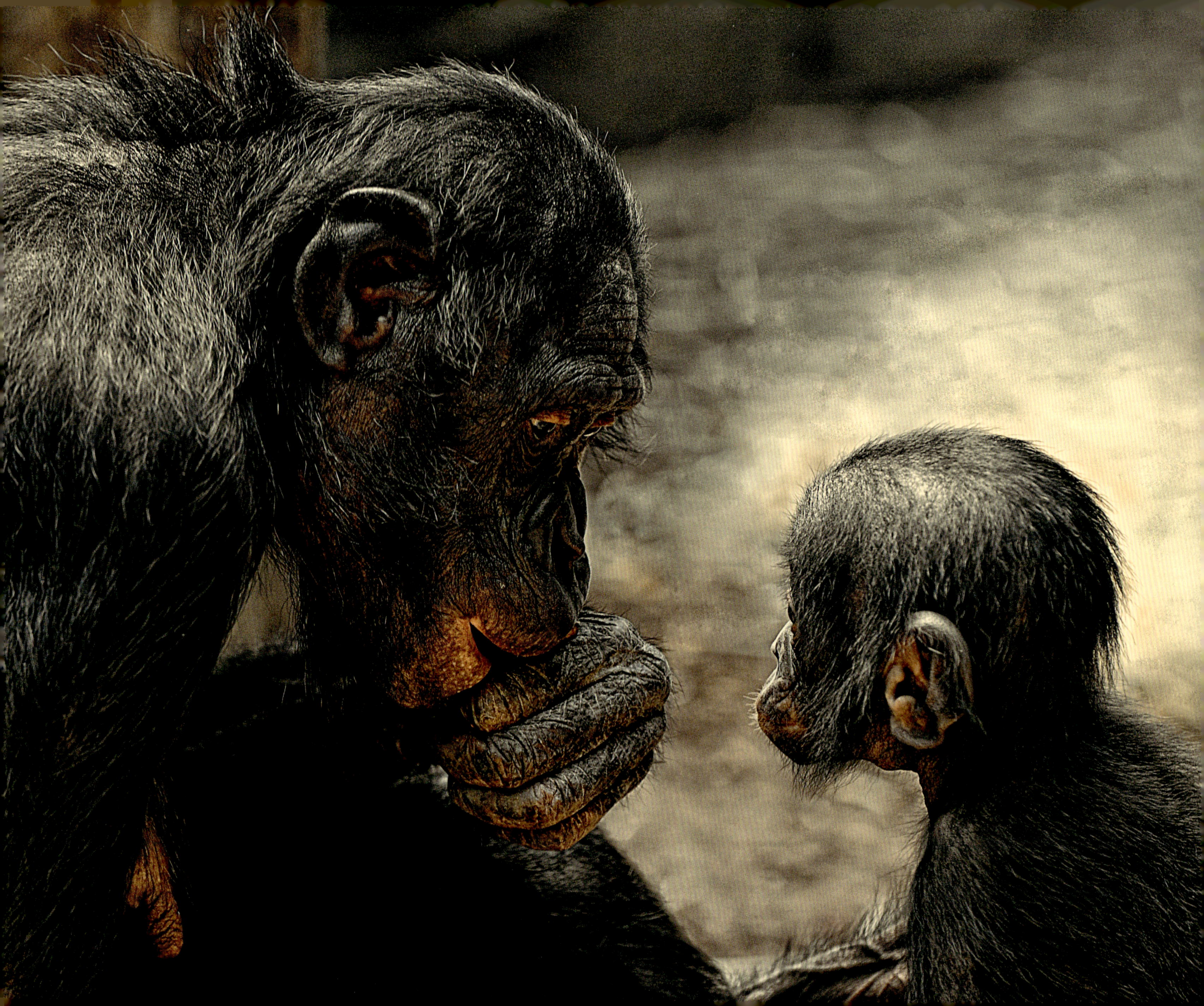

Zukunft

Future

Bonobo / *bonobo*

Bonobo / *bonobo*

10. Zukunft

Archen in der Menschenflut

Um auf dem Mars ein Fünkchen Leben zu entdecken, werden Milliarden ausgegeben. Unsummen würden bereitgestellt, würden sich auf anderen Planeten intelligente Wesen finden, die ähnlich wie wir Freude und Leid empfänden, in hochkomplexen Gesellschaften lebten und mit uns in Zeichensprachen kommunizieren könnten. Genau solche Wesen sind auf Mutter Erde beheimatet. Dennoch werben jene Organisationen, die sich ihren Schutz zum Ziel setzen, kaum mehr als ein paar Millionen Dollar im Jahr ein. Somit sehen wir praktisch tatenlos zu, wie unsere nächsten Gegenüber in der Versenkung verschwinden – durch Zerstörung ihrer Heimaten und gnadenlose Jagd.

Man sollte sich nicht in die Tasche lügen: In ihren tropischen Ursprungsländern haben größere Bevölkerungen von Menschenaffen kaum eine Chance zum Überleben. Wie andere wilde Tiere auch – gleich ob Schnecken, Fische, Fledermäuse, Schlangen, Antilopen oder Elefanten – landen Affen und Menschenaffen im Kochtopf. Dabei ist „Buschfleisch" nicht Notversorgung armer Leute. Vielmehr zahlen Honoratioren der Dörfer wie Neureiche der Städte dafür ein Vielfaches wie für Rind, Schwein oder Ziege. Überdies schleppen Flüchtlinge, Viehherden und Touristen Krankheitserreger wie Ebola, Milzbrand und Tuberkulose in die Biotope der Menschenaffen. Am schlimmsten ist der Kahlschlag des Urwalds, um Bau- und Edelholz zu gewinnen; um Plantagen von Gummibäumen und Ölpalmen zu pflanzen; um den Boden nach Erzen, fossilen Brennstoffen und Edelmetallen zu durchwühlen; um Siedlungen anzulegen, Viehweiden und Anbauflächen.

Nutznießer der flächendeckenden Zerstörung sind vor allem reiche Länder des Nordatlantik. Im Klartext: Wir. Wir waschen uns mit duftender Seife, die auf Palmöl basiert – angebaut dort, wo vor zehn Jahren Orang-Utans auf – buchstäblich – 1.000 Jahre alten Bäumen kletterten. Wir kreieren Texte über Menschenaffen auf Computern, die ohne Edelmetall aus der ruinierten Heimat der Schimpansen nicht funktionieren würden. Unsere Kinder erfreuen sich an Spielzeug aus Naturkautschuk – gewonnen dort, wo noch vor kurzem Bonobos ihr Auskommen hatten. Im Urlaub eingefangene Kopfläuse bekämpfen wir mit „Bio"-Insektizid, destilliert aus Pyrethrum-Pflanzen, die gerodetes Gorilla-Habitat bedecken.

Naturschutzorganisationen haben schon lange einen Katalog an Maßnahmen erstellt, der diese traurigen Trends, wenn schon nicht umkehren, so doch verlangsamen soll. Hierzu gehören etwa großflächiger Ankauf von Land, um bestehende Reservate zu erhalten und neue Parks zu schaffen; ein Verbot des Holzeinschlags in Biotopen von Menschenaffen; Unterbinden des Handels mit Buschfleisch und Heimtieren; bessere Ausbildung, Bezahlung und Ausrüstung von Wildhütern.

Menschenaffen sind übrigens lediglich besonders prominente Aushängeschilder solcher Schutzkampagnen, die ungezählten anderen Lebensformen, die ihr Biotop teilen, ebenfalls zugute kämen. Wer egoistischere Gründe für Erhaltungsmaßnahmen sucht, kann auch diese leicht finden. So kann das Bewahren genetischer Vielfalt zur Entdeckung neuer Arzneimittel führen. Intakte Regenwälder absorbieren überdies Treibhausgase und speisen Flüsse, die Millionen Menschen mit Trinkwasser versorgen.

Auf der Agenda von Politikern kommen Regenwälder zwar mittlerweile vor, doch fehlen politischer Wille und konkrete Mittel. In westlichen Ländern wird auch ganz gerne und aus aufrichtigen Motiven gespendet. Aber im Endeffekt wird wohl mehr unser eigenes Gewissen beruhigt, als dass sich vor Ort etwas verbesserte. Und selbst wenn Milliarden bereitgestellt würden: Korruption und Inkompetenz von Regierungen in tropischen Regionen sind weitere steile Hürden auf dem Weg zu effektivem Schutz.

Verwaiste Menschenaffen, die in Auffangstationen landen, stehen für diese Zerstörungen – und speziell für die Buschfleisch-Krise Afrikas. Alles begann harmlos, als wohlmeinende Tierliebhaber im Jahre 1970 zwei im Markt feilgebotene Schimpansenbabys aufnahmen. Zehn Jahre später, 1980, mussten bereits 21 versorgt werden, und 1990 waren es 63. Dann beschleunigte sich das Tempo, was die Gründung von 18 Reservaten nötig machte – in Westafrika in Gambia, Guinea, Sierra Leone, in Nigeria und Kamerun; in Zentralafrika in Gabon, Kongo und der Demokratischen Republik Kongo; in Ostafrika in Uganda, Kenya und Sambia. Bis ins Jahr 2000 wurden 379 Schimpansen in Stationen geschwemmt und 2010 lebten bereits 855 dort. In der letzten Dekade verdoppelte sich ebenfalls die Zahl verwaister Bonobos und die von Gorillas verdreifachten sich gar. In Asien, wo weniger die Jagd als Rodungen zerstörerisch wirken, werden gegenwärtig 1.500 Orang-Utans in Schutzeinrichtungen betreut.

Noch vor einem halben Jahrhundert bevölkerten Millionen von Menschenaffen die Dschungel. Um die Jahrtausendwende wurde berechnet, dass in der Wildnis noch 28.000 Bonobos lebten, 236.000 Schimpansen, 11.000 Gorillas und 64.000 Orang-Utans – summa summarum 446.000 Menschenaffen. Diesen Schätzungen steht eine Katastrophe um die andere gegenüber. Die Elfenbeinküste verlor in 15 Jahren 90 Prozent ihrer Schimpansen – während Menschen um 50 Prozent zunahmen. In Zentralafrika fegte eine Ebola-Epedemie eine in die Tausende gehende Urbevölkerung an Gorillas und Schimpansen hinweg. Im ostafrikanischen Nationalpark Kahuzi-Biega brach Goldgräberfieber aus, als dort das Erz Coltan entdeckt wurde – wichtiger Rohstoff für die Mikroelektronik in Mobiltelefonen, Laptops und Spielkonsolen. Für die 13.000 illegalen Ausgräber besorgten 300 Jäger Fleisch. Sie töteten, was ihnen vor die automatischen Waffen kam, sämtliche Elefanten, viele Vögel und die allermeisten der 8.000 heimischen Gorillas.

Anhand der 3.000 Stationswaisen lässt sich noch viel genauer belegen, wie gravierend die Krise für Menschenaffen wirklich ist. Nehmen wir als Beispiel die etwa 5.000 Überlebenden der nigerianisch-kamerunschen Schimpansen. In den sechs Stationen der beiden Länder landen pro Jahr durchschnittlich sechs Waisen dieser seltensten Unterart. Das klingt nicht dramatisch, bis man die Wahrscheinlichkeit, dass ein Schimpansenbaby lebend in eine Station gelangt, mit den Methoden der Jäger kontrastiert. Am Abend lokalisieren die Wilderer die Schlafstätten der Schimpansen über deren Rufe und das verräterische Knacken von Zweigen beim Konstruieren der Nachtnester. Vor Morgengrauen umzingeln sie die Schlafstätte und feuern auf alles, was sich regt. Tote und Sterbende werden mit der Machete zerhackt, ihre Körperteile über schwelenden Feuern geräuchert, um sie auf die Märkte schaffen zu können. An Babys ist kaum Fleisch, so dass es sich eher lohnt, Überlebende als Haustiere zu verkaufen.

Wieviel getöteten Schimpansen entspricht nun ein einzelner Waise, der es bis in eine Station schafft? Demographische Daten genau erforschter Studiengruppen belegen, dass ziemlich genau jedes fünfte Tier einer Schlafgruppe ein Baby ist. Statistisch gesehen müssen die Wilderer deshalb mindestens vier Schimpansen töten, damit ihnen ein Baby lebend in die Hände fällt. Die allermeisten werden jedoch selbst massakriert. Sofern nicht sogleich erschossen, klammern Babys sich an ihre getroffene Mutter – um dann beim Aufprall aus 10 oder 20 Metern Höhe zu sterben. Andere verenden alsbald an Verletzungen durch Schrotkörner. Überleben bedeutet, Zeuge beim Zermetzeln der eigenen Familie zu werden. Selbst äußerlich unverletzte Säuglinge sind davon oft so traumatisiert, dass sie ihr Lebenslicht erlöschen lassen. Andere Säuglinge sterben am Bier und den Bananen, mit denen die Jäger sie füttern, oder an Schwäche oder Infektionen. Die wenigsten sind stark genug, in Käfigen oder an Halsketten gefesselt bei Dorfhäuptlingen, in Restaurants oder Vergnügungsparks zu überleben – mit Zigaretten malträtiert oder von Kindern endlos gequält. Wenn die Schimpansen nach ein paar Jahren zu beißen anfangen, werden sie totgeschlagen oder man lässt sie verhungern. Nur falls eine Station nahebei ist, mögen ihre Besitzer sie dort abliefern – und in seltenen Fällen konfisziert ein Beamter der Naturschutzbehörde die Gefangenen. Nehmen wir an – sehr optimistisch –, dass auf zehn Massaker ein Baby kommt, das in einer Waisenstation landet. Da jedes Baby vier getötete Gruppenmitglieder entsprechen, repräsentiert dieser Schimpanse 50 Menschenaffen, die aus der Wildnis entfernt wurden. Bei sechs jährlichen Neuzugängen wird die Unterart damit um 300 Tiere reduziert – also um sechs Prozent der Gesamtpopulation von 5.000. Da Schimpansenbevölkerungen jährlich maximal ein Prozent wachsen, ist der Verlust extrem. Deshalb lässt sich berechnen, dass diese Unterart in weniger als 20 Jahren ausgerottet sein könnte.

Für andere Unterarten und Arten der Menschenaffen sieht die Zukunft kaum rosiger aus. Jene Waldinseln, die in ein paar Jahrzehnten übrig bleiben, werden vermutlich von Blauhelmen, Mauern und Elektrozäunen abgeschirmt werden, um von der UNO ausgelobtes „Weltartenerbe" zu bewahren. Die Mehrzahl dürfte sogar außerhalb dieser Freiland-Parks überleben – nämlich in Schutzstationen und Zoos.

In ihren Broschüren betonen Waisenreservate, dass sie am liebsten auf ihre eigene Schließung hinwirken würden. Wie die Dinge stehen, werden sie ihre

Schützlinge allerdings bis zum Sankt Nimmerleinstag versorgen müssen. „Auswilderung" ist extrem schwierig, weil tauglicher Dschungel praktisch nicht existiert. In „leergeschossenen" Wäldern wären die Freigelassenen tags drauf Gewehrfutter, da Schutzstatus fast immer nur auf dem Papier existiert. Zuweilen werden Menschaffen auf relativ sichere Inseln in Flüssen oder Seen ausgesetzt – aber ohne ständige Zufütterung würden sie dort alsbald sterben.

Zoos hingegen haben ein Rechtfertigungsproblem. Wenngleich moderne Tierparks sich Natur- und Artenschutz auf die Fahnen schreiben, existieren sie doch vornehmlich deshalb, damit wir ihre unfreiwilligen Einwohner bestaunen können. Eine Wahl hatten Zooaffen nicht. Lässt es sich überhaupt rechtfertigen, dass wir solche Tiere hinter Schloss und Riegel halten?

Die Frage ist sicher nicht einfach zu beantworten. Die Bandbreite der Haltungsbedingungen reicht jedenfalls von qualvoll über erträglich bis hin zu gut. Das Wort „Gefangenschaft" hat somit viele Schattierungen, von der Haft in dunklen und dreckigen Kerkern über die sterile gekachelte Verwahranstalt und das komfortable Stadthaus bis hin zum goldenen Käfig – heute oft schönfärberisch „Urwaldhaus" genannt. Den vielleicht besten Kompromiss stellen Kombinationen von Innenanlagen mit fußballfeldgroßen Freigehegen dar, die sich mittlerweile in manchen Tiergärten finden. Wichtiger noch als Platz sind aber für das relative Wohlbefinden von Menschenaffen demographisch komplexe Sozialgruppen, deren Aufbau Jahre oder Jahrzehnte dauern kann.

Dabei wird dann gerne von „artgerechter" Haltung geredet. Der Begriff ist allerdings schönfärberisch und irreführend – genauso wie „natürliche" oder „naturnahe" Haltung. Denn ironischerweise ließe sich Gefangenschaftshaltung schon deshalb genausogut als „artwidrig" deuten, weil sie lebensverlängernd wirkt. Zootieren werden beispielsweise Fortpflanzungspartner zugeteilt, was den im Freiland oft knüppelharten Konkurrenzkampf unterbindet. Auch Kindertöten wird immer schwerer gemacht. Seit sich in Zoos herumsprach, welches Schicksal noch nicht entwöhnten Primatenkindern von fremden Männchen droht, werden die von ihnen ferngehalten. Die Sterblichkeit ist im Freiland zudem höher wegen Nahrungsmangel, Raubfeinden und Krankheiten, die im Zoo ein Veterinär behandelt.

Der Begriff „artgerecht" nährt sich ohnehin aus einem statischen Naturbild, das in idealistischen Vorstellungen wurzelt. Da sich Umwelten aber ständig wandeln, züchtet die Natur, und speziell die Natur von Primaten, nicht Uniformität heran, sondern Flexibilität. Überspitzt lässt sich deshalb auch das Leben und Überleben in Gefangenschaft als „artgerecht" betrachten. Denn ganz offenbar sind Menschenaffen dazu in der Lage. Sie mögen es sogar einem Leben in Freiheit vorziehen. Lucy Temerlin, eine Schimpansin, die unter Menschen aufwuchs, mit denen sie sich in Zeichensprache verständigte, wurde „zur Belohnung" in die Wildnis ihrer afrikanische Heimat zurückgebracht. Sie fühlte sich dort, nahe ihren „barbarischen" Artgenossen, allein und verloren. „Go home", signalisierte sie daraufhin mit ihren Händen: „Ich will nach Hause".

So darf sich das schlechte Gewissen in Grenzen halten, wenn wir Freude an der Begegnung mit Zooaffen haben oder uns an fotografischen Porträts von ihnen delektieren. Denn immerhin bringt uns das unseren nächsten Verwandten noch näher. Und das ist zumindest gut für ein erweitertes Wir-Gefühl.

Bonobo / *bonobo* 177

10. Future

Arks in the Great Human Flood

Billions are spent in the hope of detecting a spark of life on Mars. Vast sums for research would be made available if intelligent beings were discovered on other planets who could feel joy and sorrow like we do, live in highly complex societies and could communicate with us via sign language. Exactly such creatures are at home on our Earth. However, organisations aiming to protect them can scarcely raise more than a few million dollars per year. Thus, we are virtually sitting on our hands while our closest kin disappears into oblivion through the destruction of their natural homes and via ruthless hunting.

One should not deceive oneself: in their tropical countries of origin, larger populations of great apes will have little chance of survival. Primates share the sad fate of other wildlife – whether snails, fish, bats, snakes, antelopes or elephants – and end up in cooking pots. "Bush meat" is not a fall-back food of the poor. Rather, the notables of villages as well as the nouveau riche of the cities will pay many times more for such game than for beef, pork or goat meat. Moreover, streams of refugees, tourists and cattle spread pathogens such as Ebola, anthrax and tuberculosis in the natural domains of great apes. Their worst enemy, however, is the clear-cutting of forest, which is undertaken to obtain timber and fine woods for construction; to establish plantations with rubber trees and oil palms; to rummage the ground in search of ore, fossil fuels and precious metal; to make room for settlements, pastures and farmland.

The most important beneficiaries of such widespread destruction are the wealthy countries of the North Atlantic rim. In other words: us. We wash with perfumed soap made from palm oil grown where only ten years ago orangutans climbed on trees that were – literally – 1,000 years old. We create texts about apes on computers that wouldn't work without ore-based material dug up in what was the natural home of chimpanzees. Our children play delightfully with toys made of natural rubber – harvested where until recently bonobos lived. We fight lice with "organic" insecticides, distilled from pyrethrum, an aromatic plant grown for export in logged gorilla habitat.

Conservation organisations have long identified measures that might, if not reverse, at least slow down this sad trend. These include large-scale purchases of land to preserve existing reserves and create new parks; a ban on logging in great ape habitats; a stop to the trade in bush meat and pet animals; and better training, pay and equipment for park rangers.

Apes are, of course, only the flagship species for such protection campaigns that would likewise benefit countless other life forms sharing their habitat. It is also easy to identify more selfish reasons to support conservation measures. For example, the preservation of genetic diversity may lead to the discovery of new drugs. Intact forests also absorb greenhouse gases and feed rivers that supply millions of people with drinking water.

To be sure, rainforests have made it onto the agenda of politicians. But political will and a concrete supply of resources are lacking. In Western countries, many – out of sincere motives – do indeed donate money to preservation causes. But in the end such contributions probably do more to reassure our own consciences than make a difference on the ground. And even if billions would be made available, corruption and incompetence of governments in tropical regions are additional steep hurdles for effective protection.

Orphaned apes who end up in sanctuaries symbolise the destruction – and especially Africa's bush meat crisis. It all began rather innocently in 1970, when well-meaning animal-lovers took in two baby chimpanzees offered for sale in the market. Ten years later, in 1980, already 21 youngsters had to be taken care of, and in 1990 there were 63. The pace accelerated thereafter, which necessitated the creation of 18 reserves – in West Africa in the Gambia, Guinea, Sierra Leone, Nigeria and Cameroon; in Central Africa in Gabon, Congo and the Democratic Republic of Congo; and in East Africa in Uganda, Kenya and Zambia. By the year 2000, 379 chimpanzees had been washed into those stations, and by 2010 the tide had risen to 855. In the last decade, the number of orphaned bonobos doubled likewise, and those of gorillas has even tripled. In Asia, where hunting takes second place behind deforestation in terms of destructive power, 1,500 orangutans are currently cared for in institutions dedicated to their upkeep.

Only half a century ago, jungles harboured millions of apes. When the new millennium began, the population numbers for wild apes were calculated as 28,000 for bonobos, 236,000 for chimpanzees, 11,000 for gorillas and 64,000 for orangutans – summa summarum 446,000 apes. These estimates were constantly revised down when one catastrophe hit after another. The Ivory Coast, in 15 years only, lost 90 percent of its chimpanzees – while humans increased by 50 percent. In Central Africa, an Ebola epidemic virtually annihilated an indigenous population of thousands of gorillas and chimpanzees. In the east African Kahuzi-Biega National Park, a mining fever ran high after the discovery of coltan ore – an important component of microelectronics in mobile phones, laptops and game consoles. Meat for the 13,000 illegal miners was provided by 300 hunters. They killed whatever came in front of their automatic weapons: all elephants, many birds, and the vast majority of 8,000 native gorillas.

By taking into account the 3,000 orphans already kept in sanctuaries, one can reconstruct in even greater detail how serious the situation for great apes really is. Take, for example, the approximately 5,000 surviving specimens of the Nigeria-Cameroon chimpanzee. An average of 6 orphans of this rarest subspecies is taken in per year into one of the six sanctuaries in either of the two nations. That might not sound dramatic until one considers the chances of a baby chimpanzee arriving alive at a sanctuary, given the methods of ape-hunters. In the evening, poachers will locate the sleeping site of chimpanzees by either listening to their vocalisations or the crackle of branches when the apes construct their night nests. Before dawn, the poachers surround the nesting area and fire at anything that moves. Dead and dying apes are hacked to pieces with machetes, their body parts smoked over smouldering fires, then transported to markets. Babies have little meat, so it is more profitable to sell those who survive as pets. How many killed chimpanzees might correspond to a single orphan who ultimately makes it to a sanctuary? Demographic data from well-known study groups indicate that every fifth animal in a nest group is a baby. Statistically, poachers must thus kill at least 4 chimpanzees to obtain one baby. The vast majority of infants, however, are massacred themselves. If not outrightly killed, babies will cling to their mothers after she has been shot, and fall 10 or 20 metres deep to then die on impact. Others will quickly succumb to pellet wounds. Survival means witnessing the butchering of one's own family. Even infants that don't suffer outward injuries are often so traumatised that they lose their will to live. Other babies die from the diet of beer and bananas hunters feed them; from weakness, or infection. Few are strong enough to survive, kept in cages or on neck chains in compounds of village chiefs, in restaurants or amusement parks – abused with cigarettes or endlessly tortured by human children. Once the chimpanzees are old enough to be able to inflict bite wounds, they will be clubbed or starved to death. Only if a station is nearby may owners hand them over – except for rare cases, when a government official confiscates a prisoner.

Let us assume – very optimistically – that for each 10 massacres, one orphan will make it to a sanctuary. Because every baby killed corresponds to 4 group members, this represents 50 chimpanzees removed from the wild. The 6 new orphans arriving into a sanctuary per year would thus represent 300 animals – or 6 percent of the total subspecies population of 5,000. Because chimpanzee communities annually may grow by only 1 percent, the loss is extreme. We can therefore calculate that this chimpanzee subspecies might go extinct in less than 20 years.

The future looks no brighter for other types of great apes. Those small islands of forest that remain in a few decades will probably be guarded by Blue Berets, walls and electric fences, to protect the United Nations' "world heritage species". The majority, however, will likely survive outside these outdoor parks – namely, in sanctuaries and zoos.

Sanctuaries emphasise in their brochures that they would prefer to work towards their own closure. As things stand, however, they will have to take care of their charges until the end of times. "Reintroduction" is extremely difficult because suitable jungle is almost impossible to come by. If released into forest that has previously been shot "empty", those "set free" would be gun fodder the very next day, since protection exists almost always only on paper. Sometimes apes are released into the relative security of islets that form in broad rivers or lakes – but, without the constant provision of food, they would soon die there.

Traditional zoos, on the other hand, have a justification problem. Although modern institutions have incorporated in-situ conservation into their mission statements, they still do exist primarily so that we can look at their involuntary residents. Primates in zoos did not have a choice. So, can it ever be justified to keep them under lock and key?

This question does not have a simple answer. For sure, the conditions of being kept by humans range from torturous via bearable to good. "Captivity" can thus mean very different things, including imprisonment in dark and filthy cages, sterile tiled enclosures, comfortable town houses or a golden cage – euphemistically called a "jungle house". The perhaps best compromise might be combinations of indoor sections with outdoor enclosures, sometimes the size of a football pitch, as some zoos now have. Even more important for the relative wellbeing of apes than space is a demographically stratified social group, which can take years or even decades to develop.

Such zoo environments are sometimes spoken of as "species appropriate". The term, however, is misleading – just as much as the expression "natural" or "naturalistic". Because captive settings may well be seen as "anti-naturalistic" – if only in that they prolong life. For example, zoo animals are allocated reproductive partners, thus preventing the often life-threatening competition prevailing in the wild. Also, infanticide is made more and more difficult. Ever since word spread in zoos about the threat that unfamiliar males pose for unrelated infants, they are kept away from each other. Mortality is likewise higher in nature because of starvation and predators – and also diseases, which a veterinarian can attend to in a zoo.

In any case, the term "species appropriate" conveys a static image rooted in idealistic notions. In nature, and specifically in the nature of primates, not uniformity but flexibility is selected for, given ever-changing environmental conditions. Apes can obviously not only adapt to a captive setting, they may even prefer it to a life in freedom. The chimpanzee Lucy Temerlin – who grew up among humans who taught her sign language – was "rewarded" by repatriation to a wild African homeland. There, near her own "barbaric" kind, she felt alone and lost. "Go home," she was seen signing with her fingers, "I want to go home."

Our bad consciences can thus perhaps be assuaged, if we catch ourselves enjoying the sight of primates kept in zoos or if we marvel unabashedly at their photographic portraits. After all, such connections bring us even nearer to our closest relatives. And that is good, if for nothing else than an extended feeling of "us".

Gorilla / *gorilla*

Gorilla / *gorilla*

Schimpanse / *chimpanzee* Bonobo / *bonobo*

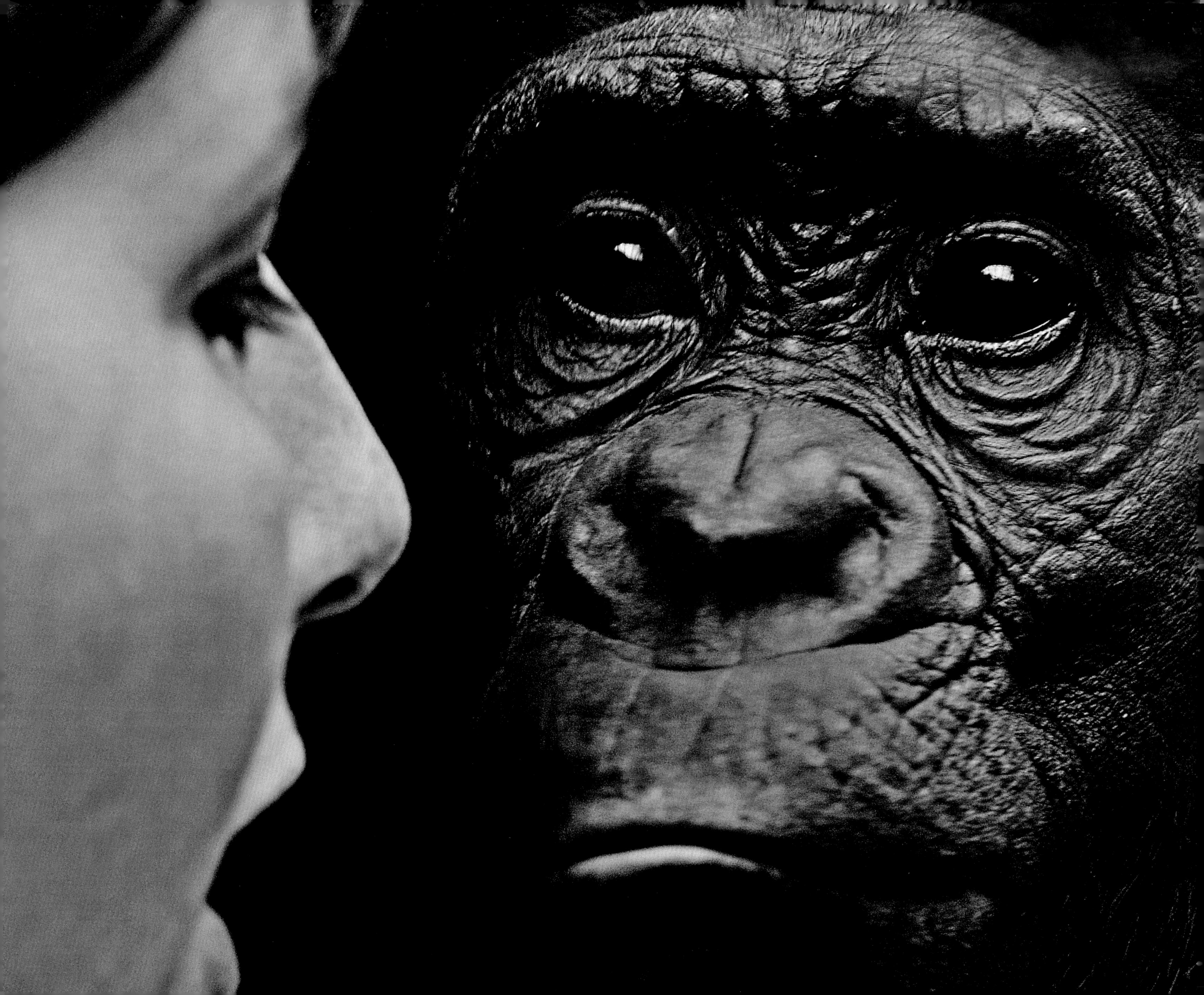

Anhang
Appendix

Literatur / Literature

1

Engels, Eve-Marie (2007). *Charles Darwin.* München: C.H. Beck

Hösle, Vittorio & Christian Illies (Hg. / eds.) (2005). *Darwinism and Philosophy.* Notre Dame: Univ. of Notre Dame Press

Janson, Horst Woldemar (1952). *Apes and Ape Lore in the Middle Ages and the Renaissance.* London: The Warburg Institute, Univ. of London

2

Campbell, Christina J.; Agustin Fuentes, Katherine C. MacKinnon, Melissa Panger, Simon K. Bearder (Hg. / eds.) (2007). *Primates in Perspective.* Oxford: Oxford Univ. Press

Paul, Andreas (1997). *Affen und Menschen.* Darmstadt: Wissenschaftliche Buchgesellschaft

Sommer, Volker & Karl Ammann (1998). *Die Großen Menschenaffen. Orang-Utan, Gorilla, Schimpanse, Bonobo.* München: BLV

Voland, Eckart (2009). *Soziobiologie. Die Evolution von Kooperation und Konkurrenz.* Heidelberg: Spektrum Akademischer Verlag

3

Arnold, Michael L. (2008). *Reticulate Evolution and Humans. Origins and Ecology.* Oxford: Oxford Univ. Press

Diamond, Jared (1992). *The Third Chimpanzee. The Evolution and Future of the Human Animal.* New York: Harper Perennial. – Deutsch: (2000). Der dritte Schimpanse. Frankfurt / Main: Fischer Taschenbuch

Enard, Wolfgang & Svante Pääbo (2004). Comparative primate genomics. *Annual Review of Genomics and Human Genetics 5:* 351–378

Schrenk, Friedemann (2008). *Die Frühzeit des Menschen. Der Weg zum Homo sapiens.* München: C.H. Beck

Wildman, Derek E.; Monica Uddin, Guozhen Liu, Lawrence I. Grossman & Morris Goodman (2003). Implications of natural selection in shaping 99.4% nonsynonymous DNA identity between humans and chimpanzees: Enlarging genus Homo. *Proceedings of the National Academy of Sciences* 100: 7181–7188

4

Galdikas, Biruté (1995). *Reflections of Eden. My Years with the Orang-Utans of Borneo.* Boston: Little, Brown & Co

van Schaik, Carel P. (2004). *Among Orangutans. Red Apes and the Rise of Human Culture.* Cambridge / MA: Belknap Press of Harvard Univ. Press

Wich, Serge A., S. Suci Utami Atmoko, Tatang Mitra Setia & Carel P. van Schaik (Hg. / eds.) (2009). *Orangutans. Geographic Variation in Behavioral Ecology and Conservation.* Oxford: Oxford Univ. Press

5

Dixson, Alan (2009). *Sexual Selection and the Origins of Human Mating Systems. Oxford:* Oxford Univ. Press

Fossey, Dian (1983). *Gorillas in the Mist.* Boston: Houghton Mifflin Co. – Deutsch: (1989). *Gorillas im Nebel.* München: Kindler

Harcourt, Alexander H. & Kelly J. Stewart (2007). *Gorilla Society: Conflict, Compromise, and Cooperation Between the Sexes.* Chicago: Univ. of Chicago Press

Taylor, Andrea B. & Michele L. Goldsmith (Hg. / eds.) (2003). *Gorilla Biology: A Multidisciplinary Perspective.* Cambridge: Cambridge Univ. Press

6

Boesch, Christophe (2009). *The Real Chimpanzee. Sex Strategies in the Forest.* Cambridge: Cambridge Univ. Press

Boesch, Christophe, Gottfried Hohmann & Linda Marchant (Hg. / eds.) (2002). *Behavioural Diversity in Chimpanzees and Bonobos.* Cambridge: Cambridge Univ. Press

Goodall, Jane (1986). *The Chimpanzees of Gombe. Patterns of Behavior.* Cambridge / MA: Belknap Press of Harvard Univ. Press

McGrew, William C. (2004). *The Cultured Chimpanzee: Reflections on Cultural Primatology.* Cambridge: Cambridge Univ. Press

7

de Waal, Frans B. M. & Frans Lanting (1997). *Bonobo. The Forgotten Ape.* Berkeley: Univ. of California Press

Furuichi, Takeshi & Jo Thompson (Hg. / eds.) (2008). *The Bonobos. Behavior, Ecology, and Conservation.* New York: Springer

Parish, Amy R. (1996). Female relationships in bonobos (Pan paniscus): evidence for bonding, cooperation, and female dominance in a male-philopatric species. *Human Nature* 7: 61–96

Sommer, Volker & Paul Vasey (Hg. / eds.) (2006). *Homosexual Behaviour in Animals. An Evolutionary Perspective.* Cambridge: Cambridge Univ. Press

8

Boesch, Christophe (2007). *What makes us human (Homo sapiens)? The challenge of cognitive cross-species comparison.* Journal of Comparative Psychology 121: 227–240

Byrne, Richard W. & Andrew Whiten (Hg. / eds.) (1988). *Machiavellian Intelligence: Social Expertise and the Evolution of Intellect in Monkeys, Apes, and Humans.* Oxford: Clarendon

Hurley, Susan & Matthew Nudds (Hg. / eds.) (2006). *Rational Animals?* Oxford: Oxford Univ. Press

Metzinger, Thomas (2009). *The Ego Tunnel. The Science of the Mind and the Myth of the Self.* New York: Basic Books. – Deutsch: (2009). *Der Ego-Tunnel. Eine neue Philosophie des Selbst: Von der Hirnforschung zur Bewusstseinsethik.* Berlin: Berlin Verlag.

Tomasello, Michael; Malinda Carpenter, Josep Call, Tanya Behne & Henrike Moll (2005). Understanding and sharing intentions: The origins of cultural cognition. *Behavioral & Brain Sciences* 28: 675–735

9

Cavalieri, Paola & Peter Singer (Hg. / eds.) (1993). *The Great Ape Project. Equality Beyond Humanity.* New York: St. Martin's Press; London: Fourth Estate. – Deutsch: (1994). *Menschenrechte für die Großen Menschenaffen.* München: Goldmann

Vollmer, Gerhard (2002). *Evolutionäre Erkenntnistheorie.* Stuttgart: Hirzel / Wissenschaftliche Verlagsgesellschaft

Walach, Harald (2009). *Psychologie. Wissenschaftstheorie, philosophische Grundlagen und Geschichte.* Stuttgart: W. Kohlhammer

Wetz, Franz Josef (2008). *Ethik Zwischen Kultur- und Naturwissenschaft* (Kolleg Praktische Philosophie Bd. / vol. 1). Stuttgart: Philipp Reclam jun.

Wise, Steven M. (2000). *Rattling the Cage: Toward Legal Rights for Animals.* Cambridge / MA: Perseus

10

Caldecott, Julian & Lera Miles (Hg. / eds.) (2005). *World Atlas of Great Apes and Their Conservation.* Los Angeles: Univ. of California Press

Cowlishaw, Guy & Robin Dunbar (2000). *Primate Conservation Biology.* Chicago: Univ. of Chicago Press

Peterson, Dale & Karl Ammann (2003). *Eating Apes.* California: Univ. of California Press

Sommer, Volker (2008). *Schimpansenland. Wildes Leben in Afrika.* München: C.H. Beck

Schutz- und Forschungseinrichtungen

Aufgeführt sind Institutionen, die sich des Tier- und Biotopschutzes sowie der Erforschung Großer Menschenaffen annehmen:
1 Primaten und Menschenaffen generell
2 bestimmte Arten Großer Menschenaffen
3 Fauna und Flora generell

1
International Primatological Society www.internationalprimatologicalsociety.org
International Primate Protection League www.ippl.org
The Jane Goodall Institute www.janegoodall.org
Pan African Sanctuary Alliance www.pasaprimates.org
Great Ape Project www.greatapeproject.org
Great Ape Survival Project www.unep.org/grasp
Ape Alliance www.4apes.com
Max Planck Institute for Evolutionary Anthropology www.eva.mpg.de

2
Orangutan Conservancy www.orangutan.com
Balikpapan Orangutan Survival Foundation www.savetheorangutan.org
Orangutan Foundation www.orangutan.org.uk
Sumatra Orangutan Conservation Programme www.sumatranorangutan.org
The Gorilla Organization www.gorillas.org
International Gorilla Conservation Programme www.mountaingorillas.org
Berggorilla & Regenwald Direkthilfe www.berggorilla.de
Dian Fossey Gorilla Fund International www.gorillafund.org
Goualougo Triangle Ape Project www.congo-apes.org
Wild Chimpanzee Foundation www.wildchimps.org
Gashaka Primate Project www.ucl.ac.uk/gashaka
Pan troglodytes ellioti www.ellioti.org
Bonobo Conservation Initiative www.bonobo.org

Institutions Dedicated to Conservation and Research

Listed below are institutions working towards welfare of great apes, habitat conservation and research into their socio-ecology:
1 primates, including apes in general
2 particular great ape species
3 wildlife (fauna, flora) in general

3
CITES The Convention on International Trade in Endangered Species of Wild Fauna and Flora www.cites.org
Conservation International www.conservation.org
Flora and Fauna International www.fauna-flora.org
Institute for Conservation Research / San Diego Zoo www.sandiegozoo.org
IUCN International Union for the Conservation of Nature www.iucnredlist.org
LAGA The Last Great Ape Organization www.LAGA-enforcement.org
North of England Zoological Society / Chester Zoo www.chesterzoo.org
Wildlife Conservation Society www.wcs.org
Worldwide Fund for Nature www.wwf.org
Zoological Society London / London Zoo www.zsl.org
Zoologische Gesellschaft Frankfurt / Zoo Frankfurt www.zgf.de

Die Porträtierten   The Portrayed

Name (Geschlecht [f = weiblich, m = männlich], Geburtsjahr, Vater und Mutter [wenn ebenfalls abgebildet]): Seitenzahlen [l = links, m = mitte, r = rechts, o = oben, u = unten], (Aufnahmeort)

Name (sex [f = female, m = male], year of birth, father and mother [if likewise depicted]): page numbers [l = left, m = middle, r = right, o = on top, u = underneath], (photo locality)

Aufnahmeorte / *photo localities:*
B (ZooParc de Beauval / F), F (Zoo Frankfurt / D), G (Walter Zoo Gossau / CH), H (Zoo Heidelberg / D), L (Zoo La Boissière / F)

Orang-Utan / *orangutan:* 27or, 153, 162, 164, 165
Charly (m *1957): 10, 76, 86, 87 (F)
Jane (f *1983): 84l (L)
Muda (m *1983): 91 (B)
Christina (f *1986): 38, 147 (B)
Moni (f *1986): 84r (L)
Rosa (f *1989): 72l, 77l, 141l (F)
Lucu (m *2005, Rosa x Charly): 141r (F)
Belayan (f *2009): 140 (B)
Pandai (m *2009, Rosa x Charly): 77r (F)

Gorilla / *gorilla:* 26ur, 27ol, 67,78, 145ul, 191
Julchen (f *1966): 96 (F)
Inge (f *1980): 97l (B)
Kabinda (f *1982): 142l (B)
Rebecca (f *1982): 30l, 31l, 150 (F)
Asato (m *1991): 94, 102r (B)
Viatu (m *1998): 11 (F),
Fossey (f *1999): 21r (F)
Kabuli (m *2004, Rebecca x Matze): 63 (F)
Mayombé (f *2007, Inge x Asato): 97r (B)

Nasibu (m *2007, Rebecca x Matze): 30r, 31r, 138, 180 (F)
Mapenzi (m *2010, Kabinda x Asato): 69, 142m, 181 (B)

Bonobo / *bonobo:* 6, 9, 11, 24, 26 (ol, or, ul, ur), 27 (ul, ur), 42, 44, 48, 78, 79, 136, 144, 145 (ol, or)
Margrit (f ca.*1952): 25, 41, 54, 120, 177 (F)
Natalie (f *1966): 19r, 139 (F)
Ludwig (m *1984): 7, 16, 21l, 22r, 23, 29, 32, 152, 157l, 161r, 173 (F)
Ukela (f *1985): 20, 28l, 137, 139r, 143 (F)
Kamiti (f *1987): 12,19l, 22l, 73, 134, 135, 170l (F)
Kutu (f *1998): 18r, 34r, 62, 80r, 81, 82, 118l, 172r, 183 (F)
Zomi (f *1998): 34, 52, 80l, 83l (F)
Haiba (f *2001, Ukela x Ludwig): 66, 121 (F)
Heri (m*2001, Natalie X Ludwig):157r (F)
Kelele (m *2004): 45 (F)
Nakala (w, *2007, Ukela x Ludwig): 28r, 129r (F)
Nyota (m *2007, Natalie x Ludwig): 75, 124, 129l, 132, 133r (F)
Bili (m *2008): 149 (F)
Omanga (f *2008, Kamiti x Ludwig): 19m 22m 70, 71, 128, 161l, 170r (F)
Pangi (f *2009, Kutu x Ludwig): 18l, 72r, 118r, 148, 172l (F)
Panisco (m *2009, Zomi x Ludwig): 83r (F)

Schimpanse / *chimpanzee:* pp. 51, 68, 145ur
Lulu (f *1973): 146 (H)
Max (m *1974–2009): 13, 17 (H)
Cess (m *1976): 74 (G)
Macouri (f *1999): 55, 106 (B)
Brigitte (f ca.*1981): 182 (G)
Ann (f *2002): 108 (B)
Madshabu (m *2007): 112 (G)
Malik (m *2007): 116, 117, 133l (G)
Oseye (f *2009): 160 (G)
Tumba (m *2009): 35, 109 (B)
Pili & Petiri (m & m *2010; Mutter der Zwillinge / mother of the twins = Brigitte): 182 (G)

Jutta Hof

Jutta Hof wurde in Dortmund geboren. Sie studierte vorderasiatische Archäologie und Ägyptologie. Jutta Hof lebte u. a. in Irland, Grossbritannien, Italien, der Schweiz und in den USA. Heute wohnt sie in Frankfurt am Main und ist als freie Fotografin tätig – mit dem Arbeitsschwerpunkt Tierfotografie.

Jutta Hof was born in Dortmund (Germany). She studied Near Eastern Archaeology as well as Egyptology. Jutta Hof lived in Ireland, Great Britain, Italy, Switzerland and the USA. Today, she works out of Frankfurt am Main (Germany) as a freelance photographer – her main focus being portraits of animals.

www.jutta-hof.de

Volker Sommer

Foto: Evelin Frerk

Volker Sommer erforscht wildlebende Primaten in Asien und Afrika und berät die *International Union for Conservation of Nature* als Menschenaffen-Experte. Er ist Professor für Evolutionäre Anthropologie am University College London (UCL) und gestaltet als Pro-Provost die internationale Strategie der Universität. Als wissenschaftlicher Beirat der Giordano-Bruno-Stiftung setzt Volker Sommer sich für einen säkularen Humanismus ein. Öffentlich bekannt ist der engagierte Naturschützer durch Radio, Fernsehen und Bücher zu evolutionsbiologischen Themen – zuletzt *Dawinisch denken* (2007) und *Schimpansenland* (2008).

Volker Sommer conducts field studies of primates in Asia and Africa and advises the *International Union for Conservation of Nature* as an expert on apes. He is Professor of Evolutionary Anthropology at UCL (University College London), and, as Pro-Provost, also develops UCL's international strategy. Volker Sommer is on the scientific board of the Giordano-Bruno-Foundation, a think-tank for the promotion of secular humanism. The dedicated conservationist is known to a wider audience through radio, television and books on evolutionary topics.

www.ucl.ac.uk/gashaka
www.ucl.ac.uk/anthropology/staff/v_sommer/index
www.ucl.ac.uk/global
www.giordano-bruno-stiftung.de

© 2010 by Edition Panorama Germany
All rights reserved | Printed and bound in Germany

© All photographs: Jutta Hof & Edition Panorama
© All texts: Volker Sommer & Edition Panorama

ISBN: 978-3-89823-435-1

Design: Marcus Bela Schmitt [Designgruppe Fanz und Neumayer]
Translations: Volker Sommer
Editorial Department: Dr. Christophe Klimmer, Wolfgang Roth
Seperations: EPS GmbH, Speyer
Printing: abcdruck GmbH, Heidelberg
Bookbinding: Buchbinderei Schaumann GmbH, Darmstadt

Edition PanoramaGmbH
G7, 14
D-68159 Mannheim
www.editionpanorama.com

No part of this book may be reproduced in any form or by any electronic
or mechanical means without prior written permission from the publisher
Edition Panorama

Diese Publikation entstand mit Unterstützung der VolkswagenStiftung, Hannover.
This publication was supported by the Volkswagen Foundation, Hanover.

Jutta Hof dankt / *wishes to thank*
Zoo Frankfurt/M., D
Zoo de La Boissiére, F
Walter Zoo Gossau, CH
Zoo Heidelberg, D
ZooParc de Beauval, F

Volker Sommer dankt / *wishes to thank*
Maren Gumnior für die Kartographie / *for cartography*
Alejandra Pascual-Garrido für Hintergrunddokumentation / *for backround research*
Kathleen Bryson für Englisch-Lektorat / *for editing the English*